A
PATTERN
OF
ISLANDS

Arthur Grimble

PENGUIN BOOKS

Penguin Books Ltd, Harmondsworth, Middlesex, England
Penguin Books, 625 Madison Avenue, New York, New York 10022, U.S.A.
Penguin Books Australia Ltd, Ringwood, Victoria, Australia
Penguin Books Canada Ltd, 2801 John Street, Markham, Ontario, Canada L3R 1B4
Penguin Books (N.Z.) Ltd, 182–190 Wairau Road, Auckland 10, New Zealand

First published by John Murray 1952
Published in Penguin Books 1981

Made and printed in Great Britain by
Cox & Wyman Ltd, Reading
Set in Filmset Plantin

Penguin Books
A Pattern of Islands

Sir Arthur Grimble, K.C.M.G., was born in Hong Kong in 1888, and educated at Chigwell School and Magdalene College, Cambridge. After taking his degree he pursued postgraduate studies in France and Germany. In 1914 he joined the Colonial Service in the Pacific as a Cadet and was posted to the Gilbert and Ellice Islands, where he remained in various positions until 1933. He was then transferred to St Vincent, Windward Islands, as Administrator, and stayed there until 1936 when he became Governor of the Seychelles Islands and was also knighted. In 1942 he became Governor of the Windward Islands. While working on the Gilbert and Ellice Islands, he became 'an almost perfect Gilbertese scholar' and was said to have been the only white man not married to a native to have been initiated into some of the Gilbertese societies.

In 1948 Sir Arthur retired from the Colonial Service, and not long after his return to England embarked on a new career. In his leisure he began to jot down narratives of some of his more personal experiences in the Gilbert and Ellice Islands, took them to the BBC and discovered that he not only possessed a talent for telling a good story but an admirable broadcasting voice as well. The result was a series of talks which became extremely popular and achieved equal success in their published form as *A Pattern of Islands*, which was made into a film in 1956. He later wrote the companion volume, *Return to the Islands*. He also contributed a series of distinguished essays to the journals of the Royal Anthropological Society of Great Britain and Ireland and to the Polynesian Society of New Zealand. Some of these early writings, many before unpublished, have been collected by his daughter, Rosemary Grimble, and published under the title *Migrations, Myth and Magic from the Gilbert Islands*.

Sir Arthur died in 1956.

This book
is dedicated to the District Officers
of the Colonial Administrative Service
and their long-suffering wives

*My acknowledgements
are due to the Wide World Magazine
and the National Geographic Magazine of America
for permission to use the material
which originally appeared in two
articles of mine in their pages*

Landing MAKIN-MEANG
Kuma
Keua
BUTARITARI

The Gilbert Islands

ABAIANG
Boat Landing
North-West
Channel
MARAKEI
South-East Point
TARAWA

MAIANA
Tebiauea

P A C I F I C

O C E A N

Western Passage
KURIA
ABEMAMA
Tabonua
Kabangaki
ARANUKA

EQUATOR

NONOUTI

TABITEUEA
BERU
NUKUNAU

ONOTOA

TAMANA
ARORAE

N

Marianas Is.

Caroline Is.
Marshall Is.
EQUATOR
GILBERT
NEW
GUINEA
Solomon Is.
ISLANDS
Ellice Is.
New
Hebrides
Fiji Is.
New Caledonia
Brisbane
AUSTRALIA
Sydney
North Is.
NEW
ZEALAND
TASMANIA
South Is.

E.G. Morton

CONTENTS

CADET IN EMBRYO

Old Man of the Colonial Office

I was nominated to a cadetship in the Gilbert and Ellice Islands Protectorate at the end of 1913. The cult of the great god Jingo was as yet far from dead. Most English households of the day took it for granted that nobody could be always right, or ever quite right, except an Englishman. The Almighty was beyond doubt Anglo-Saxon, and the popular conception of Empire resultantly simple. Dominion over palm and pine (or whatever else happened to be noticeably far-flung) was the heaven-conferred privilege of the Bulldog Breed. Kipling had said so. The colonial possessions, as everyone so frankly called them, were properties to be administered, first and last, for the prestige of the little lazy isle where the trumpet-orchids blew. Kindly administered, naturally – nobody but the most frightful bounder could possibly question our sincerity about that – but firmly too, my boy, firmly too, lest the school-children of Empire forget who were the prefects and who the fags. Your uncles – meaning every man Jack of your father's generation, uncle or not, who cared to take you by the ear – all said you'd never be a leader if you weakened on that point. It was terrifying, the way they put it, for Stalky represented their ideal of dauntless youth, and you loathed Stalky with his Company as much as you feared him; but you were a docile young man, and, as his devotees talked, you felt the seeds of your unworthiness sprouting into shameful view through every crack in your character.

The Colonial Office spoke more guardedly than your uncles. It began by saying that, as a cadet officer, you were going to be on probation for three years. To win confirmation as a member of the permanent administrative staff, you would have to pass within that time certain field-examinations in law and native language. This seemed plain and fair enough, but then came the rider. I forget how it was conveyed, whether in print or by word of mouth; but the gist of it was that you could hardly hope to be taken on as a permanent officer unless, over and above getting through your examinations, you could manage to convince your official chiefs overseas that you possessed qualities of leadership. The abysmal question left haunting you was – did the Colonial Office mean leadership in the same sense as Kipling and your uncles? If it did, and if you were anything like me, you were scuppered.

I was a tallish, pinkish, long-nosed young man, fantastically thin-legged and dolefully mild of manner. Nobody could conceivably have looked, sounded or felt less like a leader of any sort than I did at the age of twenty-five. Apart from my dislike of the genus Stalky, I think the only positive things about me were a consuming hunger for sea-travel and a disastrous determination to write sonnets. The sonnet-writing had been encouraged by Arthur Christopher Benson at Cambridge; the wanderlust had started to gnaw at my vitals at school, when I read that essay of Froude's 'England's Forgotten Worthies' – especially the part of it that pictured how Humfrey Gilbert met his end in the ten-ton 'frigate' *Squirrel*, sitting abaft with a book in his hand, 'giving signs of joy' to his fellow-adventurers in the *Golden Hinde* and roaring at them through the wild Atlantic gale that engulfed him, 'We are as near heaven by sea as by land' so often as they approached within hearing. I tried at Cambridge to cram some of my feelings about that, and the sea's lure in general, into a sonnet of dubious form –

> She called them with the voices of far lands
>> And with the flute-like whispering of reeds,
>> With scents of coral where the tide recedes,
> With thunderous echoes of deserted strands.
>
> She babbled the barbaric lilt of tongues
>> Heard brokenly in dreams; she strung the light
>> Of swarthy-smouldering gems across the night;
> She wrung their hearts with haunting of strange songs.
>
> She witched them with her ancient sorceries
>> And lo! they knew the terrible joy of ships

2

Gone questing where the moon's last footstep is,
And stars hold passionless converse overhead
    While mariners are drawn with writhen lips
Down, down, deep down, among her voiceless dead.

Arthur Benson was pained at the rhyme-pattern of the octave, but said the thing sounded sincere and showed promise. I was unwise enough to bring his kindly letter to the notice of some of my uncles. They only said he ought to have known better; after all, he had had every chance, dammit, as the son of an archbishop! So, Benson, as a moral prop, was out. But I had acquired at school and Cambridge some kind of competence at cricket and other sports, which kept them always hoping for the best. When I became, first secretary, and then, in the normal course, captain of my college cricket XI, they began to believe I really might be on my way to vertebrate life. But they could not have been more deeply mistaken. As secretary, I invariably took orders from the captain; as captain, I invariably took orders from the secretary, while the team invariably played the game as if neither of us were there. The worst of it was, I loved it. If ever I had previously entertained a notion that I might enjoy ordering people around, that experience certainly disabused me of it.

The fear of being packed home from the Gilbert and Ellice Islands in disgrace, after three years of probation, for having failed to become the kind of leader my uncles wanted me to be, began to give me nightmares. A moment came when I felt that the instant sack for some honest admission of my own ineptitude would be easier to bear than that long-drawn-out ignominy. In any case, I decided, someone at the top ought to be warned of my desperate resolve never to become like Stalky. It sounded rather fine, and lonely, and stubborn, put like that; but I fear I didn't live up to the height of it. I did, indeed, secure an interview at the Colonial Office, but my nearest approach to stubbornness with the quiet old gentleman who received me there was to confess, with a gulp in my throat, that the imaginary picture of myself in the act of meting out imperial kindness-but-firmness to anybody anywhere in the world, made me sweat with shame.

The quiet old gentleman was Mr Johnson, a Chief Clerk in the department which handled the affairs of Fiji and the Western Pacific High Commission. That discreet title of his (abandoned today in favour of Principal and Secretary) gave no hint of the enormous penetrating power of his official word. In the Western and Central Pacific alone, his modest whisper from behind the throne of authority had power to affect the destinies of scores of races in hundreds of islands scattered over millions of square miles of ocean. I was led to him on a bleak afternoon of February, 1914, high up in the gloomy Downing Street warren that housed the whole Colonial Office staff of those days. The air of his cavernous room enfolded me with the chill of a mortuary as I entered. He was a spare little man with a tenuous sandy beard and heavily tufted eyebrows of the same colour. He stood before the fire, slightly bent in the middle like a monkey-nut, combing his beard with one fragile hand and elevating the tails of his cut-away coat with the other, as he listened to my story. I can see him still, considering me over his glasses with the owlish yet not unkindly stare of an undertaker considering a corpse. (Senior officials in the Colonial Office don't wear beards today, but they still cultivate that way of looking at you.) When I was done, he went on staring a bit; then he heaved a quiet sigh, ambled over to a bookcase, pottered there breathing hard for a long while (I think now he must have been laughing), and eventually hauled out a big atlas, which he carried to his desk.

'Let us see, now,' he murmured, settling into his chair 'Let us see . . . yes . . . let us go on a voyage of discovery together. Where . . . precisely . . . *are* the Gilbert and Ellice Islands? If you will believe me, I have often been curious to know.'

He started whipping over the pages of the atlas; I could do nothing but goggle at him while he pursued his humiliating research.

'Ah!' he chirruped at last, 'here we have them: five hundred miles of islands lost in the wide Pacific. Remote . . . I forbear, in tenderness for your feelings, from saying anything so Kiplingesque as far-flung. Do we agree to say remote and *not* far-flung?' He cocked his wicked little eye at me.

I made sounds in my throat, and he went on at once, 'Remote

. . . yes . . . and romantic . . . romantic! Eastwards as far as ship can sail . . . up against the gateways of the dawn . . . coconut-palms, but of course *not* pines, ha-ha! . . . the lagoon islands, the Line Islands, Stevenson's Islands! Do we accept palms, *not* pines? Do we stake our lives on Stevenson, *not* Kipling? Do we insist upon the dominion of romance, *not* the romance of dominion? I should appreciate your answer.'

I joyfully accepted Stevenson and ruled Kipling out (except, of course, for *Puck of Pook's Hill* and *Kim*, and the *Long Trail*, and others too numerous to mention); but my callowness squirmed shamefully at romance. He became suddenly acid at that: 'Come, come! You owe perhaps more to your romanticism than you imagine – your appointment as a cadet, for example.' The truth was, according to him, that I had been the only candidate to ask for the job in the Gilbert and Ellice Islands. But for that . . . if, in fact, I had been up against the least competition . . . well . . . who could say? As I, for one, could not, he leaned back in his chair and fired a final question at me: 'I may take it, may I not, that, despite certain doubts which you entertain about the imperialism of Mr Kipling and . . . hm . . . a great many of your betters, you still nurse your laudable wish to go to the Central Pacific?'

I replied yes, sir, certainly, sir, but how was I going to tackle this thing about leadership, sir.

He peered at me incredulously, rose at once, and lifted his coat-tails again at the fire, as if I had chilled whatever it was. 'I had imagined,' he confided in a thin voice to the ceiling, 'that I had already – and with considerable finesse – managed to put all that in its right perspective for this queer young man.'

'However,' he continued, after a long and, to me, frightful silence, 'let us dot our i's and cross our t's. The deplorable thing about your romanticism is that you display it as a halo around your own head. You seem to think that, when you arrive in the Gilbert and Ellice Islands, the entire population will forthwith stop work to stand with bated breath awaiting your apotheosis as a leader among them.'

The blend of venomous truth and ghastly unfairness in this bit deep into my young soul; I opened my mouth to protest, but he overrode me: 'You permit me to proceed? Thank you. Now, believe me, your egocentric surmise is grotesquely incorrect. You will encounter out there a number of busy men interested primarily in only one thing about you, namely, your ability to learn and obey orders. These will severely deplore any premature motion of your own to order them – or, in fact, anybody else – about. They will expect you to do as you are told – neither more nor less – and to do it intelligently. In the process of learning how to obey orders with intelligence and good cheer, you may, we hope, succeed in picking up some first, crude notions about the true nature of leadership. I say "we hope" because that is the gamble we, in the Colonial Office, have taken on you. Kindly do your best to justify it.'

Though his tone had been as cutting as his words, the flicker of a smile had escaped once or twice, as if by permission, through his beard. I got the notion that the smiles meant, 'You incredible young ass! Can't you see *this* is the way round to put it to your uncles?' But when I gave him back a timid grin, he asked me sharply why. I answered sheepishly that he had eased my mind, because truly, truly I didn't want to go ordering anybody round any more than he wanted me to.

At that, his manner changed again to one of sprightly good humour. He began to tell me a whole lot of things about a cadet's training in the field (or, at least, the training he thought I was destined to get in the Central Pacific) that nobody else had ever hinted at. As I understood the burden of it, it was that I would serve my first year or so of probation on Ocean Island, the administrative capital of the Protectorate, where I would be passed from department to department of the public service to learn in successive order, from a series of rugged but benevolent Heads (all of whom quite possibly harboured a hidden passion for the writings of R.L.S.) the basic functions of the Secretariat, the Treasury, the Magistrate's Court, the Customs, the Works Department, the Police, the Post Office, and the Prisons organization. I don't know what magic he used – he certainly never spoke above a chirp; but he managed to make that arid list of departmental names roll from his lips like the shouting of golden trumpets upon my ear. I had a vision as he spoke: the halo he had mentioned burst into sudden glory around my head . . .

. . . It was dawn. I was hurrying, loaded with papers of the utmost import, through the corridors of a vast white office building set on an eminence above a sapphire ocean. I had been toiling all night with the Chief Secretary, the Treasurer, the Magistrate, the Collector of Customs, the Commissioner of Works, the Chief of Police, the Postmaster General, and the Keeper of the Prisons. The job was done! I had pulled them all through. Just in time! There in the bay below lay a ship with steam up, waiting for final orders. I opened a door. A man with a face like a sword – my beloved Chief, the Resident Commissioner himself – sat tense and stern-eyed at his desk. His features softened swiftly as he saw me: 'Ah . . . you, Grimble . . . at last!' He eagerly scanned my papers: 'Good man . . . good man! It's all there. I knew I could trust you. Where shall I sign? . . . God, how tired I am!' 'Sign here, sir . . . I'll see to everything else . . . leave it *all* to me.' My voice was very quiet, quiet but firm . . .

'. . . and remember this,' broke in the voice of Mr Johnson, 'a cadet is a nonentity.' The vision fled. The reedy voice persisted: 'A cadet washes bottles for those who are themselves merely junior bottle-washers. Or so he should assess his own importance, pending his confirmation as a permanent officer.'

He must have seen something die in my face, for he added at once, 'Not that this should unduly discourage you. All Civil Servants, of whatever seniority, are bottle-washers of one degree or another. They have to learn humility. Omar Khayyam doubtless had some over-ambitious official of his own epoch chiefly in mind when he wrote "and think that, while thou art, thou art but *what thou shalt be*, NOTHING: thou shalt not be less." Sane advice, especially for cadets! Nevertheless, you would do well to behave, in the presence of your seniors, with considerably less contempt for high office than Omar seems to have felt. Your approach to your Resident Commissioner, for example, should preferably suggest the attitude of one who humbly aspires to "pluck down, proud clod, the neck of God".'

Who was I, to question the rightness of this advice? I certainly felt no disposition to do so then (I don't remember having felt any since) and, as he showed no further wish to pursue the topic, I passed to another that had been on my mind. A marriage had been arranged. My pay as a cadet would be £300 a year, plus free furnished quarters. Did he think a young married couple could live passably well on that at Ocean Island? I pulled out a written list of questions about the local cost of living. At the word 'marriage' he started forward with a charming smile, light-stepping as a faun, whisked the paper from my hand, laid it on the mantelpiece, and turned back to face me: 'Ah . . . romance . . . romance again,' he breathed, 'a young couple . . . hull-down on the trail of rapture . . . the islands of desire . . . but there is method, too . . . let us look before we leap . . . the cost of living! A business-like approach. Very proper. Well . . . now . . . hmm . . . yes . . . my personal conjecture is that you should find the emoluments adequate for your needs, provided always, of course, that you neither jointly nor severally acquire the habit of consuming vast daily quantities of champagne and caviare. Remember, for the rest . . . in your wilderness . . . how the ravens fed Elijah . . . or was it Elisha?'

And that was that about the cost of living. I was too timid to recover my list from the mantelpiece.

Thus finally primed in the Colonial Office for exploding as a bottle-washer upon the Gilbert and Ellice Islands, I sailed with Olivia from England on March 6th, 1914.

Pacific Tramp

We reached Australia in a liner designed for the delight of passengers; we wallowed out of Sydney harbour, towards the end of April, in a craft of more romantic dedication. She was Burns, Philp and Company's steamship *Moresby*, a typical Pacific tramp of those days – 1,300 tons register, thirty-three years old, but still A1 at Lloyd's and still game to plug her stinking way at the rate of six knots an hour through any weather to any palm-green shore where pearl-shell or bêche-de-mer, shark-fins or copra were to be picked up. By the time we met her, her battered hull, surviving god-knows-how-many hurricanes at sea

8

and casualties by reef or shoal, had puffed with unconquerable patience across three-quarters of a million miles of empty ocean (by the captain's reckoning) and pushed its grimy nose through every remotest archipelago of the Pacific. The captain, a minute Cockney as way-worn but steadfast as his ship, would talk to us for hours about her achievements, his brown eyes tender with love; but the chief of all her virtues for him was her iron hull.

'Look at those lovely plates!' he would exclaim, pointing to the incredibly buckled decks. 'All bent to hell, but not a leak in 'em anywhere! Because why? They're beautiful soft iron, not this here cheap steel. She can knock her way into lagoons through horses' heads and coral mushrooms . . . crack-crack, like that, port and starboard, the dear old what-not, just taking a few more dents in her old bottom but never springing a blanky leak anywhere.' A sweet old lady she was, he always finished up, a sweet old lady. She must have been, in her fashion, for the memory of her still tugs somehow at my heart; but she had not been designed for the comfort of land-lubbers like us, nor had her business occasions sweetened the smell of her for our kind of noses. She reeked of dead shark, putrid oyster and rancid copra from stem to stern of her aged body, and the ruinous wooden hutch on the forward well-deck where we tried to sleep was undoubtedly the chief concentrating-point of all her odours. Then, too, there were the cockroaches.

Those three-and-a-half-inch monsters, fattened on the oily refuse that clotted every crevice of the holds, swarmed up at night into our bunks, looking for a change of diet. Pacific cockroaches eat feet. They would willingly devour any other exposed part of the human body, for that matter, if one let them; but the tickle of a dozen or so on a hand or face usually wakes a sleeper before they can get down to a meal. A foot, though, is a different proposition; the thick skin on the sole is insensitive, and the victim feels nothing until they have gnawed that down to the quick. When he does wake, the ball and heel have been stripped pink, and he hobbles for the next week or so, to the exquisite enjoyment of all true sailormen and shell-backs. I know, because it happened to me in the *Moresby*. It was then that I heard for the first time that side-splitting joke, so gloatingly reiterated by shell-backs for the comfort of green-horns: 'Take it easy, son: it's only the first ten years in the islands that's hell!'

We did learn later to accept cockroaches as domestic pets (or almost) for, in the Gilbert Islands, whenever foul weather threatened, whole rustling clouds of them would come flying into the house for refuge. Once lodged, they stayed for weeks; so we decided at last to count them in as an essential ingredient of Pacific romance – it was either that, or die of daily horror – and our only incurable pedantry about them in the long run was to keep them, if or when possible, out of the soup. It was fortunate, nevertheless, that we did not reach this stage of civilization in the *Moresby*, because, but for our first maniac terror of the brutes, we might never have slept on deck. The captain had strong ideas about the propriety of such a thing for a young woman. Nothing but our most haggard entreaties persuaded him to let us, at last, drag our mattresses up to the boat-deck amidships. Once we were there, however, he gave us a tarpaulin sheet for extra cover against rain squalls. We needed it a lot at first, but the weather cleared as we slid past the Santa Cruz group; and then we found out what it was to lie at night over-leaned by nothing but a firmament of flaming stars – for the tropic stars did flame for us, just as the travel books had promised. The nights were amethyst clear and cool. Eddies of warm air, loaded with earth scents and jungle dreams from islands beyond sight enmeshed us and were gone again. The swing of the old ship was so quiet, she seemed to be poised moveless while the stars themselves were rocking to the croon of the bow-wave, back and forth above her mastheads, as we lay tranced with watching.

There were Gilbertese deck-hands in the crew, copper-skinned boys, thick muscled and short in the leg but as active as cats in the rigging. They were shy with strangers, stern featured and remote-looking when they worked alone. We thought them dour folk until we saw them get together. That was somewhere on the edge of the tropics, when the trousers and jerseys that had veiled the glorious moulding of their bodies had been discarded for the belted waist-cloths, trimmed to the knee, of ordinary island wear. They had been called to the forecastle-head to heave an anchor inboard for cleaning. We saw them cluster in silence, a group of bronze statues by the catheads, while the boatswain's mate, an Ocean Islander, interpreted the first mate's talk. There was hardly a move and never the hint of a smile among them until the officer walked away. We wondered why he had left them standing so unresponsive there; but 'you watch 'em' said the captain. Magically, as he spoke, the tough masks relaxed and were turned with grins towards one man of their number – not their official leader, the boatswain's mate, but a massive, towering fellow, who still stood utterly smileless. The captain said he was their licensed wag: it was up to him and nobody else on board to start things humming. He had his joke all ready cooked up behind those brooding eyes. It was a crack, as we heard later, of the most joyous ribaldry about the ancestry of anchors; he delivered himself of it in a high feminine shriek, tottering towards the side in perfect simulation of senility. The air suddenly rang with answering laughter; the crew leapt alive; the anchor came aboard in no time to the accompaniment of hoots and horse-play. When the job was finished, they stood around holding hands and chattering for a while, to look at what they had done, like satisfied children or artists well pleased with their handiwork. Then, one by one, they drifted off to their separate tasks, each wrapped again in the cloak of his austere silence.

One evening, we heard them singing on the forecastle-head. We could make out, from where we listened, a circle of sitting shapes, their torsos stippled in black against the night sky. Their heads and shoulders were bowed, their voices muted; the queer inflections of their chant were cadenced, even for our alien ears, with grief beyond bearing. We knew it could not be one of the ancient island sagas of war or wonder-voyage that we had read about. We were to hear many of those later, triumphantly intoned, in the packed meeting-houses of the Gilberts; but this was a new song and a sad song made by one of the crew for love of his cruel lady. I got the words of it from Teburea, the boatswain's mate, before we left the ship. He wrote them down for me and I still have the paper; here is the ungarnished translation of them:

11

I am sore-hearted for you,
Do not make me kill myself.
How great is my frustration
Because you give me no reward!
I am sad, I am sad,
But I can hide my sadness from you,
If you will only say that one day
Perhaps I shall have my reward.

Teburea told me that the suffering poet could not, for shame of seeming boastful, himself join in the singing. His part was to teach his song to friends who loved him, and sit weeping in their circle while they sang it for him. They too wept as they sang, Teburea said, because they knew their tears would make their friend a little happy, and because the words were very beautiful, and because all of them were sick for their own sweethearts, over there across the sea to eastward. Or perhaps, if they were not sick for sweethearts, they wanted to see their fathers and mothers again. 'Me sick, too, for my old man,' Teburea finished simply (I know now that he meant his adoptive grandfather), 'he love me too much; me love him too much, too,' and walked away.

It began to dawn on me then that, beyond the teeming romance that lies in the differences between men – the diversity of their homes, the multitude of their ways of life, the dividing strangeness of their faces and tongues, the thousand-fold mysteries of their origins – there lies the still profounder romance of their kinship with each other, a kinship that springs from the immutable constancy of man's need to share laughter and friendship, poetry and love in common. A man may travel a long road, and suffer much loneliness, before he makes that discovery. Some, groping along dark byways, never have the good fortune to stumble upon it. But I was luckier than most. The islands I had chosen blindly, for the only reason that they were romantically remote, were peopled by a race who, despite the old savagery of their wars and the grimness born of their endless battle with the sea, were princes in laughter and friendship, poetry and love. Something in the simple way Teburea had spoken of that love song and the singing of it gave me a sudden inkling of things to come. I felt in my bones I was going to a place that, for all its remoteness, would prove to be no strange land for me.

Island of Dust and Dreams

We raised Ocean Island, via Solomon Island ports, on the morning of our seventh day out of Sydney. It was one of those burning days of the doldrums, when the sea is glassy but not still. The solemn swells that came pulsing up out of the south were unruffled by any breath of wind, but the huge heave of them told of storms far away. The ship swung dizzily from valley to burnished mountain-crest and back again to shining valley as she laboured her way up to the island. We heard the boom of the breakers from miles off shore as they crashed upon the reef. It was a sound new to our ears, a note of majesty once heard, for ever remembered. It seemed unbelievable that the sweep of that thunderous attack could fail to engulf the tiny hump of land – not 2,000 acres of it in all – so forlornly crouched between the vastitudes of sky and sea.

The shudder of Ocean Island's narrow reef to the shock of the surf is familiar to people who live there. The old fishermen who used to dwell in the water-side villages would whisper to each other, when they felt it, 'Behold, Tabakea moves a little!' Tabakea was the great turtle at the bottom of the sea, who balanced on his back the thin column of rock that carried their home like a coral mushroom-head on its top. One day, they believed, Tabakea would move too much, and Baanaba (The Rock-Land – that was their name for it) would topple over and be engulfed in the roaring waters. But the thought did not trouble them mightily, for they knew that their hero ancestor, the far-voyager, the all-conquering warrior and lover, Au-of-the-Rising-Sun, who had pinned Tabakea down when his people had made the place their home, would see them safely through the end. Every new dawn was his repeated guarantee of that. So, when someone whispered, 'Tabakea moves a little,' it was enough to answer, 'The Sun rises!' for everyone to be comforted again. And, awaiting the end, they treated the imprisoned giant as a friend and helper, as was only proper, because he too was an ancestor; the Turtle had been the god of the men whom the People of Au had overwhelmed, and so also the god of their widows and daughters. These had been taken to wife by the womanless invading horde for the raising of a new stock of Baanaba. But their subjection had not made them false to the faith of their fathers; their constancy saw to it that the children they bore to the invaders should inherit the cult of the Turtle not less than the cult of the conquering Sun-hero. Though Au remained the triumphant Lord of Heaven (*Taumarawa*, the Holder-of-the-Skies), Tabakea sidled his way through the nurseries at sea-level, so to speak, into the daily life of the people. He became *Tau-marawa*, the Holder-of-the-Ocean. It was to him that the new generation turned to pray for good fishing, and, above all, for safe goings and comings through the dangers of Baanaba's terrible reef.

The fisherman's notion that the land was perched on a column of rock was not so very wide of the truth. Ocean Island is nothing but the tip of a vast pinnacle upthrust out of the depths. At two cables' lengths out from the reef in Home Bay, there is a little ledge a hundred fathoms down, over which ships can tie up in fine weather to colossal buoys that carry the world's deepest moorings. Only a bare half-dozen cables' lengths farther to seaward, the bottom has plunged to nearly two thousand fathoms. In other words, the hundred-fathom mooring-ground is a mere niche by the pinnacle's crest, chipped out of a two-mile precipice that soars almost sheer from the ocean's abysses. It may be not even a niche, but a cornice of reef-coral overhanging the black deeps. If that be so, it follows that the island's cliffs have slipped six hundred feet lower today than once they stood, for the polyp that builds reef-coral is a creature of the light – its extreme living depth is within one hundred and twenty feet of the surface. It is sure, in any case, that the towering pinnacle has been the plaything of vast movements in the ocean's depths.

Aeons ago, its crest must have lain under water, yet just near enough to the top for the reef-building polyps to live there, for it was capped in that age with a platform of coral rock. Perhaps, when the reef broke surface after countless centuries of growth, the grinding of the surf for countless further centuries of disintegration formed a bank of coral sand upon it; or perhaps there was simply a sudden upheaval of the peak to tremendous heights above the sea. Whichever it was, that solitary perch in the midst of the mighty waters became the sanctuary of unnumbered sea birds. There were so many of them and they stayed for so long, that their droppings covered the coral platform with a bed of guano forty feet deep and tens of millions of tons heavy.

That was the age of birds; it was ended by a subsidence; the island disappeared, and the age of fishes began. One relic that remains for man out of the era of engulfment is the fossil tooth of a shark so enormous that a motor lorry could be driven through its reconstructed jaws. The heaped bird-droppings, overlaid by the rich refuse of the depths, suffered a sea-change from guano into phosphate of lime. Then again the ocean's bed was convulsed, and the coral platform with its load of precious phosphate was pushed three hundred feet above the water. It did not sink again. New generations of polyps got to work to build a cornice of reef around the island's foot; birds flew in from places afar bearing seeds in their feathers; the land was covered in scrub that rotted, and grew, and rotted again, to form a topsoil of black earth; a forest of great calophyllum trees appeared on the heights.

Maybe it was not so very many millions of years after the last upheaval that seafaring men – the people of Tabakea, the People of Au, and who knows what other land-hungry swarms before them – arrived and built their villages above the south-west facing bay. Only a few score centuries more were to pass from then until the Pacific Islands Trading Company, scouring the archipelagos for cargoes of guano, chanced upon the vast deposit saved on Ocean Island out of the gulfs of time.

The Company, never a very rich concern, was tottering towards financial collapse in the late eighteen-nineties. Its old ship, the *Ocean Queen*, sailing out of Melbourne, Australia, had helped to rake all the known guano-islands of the Western Pacific clean of their deposits by that time; persistent search had failed to discover any worth while new sources; a day came when the directors knew that a single speculative voyage would probably land them in the bankruptcy court. They decided to go out of business before worse happened. It was a bleak look-out for everyone at the table. They called in young Albert Ellis, the supercargo of the *Ocean Queen*, and broke the gloomy news to him.

But Albert had a bright bee in his bonnet. Their sad looks only made it buzz the louder. 'Wait a minute . . . wait a minute!' he shouted, dashed out of the room and returned at a run carrying in his hand a queer-looking chunk of putty-coloured rock. Everyone recognized it. He had used it for several years to prop open the door of his office. 'This,' he said, 'was given me by a friend, who picked it up at Ocean Island. I believe . . .'

'Yes, yes,' they cut him short wearily, 'you needn't go on.' He had said the same thing before, a dozen, a hundred times. He believed the rock might have phosphate of lime in it. But they believed otherwise. They were so certain he was wrong, nobody had ever even thought of having the thing analysed. They scoffed at his plea for an analysis now, at the eleventh hour. 'Fortune doesn't play fairy-godmother tricks these days, boy,' they said. 'Now drop it and hop it.'

But he was not to be put off this time. He could ill afford to pay for an analysis himself, but he rode his hunch and took the rock to an expert.

A week or so later, he stalked into the directors' room again and reported what he had done. 'I'm not asking for a refund of the fee,' he told the astonished board, 'because I think you're going to raise my pay quite soon.'

'My poor boy,' answered the fatherly managing director, 'you shall certainly have your money back. Foolish as you were, you acted in our interests and you shan't lose by it. But we can't raise your pay. The firm is closing down.'

'Oh-no-it's-not!' shouted the irrepressible Albert. 'You just take a look at this report,' and slapped the paper on the table. The analyst had recorded a ninety per cent phosphoric acid reaction to his tests. The rock was made of the purest phosphate of lime yet discovered in a natural state by man.

On the strength of that report, a Melbourne bank granted an

overdraft that enabled the Company to send the *Ocean Queen* prospecting up to Ocean Island. She returned, her holds crammed with the putty-coloured rock, bought piecemeal from the Baanabans in exchange for tobacco, beads, knives, prints, and calico. The profits from this first yield paid for a better-fitted second voyage; and so on; the business never looked back. The Pacific Islands Trading Company became the millionaire Pacific Phosphate Company; this, in its turn, was converted into the British Phosphate Company, which again, a few years later, became the British Phosphate Commissioners, a nationalized industry owned jointly by the governments of Britain, Australia and New Zealand. Albert Ellis finished his career as Sir Albert, a Knight of the Order of the British Empire and Phosphate Commissioner for New Zealand.

The romance of the Company, however, was far from being the first point to strike us as the old *Moresby* brought us lurching into Home Bay. What stood out initially was a dreadful, corrugated-iron factory building above the water-front, from which enormous clouds of dust were being thrown sky-high. It was the crushing-mill of the Company, busy pulverizing its daily quota of a thousand tons of phosphate rock for the export market. The dust it flung up drifted heavily down the still air, to load all the greenery of the island's flank with a grey pall. Its belchings seemed to us as grossly out of place as a series of eructations in the face of the infinite. Yet the major impertinence was ours; the unmannerly monster we saw before us was helping to keep a million acres of pasture-land green in Australia and New Zealand; and, but for its disfiguring industry on Ocean Island, there would have been little enough revenue to maintain services for the thirty thousand Gilbertese and Ellice folk who lived by their bright lagoons in the atolls to east and south. But, though the first shock of our disappointment was tempered by no such mature reflections, we did not have to stand nursing our peevishness for long; a boat was riding the mighty procession of swells a mile off shore, awaiting our arrival. The ship swung to give it a lee, and Methven came aboard.

Stuartson Collard Methven was the Officer-in-Charge of

Police, Ocean Island. It was not his business, as such, to board ships for the Customs, or the Post Office, or anybody else. But there were Ellice Islanders in the police force, and no race in that ocean of sea-princes ever produced a more superb breed of surf-riders than theirs. So it was a hand-picked crew of Ellice Island policemen who manned the government's boat for every purpose, and where they went Methven went too, in whatever weather. That is the sort of man he really was; he and his wife Ruby were to be our very dear friends a little later; but he was not actually bursting with *bonhomie* that day. The mails from the *Moresby* were, of course, worth coming out for, but the idea of hoiking ashore a curio called a cadet – a phenomenon until then most happily unknown in the Central Pacific – *and* his wife (heaven pity her whoever she might be), *and* their frightful luggage scratching the boat's beautiful paintwork to hell . . . well, I ask you, he said. We know he said it, because Ruby told us so in due course, and anyhow, we saw it sticking out of every angular Scottish inch of his six-foot-three, as he walked up to us like a one-man procession in resplendent ducks.

'I am Methven,' he opened, and added after a pause, 'the Police Officer,' with the courteous grimness of an executioner announcing his functions. 'If you are the new What's-It from England I'm to take you ashore. Will you please introduce me to your wife . . . Thank you . . . And is that your dunnage down there?'

When I explained that there was still a big box to come from the baggage room, he exclaimed, 'Oh, my God!' in a high, shaken whisper, and walked away to give some orders. On his return, he said, 'I suppose you've seen to the Way Bill,' and when I asked what the Way Bill was, he whispered 'Oh, my God!' again, falsetto, but allowed me to gather that the thing was a kind of receipt for the mails, which I should have saved him the trouble of signing. So I went and did it at once, and that was my very first official gesture in the service of His Majesty overseas. I felt the job had been done with considerable *éclat* until Methven asked me if I had counted the mail-bags I had signed for. When I said I hadn't, he exclaimed 'Oh, my God!' yet again, but this time on a bass note strangled with suffering.

The top end of a Jacob's ladder hung over a ship's side is the only part of it made fast to anything. It follows that, when the ship rolls towards that side, the bottom end swings gaily out over the depths, only to crash back against the plates when the roll is reversed. The terror of the landsman at the bottom end is the greater or less in proportion to the extravagance of the rolling. Olivia was near the bottom when the prize-winning outward swing happened. The accompanying downward plunge caused an uprush of air beneath her skirts which lifted them over her head. Skirts were worn voluminous in those days; Olivia's got so firmly entangled with her hat that the downward draught caused by the following upward rush failed to dislodge them. She groped her way blind after that, through a series of sick swings and crashes, until her questioning feet found no more steps to step upon, and she was left dangling in the void by her hands only, for somebody to do something about. It was Methven who did it. He grabbed at one of her wild legs as they swung out at him, and gave a good strong jerk. She came apart from the ladder like plucked fruit, and hurtled down upon him. I saw him crumple under the impact and collapse beneath her in the stern-sheets. His only remark when I got into the boat was that women ought to be careful to wear bloomers for occasions of that sort in the Pacific. I agreed with him cravenly. Olivia either did not hear him or was past caring, for she was being sick into the deep blue waters.

The swells got steeper where the bottom rose towards the reef. As their racing slopes snatched up our stern and tossed it high, the oarsmen fought to keep pace with the forward 'scend of them, and the boat drove on, impossibly tilted, into valleys that forever fled away from under the plunging bows. But the bronze giant at the steer-oar stood easily poised on the tiny locker-deck behind us. His bare feet braced against the gunwales, he swung in lovely rhythm to the heave and thrust of the seas upon his oar, and sang aloud for the joy of his mastery as he brought the boat swooping like a gull towards the boat harbour. His voice cut across the crashing diapason of the surf with the gay challenge of a clarion. When we came to the very edge of the reef – so near it seemed nothing could stop our onrush into the maelstrom – he called of a sudden, 'Easy!' The crew lay on their oars and waited. The passage into the boat harbour, a narrow channel blasted through the reef, was a few lengths ahead, its entrance wide open to the giant seas. The lesser surfs were breaking short of the entrance, and the back-suck from the brimming harbour basin – we could hear it snarling – fought their furious invasion to make a hell's cauldron of the passage. No boat could live in that raging battle of waters. The only safe way in was to ride on the crest of a wave so big that it would sweep the boat well down the passage before being undercut by the back-suck. We lay rearing and plunging while the steersman picked his wave. It came, house-high: 'Pull!' he yelled as its forefoot lifted the stern. We shot forward; the crest swung us towering; the crew spent their last ounce of strength to hold it; we held it – we were riding Leviathan – we were flying – we were halfway down the passage. The crest began to topple and foam overside. The wave hollowed itself for breaking, and the boat's nose was pushed out into the void over its forefoot. There was a sizzling downward rush through ruin as it collapsed; the sea came boiling in over the gunwales; the life went out of the boat; we were labouring, half waterlogged. But we were safe in the still water of the boat harbour.

Methven had sat bolt upright through all this, with a look of petrified correctitude upon his countenance. It somehow emanated from his total silence that the people of his clan regarded the demeanour of a royal mummy as the only proper one to adopt in the presence of the sea's contemptible nonsenses. Nevertheless, we supposed he actually had noticed something a bit out of the ordinary that day, because he did turn to the happily smiling steersman and murmur, 'Nice work, Sergeant Kaipati, very nice indeed!' before we tottered up the steps of the boat jetty.

From the boat jetty we climbed again, up the steep incline of a narrow-gauge cable-way which handled all the Company's imports in those times. The first terrace in the island's westward slopes was at the top. There stood the Company's trade store and office. Strung out farther to the left, above the curve of Home Bay, were the electric power house; the machine shop, the crushing mills, the drying plant, the cold storage works, and the locations of the thousand or so Gilbert Islanders, Ellice Islanders and Japanese who worked under indenture as mechanics or boatmen, carpenters or miners for the Company. The bungalows of the European staff – forty or fifty of them maybe – straggled up the hillside above, pleasantly scattered among trees. But along the flagrant quarter-mile of factory buildings and workshops, hardly a green thing was to be seen.

We passed through the brazen heat and clamour of it ridiculously perched upon minute flat-cars furnished with benches far too high for safety. These were pushed by poles in the manner of punts – but at breakneck speed – along a narrow-gauge railway line. The benches were built to suit the length of Methven's legs, but not ours. He was propelled ahead of us alone, sitting purchased by his heels, whatsoever the angle or velocity of his car, as firm and majestic as a monument of Caledonia. We rocketed after him together, legs flying, and clutching at each other despairingly for lack of any other hold. Fat, apricot-coloured children near the line laughed with delight as we went whizzing by. I mention the journey because it was the occasion of my first considered resolve upon a matter of dignity in the service of His Majesty. I decided that, if it was given me to survive, I would have the height of at least one bench lowered, so as to accommodate it to the length of my own particular legs, not Methven's.

But the pace slowed as we took the slight gradient beyond the locations; suddenly, too, we were out of the torrid glare and running in the latticed shade of palms. The din of machinery was magically snuffed out as we rounded a bend; the dwellings of a Baanaban village over-arched by palms came in sight on the seaward slopes below us. We caught glimpses, through twined shadow and sunlight, of crimson and cream hibiscus, of thatches raised on corner-posts, of neatly matted floors beneath them, of bronze bodies in brightly coloured loin-cloths. We heard the chatter of laughing women and the shouts of children across a murmur of surf that rose muted through the trees. Scents of gardenia and frangipani floated up to us mixed with savours of cooking. The grim civilization of Home Bay lay forgotten, as though a thousand miles away. The village was gone again in half a minute, but its spell stayed with us. We felt we had passed, in that flash of time, through a miraculous gateway opened for us into the real, the homely heart of the Pacific.

We reached the government siding and got down from our cars. A hundred yards up-hill from there, we came upon a squalid-looking wooden bungalow, without side-verandahs, perched among rocks. The rear edge of its floor squatted up against the hillside; the front edge was propped, visibly sagging, on concrete stilts. Part of the space between the stilts had been boxed in, and the hutch so formed, said Methven, was the Post Office. On the top side of the floor were all the other offices of the Headquarters Administration of the Gilbert and Ellice Islands Protectorate, a total of three rooms. A typewriter had been installed in one of them. Nobody yet knew how to use it. It awaited introduction to me, but the pleasure would have to be delayed until Monday, as this was Saturday afternoon.

So this was the vast white office building with corridors, *et cetera*, of my vision in London. But no – Methven must be pulling my leg. How could all those departments that Mr Johnson had reeled off – the Secretariat, the Magistracy, the Treasury, the Customs, the Public Works, the Police Administration, the Prisons Organization, not to speak of the Resident Commissioner's personal group of Secretaries and so forth – I mean to say, I said, how could so many senior officers with their senior assistants, their junior assistants and all their respective clerical staffs possibly be crowded together into three little rooms?

It clearly pleased Methven to answer that one. This wasn't a rabbit-warren like the Colonial Office, he explained. People *worked* here. There was first the Old Man (in other words, the Resident Commissioner) who operated as his own Chief Secretary, Private Secretary, District Officer and Magistrate, except, of course, when his wife interfered. The Secretariat, as I had called it, consisted of a Clerk. Presumably, when I spoke of the Treasurer, I meant the Accountant, who comprised the entire financial personnel, besides being the Postmaster General, the

Collector of Customs, the staff of Landing Waiters, the Immigration Officer, and what-not-else of the kind. That made three Europeans, then came himself: he as Police Officer, was in charge of the Prisons too, and, as the prisons supplied a labour force, it followed that he also functioned as Superintendent of Public Works, Chief Sanitary Inspector, Conservator of the Water Supply, and manager of about a million other things that pertained to the upkeep and welfare of the government station. Fifth, there was myself, who (as everybody hoped) would be fairly divided between all of them from the word go, and not merely collared as a private slave by the Old Man.

I gathered from his tone that there was a good deal of local feeling about that.

We learned, further, as we trudged past the Police Barracks and Prison, up the steep mile to the Residency, that the rest of the Protectorate's European staff consisted of a doctor employed on Ocean Island by the Company, but subsidized by the Government for public health duties; another doctor in charge of a Government hospital in Tarawa, 250 miles to eastward; and four District Officers scattered singly, at distances ranging from three to five hundred miles away from us, up and down the chain of the Gilbert and Ellice groups. It came to me then that, however else we might be maintaining dominion over palm and pine in this particular corner of the Empire, we certainly were not doing it by weight of numbers. This, in some strange way, easily compensated for the loss of my dream-office teeming with busy bureaucrats. And, besides, there was the music of the lovely island-names that had rolled from Methven's tongue – Butaritari, Tarawa, Abemama, Funafuti – Abemama above all, where Stevenson had lived a while and written. I mentioned his piece on the Gilbert Islands to Methven; 'Never seen it,' he replied (Oh, sprightly shade of Mr Johnson!). 'Here's the cricket field and there's the Residency straight ahead.'

We had reached an open plateau overlooking the tremendous emptiness of the ocean to south and west. The northern edge of the cricket ground lay cool beneath a green bank fringed with coconut palms. Behind the palms stood the Residency, a pleasant white bungalow, backed by a towering forest of calophyllum trees. A slim white-clad figure was waiting for us at the top of the broad front steps.

'That's the Old Man,' said Methven: 'he won't ask you to tea. Come and have some with us when he's finished with you.' His voice was warm of a sudden, but he left us to go forward alone.

Old Man of Ocean Island

Edward Carlyon Eliot, the Resident Commissioner, was struggling at the time of our arrival to improve the conditions that governed the mining of phosphate on Ocean Island. His aims were to secure for the Baanaban villagers an increase of the tonnage-royalties paid into a trust fund for their phosphate, and to set up guards against the premature encroachment of the diggings upon their villages. He won his fight eventually in the teeth of much official misunderstanding. Fifteen years later, as Resident Commissioner myself, I was called to add a little to the foundations he had laid, and others added more after me. But it was mainly due to his courage and foresight between 1913 and 1920 that the Baanabans of 1945 found themselves in a position to buy an exquisite new home for themselves in the Fiji group and to migrate there in their own good time. I was greatly fortunate to have him as my first chief, for he was a personification of the protective spirit which did inspire the best servants of autocracy with benevolence in the field, whatever may be said today about the system of their allegiance.

He was healthy for me in another way, too, though the pleasure of it was at the time not so obvious. The prospect of having a cadet to lick into shape did not entrance him. There were reasons for this. His parents had not been rich and, as a youth, he had been obliged to forgo for the sake of a brilliant elder brother in the Diplomatic Service a number of things that it hurt him to miss, including his hope of a university education. I never heard him complain of it, but the handicaps he had suffered and the very success with which he had overcome them had affected his attitude towards beginners. He had started his own official career, while still in his teens, as a clerk of the fifth grade in the civil service of a Caribbean colony. From that 'back-stairs entrance to the Colonial Administrative Service', as he bitterly chose to call it, he had fought his way up by the time he was forty-one to be Resident Commissioner of the Gilbert and Ellice Islands. His achievement had shown him that a university degree was by no means an essential preliminary to getting on in his profession, which was all to the good; but it had also left him with a basic contempt for beginnings less difficult than his own. His generosity, so ready in other directions, was not predisposed in favour of young men like myself, who came out from Downing Street (so he said) with reach-me-down official futures all ready packed in our suitcases.

Another neat thing he used to shoot off about my species was that we thought we had been despatched across the starlit foam with special warrants in our pockets to dispense celestial wisdom direct from the Colonial Office to the benighted inhabitants of the Empire. As a matter of fact, there was a good deal more in this than an ironic twist of phrase. We were not at that time sent out trained in advance for liaison-work in the field as cadets are trained today. Nor were the senior administrative officers in the Colonies who had themselves started as cadets always careful to bludgeon us into habits of co-operation with other departments. On the contrary. The result was the spread of a poisonous kind of snobbery throughout the administrative branch, which encouraged its members, young and old, to regard themselves as unquestionably superior, clay for clay, to the members of other branches. The internal frictions engendered by this attitude militated heavily against the effectiveness of inter-departmental collaboration in the field, often to the incalculable cost of colonial populations. A good many years were to pass before a system of pre-service training designed to avoid these evils came into being. But pending that kind of improvement from the Downing Street end, my Resident Commissioner was certainly taking no chances with the likes of me. He did not, of course, cram everything down my throat at our first talk; nor, as far as I know had he any prepared series of deflationary utterances laid up in pickle for my education over the weeks and months to come. He proceeded, rather, by the catastrophic method. His most instructive sallies – I mean the ones that sank in deepest – always leapt out of him impromptu under the goad of my many stupidities. Nevertheless he did give me quite an insight into his feelings on the day of our arrival.

While Mrs Eliot talked to Olivia on the front verandah, he took me into his office and sat me before his desk. He was a neat, slim man of medium height with the very black hair and rather Phoenician features one sometimes sees in Cornwall. His slightly close-set dark eyes, overhung by thick, straight brows that almost met above the narrow nose, were as watchful and veiled as a poker player's. He had a habit of twitching his toothbrush moustache and sniffing twice, staccato, from time to time as he examined people or things. Going with his saturnine looks, it always struck me as strangely sinister.

I remember he asked me first if I played cricket. When I said I liked it, he replied, 'Well, that's *one* good thing, anyhow!' in a way that left me wondering what next. I did not have to conjecture long. He went on, with irritation in his voice, 'You know, Grimble, you ought not to have been sent here really. This isn't the sort of place for a cadet. I didn't ask the Colonial Officer for one. I asked for an experienced man – someone who knew about men and affairs.'

There wasn't much I could say to that. I sat sweating while he gave me his ideas about the right man for the job. What he wanted was someone who had knocked around . . . not an official . . . preferably a fellow who had done a bit of trading and planting somewhere. A sahib, naturally . . . right kind of breeding, right kind of school . . . all that. But definitely not a cub from a university. Above all, *not* a heavenly-born selection from the Colonial Office.

I forget what I replied to this (if anything), but I recollect asking him if I could get lessons in Gilbertese from someone on the island, and the request seemed to brighten him for a little. He said the Government would pay the official interpreter to teach me. He turned gloomy again, though, in the course of wondering how the Colonial Office thought he was going to train me in other ways. He supposed he would have to take me to sessions of the Magistrate's Court and the Native Court, for one thing; and then I could learn a bit about correspondence from the clerk at head office, and book-keeping from the accountant, and police and prisons stuff from Methven, and so forth and so on. They could doubtless teach me a few odds and ends not yet revealed to either Cambridge or the Colonial Office; and outside the Government staff there were, of course, plenty of other people on the island aching to teach me what was truly what.

I remember that his last words gave me another of those sudden visions I used to get. It was not as sanguine as the one I had had with Mr Johnson. I saw myself standing (for some peculiar reason) on the sun-smitten railway line above the crushing mills, hemmed in by a circle of Company's men with hairy forearms and noble looks enhanced by the walrus moustaches of my uncles. They held themselves erect in silence, arms folded, looking at me with contempt in their eyes for my gross ignorance of everything a real man should know.

As a matter of fact, I could not have been more mistaken about the Company's staff. Olivia and I were to find out almost at once that our ignorance could not have fallen among friendlier neighbours; only the vision was depressing in its moment. But for all that, there was a lot of comfort, too, in what Mr Eliot had said. He obviously had no ambition to collar me as his private slave; I wasn't to suffer the strain of continuous proximity to the deity, and there wasn't going to be any fighting over my body. What with the relief of this thought, plus the fulfilment of Mr Johnson's promise that I would start off as a washer of bottles for bottle-washers, plus the happy spell our first sight of a Baanaban village had laid upon both of us, I left the Residency reflectively, perhaps, and somehow not game to tell Olivia quite all the Old Man had said, or the way he had said it, but by and large a reasonably happy young man.

CADET IN ACTION

The Bottle-washer

The comfortable course of my education as a Bottle-washer for bottle-washers was very early interrupted by tragedy. Only three weeks after our arrival at Ocean Island poor kindly Darbishire, the clerk in charge of the Resident Commissioner's office, died of dysentery, and I had to act in his stead until we left Ocean Island for the Gilbert group nearly two years later. A fortnight after Darbishire's death the accountant had to go on sick leave. According to him, the anxiety of having me near his books had a lot to do with his condition. Nevertheless, the Old Man made me responsible for the next six months, jointly with Methven, for the local book-keeping and customs work. The chaos we made together of the book-keeping, and the names we called each other in the process, cemented the warmest of friendships between us.

The combination of office chores, attendance at magistrate's sessions with the Old Man, and getting ready for my examinations in law and language made a fairly hard day's work as a rule, but not quite as hard as it might sound to a modern ear. There was no wireless station yet on Ocean Island. Our overlord, the High Commissioner for the Western Pacific, was 1,200 miles away in Fiji – a month's distance by mail via Sydney. Besides our business, he had the affairs of the British Solomon Islands, the British New Hebrides and the native kingdom of Tonga to attend to, and he was always busy, too, with his other job as Governor of Fiji. What with one thing and another, he did not overload us with questions of detail, and I was not usually so burdened with clerical duties in that ramshackle office squatting on the hillside that I could not squeeze in a little field work.

Field work meant for me, among other things, picking up what I could of building methods. District Officers had to design and put up a number of things like houses and boat harbours for themselves in those days, and the Old Man's idea was to get Methven to educate me a little in such matters before I began to run away with Empire-building on a grand scale. It was a very good idea, and I liked it, if only because I nursed a notion that I had a real flair for public works. But it was anxious going for Methven, and it occasionally cost the taxpayers a lot of money. The termination of my course of study came rather suddenly in connexion with a matter of water-supply.

Water was a problem on Ocean Island, as everywhere else in that droughty Group, and Methven was doing his best to cope with it. New 20,000-gallon storage tanks of concrete were being laid down all over the Government station as fast as they could be built. One of the first out-door jobs I had to learn was how to blast twenty-foot pits for them in the rocky earth. The actual work was not difficult. You got someone to drill holes in several rocks; you pushed sticks of gelignite, with detonators and fuses attached, into the holes; then you tamped them in, lit the fuses and ran for your life.

I chose the Residency backyard for my first independent blasting operation. A cistern had been ordered for it, and I thought it would be a nice surprise for everyone to find a beautiful, big hole all ready for the concrete work. My only real mistakes were that I chose a Saturday afternoon, warned nobody, put down 100 per cent too many charges, and used 100 per cent too much gelignite in each of them. The initial result was an aggregate explosion of volcanic force. The surface of the backyard rose bodily into the air, to overhang the Residency in the form of a black cloud. Boulders of gigantic size rained from the cloud and fell crashing through the roof into the dining-room. The Resident Commissioner and his lady were taking their siesta at the time. They addressed me at once and both at once from the back verandah, in their underclothes. But they did not continue long, for this was not the end. One of the fuses had burned slower than the rest. A second explosion – trifling compared with the first yet still a thunder-blast – roared out. My chief and his partner fled to cover, and so did I, in the opposite direction.

The next morning, after an interview which need not be recorded, my Chief addressed the following minute to Methven –

O/C POLICE AND PRISONS, OCEAN ISLAND
Please note that I have today prayed Mr Cadet Grimble, in the interests of public safety, to abstain from indulgence in public works of any kind. Mr Grimble has kindly assented to my petition. You may accordingly regard his course of education in this direction as now concluded. As to his training in other outside duties, please be good enough to see that his genius is henceforward kept exclusively engaged in the boarding of ships under your most rigorous personal supervision.

E.C.E.

Methven considered this document to be so educative in itself that he invited me to take a copy of the text before returning it to the Old Man, endorsed –

RESIDENT COMMISSIONER
Noted for immediate action. Thank you, Sir, sincerely.

S.C.M.

*

A mile inland from the Residency, due north through the deep forest of calophyllum trees on the island's crest, was Buakonikai, a village of four hundred souls. The other seven hundred Baanabans were distributed between Tabwewa, Tabiang and Uma, which stood sheltered among coconut-palms along the rocky south-west coast. Tabwewa and Tabiang were perched on the steep hillside above small, beached coves, but Uma on the southern promontory of the island (we called it Solomon's Point) was different. Its brown lodges went right down to the sea-shore, for the point had collected a big flat of sand from the tide-rips that scoured Home Bay, and space was there for men to dwell near their canoe sheds.

Except that there was no lagoon, Uma nestling so snug by the waterside was very much like a hundred other villages I was to see in the Gilbert Islands later, and it will do well enough for all.

Above the beach, just within the shade of the seaward-leaning palms, were the cook-houses and canoe sheds, mere thatches raised on stilts, the cool and quiet resorts dear to the aged. If ever you wanted an old man to talk to, you would always find one dreaming the drowsy hours away where his beloved canoe lay housed. If it was an old lady you sought, you would discover her, as like as not, in the screened cook-house, guarding the earth-oven of her household from the wicked spells of enemy sorcerers.

Deeper among the trees, the *mwenga*, or dwellings, stood ranged with careful art on both sides of a broad main street that followed the shoreline, the deep eaves of their thatches falling to within a boy's height of the ground. Their floors of coconut-leaf midribs laid across joists were raised like decks two or three feet clear of the soil, to let the cool air breathe below them. There were no walls to shut out the sane winds of heaven, only screens of plaited leaf hung within the eaves, ready to lower against prying eyes or stormy weather. Two trees supplied all the material needed for building these airy lodges; thatch, rafters, joists, and corner-posts came from the pandanus; the coconut-palm gave leaves for the screens and fibre for string to lash the parts together, as well as midribs for the decking. There were no nails, no dowel-pins. Where the main timbers crossed or were spliced, the barred and chequered patterns of the lashings were the pride of the builders.

The mwenga were set back five yards or so from the roadside, with white-shingled spaces before them. Palms stood in the wide intervals between home and home, their crests spreading arches of latticed gold and green above the silver-brown thatches. There was dappled shadow and sunlight below. The deep green of bread-fruit trees and the flaming vermilion of poinsiana made an avenue down the roadway. Everywhere there were *crinum* lilies at your feet, that grew like tiger-lilies, but waxen white, in orderly shingled borders and clustered in starry clumps up against the tree-trunks. Crimson of hibiscus and scarlet-gold of Barbados pride burned insolent and tender round the lodges. The weft of frangipani perfume stealing across a warp of sea-scents from the reef made a net of fragrances, languid and sharp together, that enmeshed the life of the village day and night.

Walking down the bright avenue, the white man had no need to pry if he wanted to see the villagers at home. The people did not use their screens to shut out friendly eyes or conversation. Men back from fishing or cultivation loved to loll at ease on ther floors, smoking and bandying talk from house to house. Women and girls sat brushing their hair, braiding flower-chains, changing garments, bathing children, plaiting mats, chattering all the time, but alive to the littlest thing that passed in the village street. If you wanted a silent and reflective stroll, you avoided a village, for it was almost beyond human power to resist the temptation of their charming and curious gossip. Everything was news for the villagers, especially the women.

You might contrive to avoid sitting or standing talk, but there was always that bare minimum of conversation you must give to everyone who greeted you. The form of exchange never varied:

Villager: 'Sir, thou shalt be blest. Whence comest thou?'
Self: 'Sir (or Woman), thou shalt be blest. I come from the south.'
Villager: '*Aia!* And whither goest thou?'
Self: 'I go northwards.'
Villager: '*Aia!* And what to do in the north?'
Self: 'Just to walk.'
Villager: '*Ai-i-ia!* We shall meet again.'
Self: 'We shall meet again.'
Villager: 'So good-bye.'
Self: 'Good-bye.'

And if you met the same person again on your way back, which was most probable at the idle hour of the sundown stroll:

Villager: 'Sir, thou shalt be blest. Art thou back?'
Self: 'Sir, thou shalt be blest. I am back.'
Villager: 'And whither now?'
Self: 'I go to my house.'
Villager: 'To do what in thy house?'
Self: 'Just to sit down.'
Villager: '*Ai-i-ia!* We shall meet again.'

33

Self: 'We shall meet again.'
Villager: 'So good-bye.'
Self: 'Good-bye.'

*

I ventured once in the very early days to tell the Old Man that I found these exchanges a little redundant. He bent his thin dark look on me; 'You probably think, Grimble, that you're here to teach these people our code of manners, not to learn theirs. You're making a big mistake.'

He only gave one of his curiously narrow-nosed double-barrelled sniffs at my denial, and continued: 'Well . . . I'll tell you something that happened to me not long ago. I carpeted the Tabiang *kaubure* (village headman) the other day to complain to him about the old men's habit of hawking and spitting when they get excited in the Native Court. I told him he must talk to them about it. My grievance was that a sudden outburst of that kind had drowned my voice when I was speaking to them . . .' He broke off to tell me coldly on a point of my own manners, that he would proceed when I had wiped that grin from my face.

'If I had put the thing to him as an offence against hygiene,' he continued, 'the kaubure would have got on their tails at once, but I didn't. All I talked to him about was the breach of courtesy to me. And this is what he did. He came forward to my desk and laid his hands on mine. Then he looked me straight in the eyes and said, "How can I speak for you to the old men of Tabiang when you did what you did there only yesterday? Even you, who hold us in the palm of your hand?" '

It appeared that, in walking through Tabiang the day before, he had passed between two women – the wife and daughter of an elder – as they were chatting to each other across the road. Seeing them in conversation, he should have stopped before crossing their line of vision and asked permission to go on. There was a proper formula of words for that: '*E matauninga te aba?* (Are the people offended?)' Had he used it, he would have been assured at once that nobody could be the least bit offended. But even then, it would have been proper for him to pass forward with head and shoulders bowed well below their eye-line. His

34

omission of these formalities had been the more astounding to the people because of his exalted rank among them. They had a proverb, 'Small is the voice of a chief,' which meant, in general, that gentleness and courtesy should walk hand in hand with power.

'The kaubure told me all this so quietly,' went on the Old Man, 'that I felt a fearful bounder. Of course, I asked him to take my apologies to Tabiang, and all was well again. But it was lucky for me he had the guts to talk as he did. Sometimes they don't talk, but keep it bottled up, and then things happen, and they get the blame in the long run when the initial fault was really ours. You may walk round the villages satisfied you're a hell of a fellow, while all the time they're thinking what a mannerless young pup you are . . . yes, and forgiving you too, and staying loyal in spite of everything. Let that sink in, and go and learn a bit about them. Yours is the honour, not theirs.'

He made me feel as if the brick he had dropped had been mine, not his.

*

The loving kindness of the Baanabans, in common with the whole Gilbertese race, towards Europeans sprang from no feeling of inferiority, but on the contrary, from a most gracious sense of kinship. Their chief ancestral heroes had been, according to tradition, fair-skinned like ourselves. Au of the Rising Sun with his sister-spouse Tituaabine of the Lightning; Tabuariki the Thunderer and his consort Tevenci of the Meteor; Riiki of the Milky Way, Taburimai the White King, and the woman Nimananoa, the Navigatress – all of these heroic beings, sprung from the branches and roots of a single ancestral tree, were of the red-complexioned, blue-eyed strain called 'The Company of the Tree, the Breed of Matang', from which the race claimed descent in the male line. The Land of Matang, where they dwelt eternally, was the land of heart's desire, the original fatherland, the paradise sweeter than all the other paradises, never to be found again by the children of men. Sometimes its forests and mountains might be glimpsed in dreams, but when the dreamer strove to land upon its smiling shores, they faded

35

away before him and he was alone on the empty waters. Yet, though Matang was lost forever, a cherished tradition said that Au of the Rising Sun had promised to return to his children one day, wherever they might be, with all the heroic Company of Matang around him. So, when white men were first seen in the Gilbert Islands nearly two hundred years ago, the people said (I quote the words of old Tearia of Tabiang, which themselves had become traditional), 'Behold, the Breed of Matang is returned to us. These folk are also of the Company of the Tree. Let us receive them as chiefs and brothers among us, lest the Ancestors be shamed.' Europeans have been called *I-Matang; Inhabitants of Matang* – ever since, and treated always, whatever their faults, with the proud brotherliness due to kinsmen.

*

I worked hard at my Gilbertese, and could make a crude show of talking it in four months. It was time then, the Old Man thought, for me to start learning about native customs. He told me to take lessons first of all from the kaubure of Tabiang village who had so gently reproved him. As a beginning, I prepared a list of questions about how a guest was received by the best Baanaban families, and how he ought to behave in reply. Nothing could have been more apt, as it turned out. Armed with the questionnaire, I went to the kaubure's house-place in the village an hour or so before sunset on the day arranged.

A little golden girl of seven, naked save for a wreath of white flowers on her glossy head, invited me to mount upon the raised floor of the mwenga. As she spread a fine guest-mat for me to sit upon, she told me her name was Tebutinnang – Movement-of-Clouds. Seated cross-legged on another mat, she explained with gravity that her grandfather had charged her to entertain me with conversation, should I arrive before his return from fishing. He would not be very long now; would I like to drink a coconut while she went on entertaining? When I said yes, please, she climbed down from the floor, brought in a nut which she had opened under the trees outside with a cutlass-knife almost as long as herself, sat down again, and offered it to me cupped in both hands, at arm's length, with her head a little bowed. 'You shall be blessed,' she murmured as I took it. I did say 'Thank you' in reply, but even that was wrong; I should have returned her blessing word for word, and, after that, I should have returned the nut also, for her to take the first sip of courtesy; and at last, when I had received it back, I should have said, 'Blessings and Peace,' before beginning to drink the milk. All I did – woe is me! – was to take it, swig it off, and hand it back one-handed, empty, with another careless 'Thank you!'

She did not rise and run off with it as I expected, but sat on instead, with both arms clasping the nut to her little chest, examining me over the top of it.

'Alas!' she said at last in a shocked whisper, 'Alas! Is that the manners of a young chief of Matang?'

She told me one by one of the sins I have confessed, and I hung my head in shame, but that was not yet the full tale. My final discourtesy had been the crudest of all. In handing back the empty nut, I had omitted to belch aloud.

'How could I know when you did not belch,' she said, 'how *could* I know that my food was sweet to you? See, this is how you should have done it!'

She held the nut towards me with both hands, her earnest eyes fixed on mine, and gave vent to a belch so resonant that it seemed to shake her elfin form from stem to stern.

'That,' she finished, 'is *our* idea of good manners,' and wept for the pity of it.

Her grief was the more bitter because this was the first time her grandfather had ever charged her to receive a guest of his. I could not have let her down more abysmally. But one redeeming course seemed still open: I begged her to give me another chance when grandfather came in, and luckily the idea appealed to her. On his arrival, she sat him on his mat, smiled at me and clambered down from the floor to fetch a nut for each of us. I made no mistakes that time; the volume of my final effort shocked me, but it pleased grandfather profoundly and Movement-of-Clouds clapped her little hands for happiness of heart.

It was in my orders to submit written reports on these lessons to the Old Man. In that way, he said, he could keep track of my doings in the villages. I wrote rather fully about the coconut incident, under the heading 'Honourable Eructation', and for some reason of his own he wanted to check up on it. So, one day, we went together by appointment to the village headman's house for an official try-out, but without announcement of the basic motive. A visit from the Resident Commissioner was a big event, and a lot of relatives were there, the women – even small Movement-of-Clouds – all horribly dressed in mission-school Mother Hubbards. I found that rather daunting; also, the presence of my chief threatened to inhibit my output of good taste at the crucial moment. But when I heard the pusillanimous little compromise of a noise, like a politely frustrated hiccough, that he emitted on handing back his nut, I felt that the crumbling prestige of the Men of Matang was mine alone to save in that exquisite village by the sea. It turned me into the champion of a cause – yes, and my effort was indeed the effort of a champion. Au of the Rising Sun himself could not have bettered it. It astounded even our hosts. Movement-of-Clouds shrieked for joy; the rest were convulsed with mixed passions of laughter and fulfilment; people from other houses came crowding round to share the joke; soon, the whole village was rocking with my excess of good manners; and through it all, I, the undoubted hero of the piece, sat gabbling in vain to convince my livid chief that it was one of nature's relieving accidents, the trick of an ailing stomach, an act of God, anything, anything that might serve to save me for a moment from the glare of his cold eyes.

*

People are fond of saying that you only have to set your mind on a thing firmly enough and long enough for it to come your way at last. My own experience in the service has (doubtless healthily for me) not always corroborated this encouraging doctrine, but I have found that Circumstance – or Providence, or whatever else you like to call it – has a way of returning quick and funny answers to a man's more unreasonable disgruntlements. I was taking a sunset walk one day, after about a year on Ocean Island, in a state of noble discontent. World War I, which we called the

Great War then, was nine months old, and I was to be allowed neither to join up nor to go and do a real he-man's job in the Gilbert group. I had no title whatever to go to an out-district, as I had not yet passed my final examinations; but the luxury of life on Ocean Island (with its electric light, frozen meat, fresh vegetables – all from the Company – and mails every month or so) struck me as unworthy of the times. So also did the mainly clerical nature of my duties. I felt that the Colonial Service was turning out, for me, a very soft kind of service. With these thoughts in mind, I came to the inland village of Buakonikai, embowered among its palms and breadfruit trees on the crest of the island.

Looking ahead down the main avenue between the lines of dwellings, I saw a crowd collected in the open space up against the village *maneaba* (speak-house). The gathering was unusual for that time of day, because the sunset hour belonged by custom to the evening meal. They stood in a wide ring, so intent upon something at the centre that nobody noticed me until I touched an elderly man's shoulder. But, when he turned and saw me, he caught my hand in his and drew me forward.

'Look, all of you!' he cried, 'the Young Man of Matang has arrived!'

They evidently felt that my arrival had solved some problem for them, and when they had made a way through for me, I saw what it was.

A naked man of quite outrageous size (or so it seemed to me) was squatting on his heels at the centre of the circle. His shoulders were crouched forward so that his armpits were propped by his knees. His lank hair was in wild disorder, and he had smeared dust on the sweat of his face. A small knife dangled idly from his left hand; in his right was a cutlass, with which he was slashing around at objects in the air apparently visible to himself, though not to us. His teeth were bared in a rictus that struck me as even more sinister than the worst my Old Man had ever directed at me. But he took not the smallest notice of the crowd. It was as if we were not there for him, except that it stuck out of him about as plainly as death that he was alive to every movement we made.

'This man is mad,' explained my companions, quite unnecessarily, and added, 'we hope you will now bring him to reason for us.'

It appeared that bringing him to reason meant leading him to some place where he could be safely guarded until the fit was over.

'He will not resist you,' they assured me comfortably: 'Ourselves he would resist, for he has taken up his knives against us, and it would shame him now not to use them. Therefore, if we go to take him, we must use sticks and knives for our own defence; and this would not be suitable, for we are many, and he is mad, and we should probably kill him, and he is our brother.'

Their conviction that he could not possibly dream of doing violence to me was based upon the one fact that I was a Man of Matang. Not even a madman could forget that, they said. All I had to do was to approach him, take his hands in mine and say, 'Sir, I beg you to come with me.' The point was, I must not forget to use those words 'I beg you.' The high honour of being thus formally entreated by a chief of Matang would probably heal his sick mind at once, as well as oblige him to obey my every wish after that. The bigger the audience, of course, the more excellent the honour would seem to him. They would, therefore, sit in a semi-circle before him, while I went forward to do the doings.

They rushed around collecting fallen coconut leaves to sit upon, while I was left standing to survey my problem. He was still squatting and slashing the air. He must have heard every word of the excited talk, but he gave no sign whatever of appreciating my honourable intentions. The quality of his grin seemed, if anything, even more threatening than before. I could not help feeling that his chivalry towards me was definitely inferior to that of his fellows towards himself. I must confess also to wondering how soon it would be decent for me to get those saving words 'I beg you' said. Was it absolutely *de rigueur* for me to walk right up to him and lay my hands on his before uttering them? Surely this was a most unreasonable stipulation. But my craven thoughts were cut short: 'We are ready,' called a voice, and the babble of talking ceased. The courteous ceremony was now open.

I trod the first fifteen yards or so as delicately as Agag before his murderous Prophet. My eyes saw nothing but the whirling knife. If he didn't stop flourishing it when I got near him, what was I going to do? Walk right into it? My legs began to feel more stick-like even than they were. Oh, *shut up*, shouted my mind, and blacked out. I had no thoughts whatever for the last few paces.

He kept it up, with his teeth bared, until I was within a yard of him. Then he suddenly relaxed and smiled up at me. As I laid my hands on his wrists, I thought I had never seen such a welcome smile in my life before; but I did wish he would drop those knives. He did nothing of the kind; after I had said my piece, he got up, still holding them, and flung his arms round my neck. I heard a murmur of joyful approbation burst from the audience. This was evidently a good show, so far. But for that reassurance, I should have struggled to break out of his grip, for it was throttling me, and the little knife was round by my left ear, and the big one was searching my right ribs, and he was making inarticulate noises in his throat. The longer it went on, and the unhappier I felt, the happier the crowd became, and the longer it went on. When at last he found words, it was to bawl over my shoulder, 'O, Young Man of Matang, I love thee, I love thee!' This was the only protestation of its kind I had ever received from a male, and I did not really enjoy it; but the villagers groaned with delight, 'O, joy! O, blessings! He loves, he loves the Young Man of Matang,' and that encouraged him to further declarations of affection. My face was by this time purple and my hair, in every sense, on end. I don't know how much longer I could have borne the ignominy and terror of it; I don't think the audience would ever have intervened to cut short that riot of improving emotion. It was a sudden new arrival among them that saved me. The first thing I knew about it was the voice of a little girl shrilling from behind my back, 'Shameless, shameless Barane!' At once, my neck was released from the strangle-hold. I flung his limp arms from my shoulders. Barane stood alone with hanging head before the little girl. She was about twelve years old, and flaming with righteous anger. They told me she was his mother's brother's daughter, and he had been her special charge for several years. She certainly knew how to order him about.

'Give me those knives at once,' she shouted, and he surrendered them.

'Now tell this company you are sorry.'

He did.

'Now tell the Young Man of Matang you are sorry.'

He hesitated a little, and then murmured, 'I love, I love the Young Man of Matang. I wish him to go with me.'

'He shall lead you home,' she replied, without consulting me, 'take hold of his hand.' The order was addressed as much to myself as to him. I meekly obeyed it. It would be hard to say which of us looked the more sheepish as she drove us together, hand-in-hand before her, down the village street. I felt I must surely be living up to Mr Johnson's doctrine about the humility of leadership, but the thought gave me little or no sense of dignity.

When he was safely installed at home, I ventured to ask a group of villagers why they had not thought of fetching the little girl at once, instead of giving the job to me, a stranger. They had a perfect answer to that, from their point of view. Their case was that they certainly would have fetched her in the ordinary course, but my sudden arrival had placed an obligation on them. As a chief of Matang, I had the right to the first word and the last word in all things; therefore, the only possible course in politeness was to surrender to me the honour of handling the situation for Barane's family. And besides, it was somehow *kamaiu* (enlivening) when a Man of Matang shared their difficulties with them – much more kamaiu than when they worked alone. I gathered from this that they felt I had enjoyed the evening's fun as much as they had. I did not trouble to disabuse them and, for the rest, what objection could I possible have urged against their generous courtesy of heart towards my race?

*

I had few chances of making mistakes as a boarding officer under Methven's supervision, because it entailed little but sitting in a beautiful thirty-two-foot surf-boat while the peerless crew of Ellice Islanders did all the skilled work. But the business was exciting, as it took in the landing of mails and small cargo for the Government, and this meant going out in all sorts of weather. In the westerly gales that blew up between September and March, the ships in the unsheltered bay lay plunging like frightened stallions a mile or more clear of the yelling reef. It was a hard row out to them in the teeth of wind and sea, and tricky work taking in such things as crates from their slings; also, the surf in the boat-passage could be theatrical beyond imagination; nothing short of perfection in a boat's crew was needed to negotiate it with heavy goods aboard.

The crew was indeed perfect, but when Methven was around he never would allow me out alone in dirty weather, which sometimes embittered me exceedingly. When I claimed to be, after all, an adult, he only laughed raucously and called me 'The Young Blaster' – not *a* young blaster but *the* young blaster, with reference to the backyard incident. But towards the end of 1915 he went over to Tarawa for a while, and I got a real chance of distinguishing myself.

Two days before Christmas, the old *Moresby*, bound for the Gilbert group, came weltering into Home Bay and signalled, about 4 p.m., that she had on board a new porcelain bath and three cases of whisky for the Residency. Would we take delivery at once, please, as a westerly blow had started and the captain wanted to make for Tarawa lagoon that night.

The boat-passage looked awful to me, and I don't think I should have tackled it only for the sake of the Resident Commissioner's bath. But the whisky was another matter; the station was dry of anything but beer, and the cheeriness of our Christmas season depended on the landing of those three cases; they were not for the Old Man alone, but for all of us. A full-blown District Officer, Charles Workman, was staying at the Residency. I had particularly in mind what he might say if I let the stuff go. So out we went.

We found the bath waiting for us in the ship's slings. Have

you ever tried to catch a bath in a boat from the davits of a ship rolling twenty-five degrees? There it goes at one moment, hurtling up and away from you as the vessel wallows to windward; and there it comes now, roaring down at you with the whole ship's side, as she takes her leeward lurch. There is just an occasional second or two between rolls when you can snatch it aboard without scuppering yourself. We waited half an hour for our chance in that brutal seaway; but we did get away with it when it came, thanks to the superb boat's crew. I was so braced with the thing, I sang aloud with the steersman as we shot the harbour entrance. 'This is the life,' I thought when I read the note that awaited me on the boat jetty. The Old Man had watched us through his telescope; he had written to thank and congratulate all of us. 'And please,' his letter ended, 'have the whisky brought straight up to the Residency, and join us in a drink.' It was the proudest moment of my life – except that the whisky was not there. It was in the ship. In the excitement about the bath, I had left without it.

There was only one thing to be done. Dusk was falling when we got out to the ship again. We clawed the three cases aboard somehow, and started off on the homeward pull . . . and we pulled, and we pulled, and we pulled, and we gained not a yard shorewards. No boat in creation could have made it against that current. We were in the wrong end of a tide-rip that was scouring the bay. We found ourselves being swept round Solomon's Point into the open Pacific. In the end, after dark, the ship had to take us all on board, and I slept the night there, except when the captain came to abuse me. It was only at three o'clock the next afternoon that the weather abated and the captain got rid of us. The ship was standing away round the point as we landed.

'Well,' I thought, 'we've done the trick, anyhow. It's still Christmas Eve, and here we are with the goods.' Yes, that again could have been one of my life's high moments – if the whisky had been there. But it wasn't. The boat captain and I scrabbled through every nook of the boat, but it just was not there. And then the piteous truth came out; two men of that devoted crew had risked a lot the night before to get the liquor safely back on

44

the ship when I had gone aboard. Only, they had forgotten to say so before our return to shore. Not a thing could be done about it now. There was the whisky steaming away to Tarawa.

When I got to the Residency, they were all there, the married ones with wives annexed, waiting to greet me. Olivia was there, too. They cheered me from the front steps as I crawled up to them. They clapped me on the back. They were waiting to divide the whisky. 'My word, young Grimble,' they said, 'we'll drink the first one for you when it arrives.' Olivia looked so proud. But forgive me. I cannot go on. In the years that followed, Olivia never once reminded me of that day. Never, at least, until I became a Governor. But then, Governors *need* that kind of reminder.

Lost Paradise

Movement-of-Clouds, the little girl of Tabiang who had taught me party manners, had a grandmother, Nei Tearia, renowned for her authority as a teller of histories. Tearia was a straight, gaunt old woman, high-nosed and keen-faced as a Red Indian warrior. When she went shopping at the Company's trade-store, she would cover herself with a frilled Mother Hubbard of white cotton. But at home in her own lodge, she went proudly naked save for a short kilt of smoke-cured weeds about her waist. She told her stories in a low recitative, sitting very erect, eyes closed to look into the past, while Movement-of-Clouds gently brushed her flowing mane of silver hair. There were scarlet flowers in her ear-lobes whenever I went to see her.

When I had known her for about a year, she told me the myth of man's expulsion from the Happy Land of Matang. Fifteen years later, when she was well over seventy, I took the script back to her for checking. She repeated the story at that second sitting word for word as she had given it before, and I complimented her on the feat. Her austere face was lit by a smile, but she replied soberly (I took down her words), 'Sir, and shall it be otherwise? Each *karaki* (history) has its own body from the generations of old. These are the words of our grandfathers' fathers, and thus we pass them on to our children's children.

How should I change the words that my grandfather gave me as the contents of my mouth?'

Her story of the expulsion from Matang is the myth of a dread being called Nakaa the Judge, the keeper of the gate of death, the law-giver, whose sentence of old drove men forth from the Happy Land and first brought death among them. It is, in parts, astonishingly like the tale of man's fall in Eden; but the grandfather from whom she had it was never christianized, and, for the rest, I found its main elements widely enough known among pagans up and down the Gilbert group to put its native purity beyond doubt. Its moral teaching and the conception of Nakaa as a judge were basic to the ancestor-cult of the Gilbertese theogony.

The godlike beings who sprang with Au of the Rising Sun from the branches and roots of the Tree of Matang (or the Tree of Samoa, as the uninitiated called it) were democratic deities; there was no competition for supremacy among them. But this had not always been so. Far back in the history of the Gilbertese forefathers – or one branch of them – Au had been the head of a theocracy.

Traces of the sun-god's former glory were still easy to see in my day. His clan, significantly named Karongoa of the Kings, enjoyed sacred privileges at every ceremony held in the community speak-house called the Maneaba of Karongoa. Under the shade of that roof, the first portion of every communal feast, the first word and the last word in every debate, belonged to its members. The stud of coral in the middle of the Maneaba's eastern side, against which the clan had its immemorial sitting place, was called faai – the Sun. No man dared contradict a final word whispered – it must always be whispered – from that seat, for fear the Sun might pierce his navel. Although, in ordinary life, the men of Royal Karongoa might be reduced anywhere, by the accidents of faction warfare, to a state of indigence and even bondage, custom still preserved their ritual pre-eminence intact within the precincts of their own maneaba.

The picture reflected as in a glass, darkly, from these stubborn remnants of power outworn, backed by the proud name of the clan, is that of a caste of royal priests who enjoyed sacred privileges and dictated final wisdom in whispers from before an altar-stone in the temple of a sun-god named Au. There is much to support the inference in the secret myth of Au's rise into heaven from the depths, in the names of Au-North and Au-South for the northern and southern solstices, in the hidden rituals that governed the building of the maneaba of Karongoa, in the rites performed by the elders of the sun-clan for the fructification of Au's tree, the pandanus and the eating of its first-fruits.

But the key truths were held concealed down the ages by the clans of the Sun and the Moon, to whom they belonged, and Au – save for his fabled promise to return one day to his people, and the glamour that folk-lore shed upon him as the prince of lovers and far-voyagers – was neither greater nor less for the clans at large than any other hero-god born of the Tree of the Ancestors. Each clan of the Company of the Tree cultivated the guardian spirit of its own branch.

There were a number of offences which angered the tutelary shades and closed their ears to a man's entreaties for good crops or *te mauri*, which is to say, the blessed state of health, prosperity and freedom from the threat of evil spells. The heaviest moral crimes were those of incest and of dishonouring the paternal totem, of desecrating the shrines or refusing to honour the bones of recently dead ancestors, and of failing to perform the pious rituals for straightening the way of a near kinsman into paradise.

Yet, though the ancestral gods made it their business to avenge such sins among the living, they took no part in the judgement of the dead, and none among them was regarded as the originator of the moral code. The law-giver and ultimate judge was Nakaa. Nakaa the Judge was neither fruit of the ancestral Tree nor progenitor of any human stock, but absolute spirit. All wisdom was his. His unsleeping eye could count even the waves of the sea or the grains of sand upon the beach. Not even the Spirits of the Tree themselves could stand before him without fear. It was as much for dread of his eye as for anger of their own that they executed his justice upon living men and women. And when a man died, it was not they, but Nakaa, whom his lonely ghost had to face.

Nakaa sat forever at the narrow gate between the lands of the living and the dead. He held a net in his hand to ensnare all who approached the gate, and beside him was a pit with a row of stakes at its lip. Strangulation in the net was the fate of the ghost whose living kin had neglected to do over his dead body the rituals ordained by Nakaa. Impalement upon the stakes was the price paid in the end by the neglectful kin. The same awaited the incestuous and the eaters of their totems, the desecrators of shrines and those who honoured not their fathers' bones. Strangled and impaled alike were flung into the pit. But the strangled were at least dead forever. The impaled writhed in endless torment down in the nether blackness.

But there was reward for the virtuous. If the ghost was sinless, not even Nakaa could deny him passage to the Land of Shades. He passed through the gate, and onward thence across the sea, to be gathered with his ancestors in the lands of Bouru and Marira, Mwaiku and Neineaba, below the western horizon. Only the perfection of Matang could never be his, because of man's disobedience to Nakaa in the beginning of time.

'Thus runs the history,' said Tearia.

'In Matang of old dwelt Nakaa the Judge, and he had lordship over all the people. The spirits of Matang also bowed before him, for they feared to look into his eyes. But no land ever seen by man was as beautiful as that land. It was great, it was high: many were its mountains; all manner of trees were there, and rivers of fresh water. The trees were heavy with fruit; there were lakes also with abundance of fish. No hunger, no thirst were in that place, never an ill wind visited it, and the people knew not death.

'Nakaa had his dwelling below a mountain, in a spot that was very fruitful. And behold! he planted two pandanus trees there, very wide and tall. One tree stood in the north, the other in the south. He said, 'The men shall be gathered under the tree in the north and the women shall be gathered under the tree in the south.' And so it was; the men turned north, the women turned south; each company turned away with its own happiness; and there was neither death nor grey hair among them.

'But there came a day when Nakaa was to go on a journey. He gathered the men and the women together in the midst between the trees, and behold! they looked on each other's bodies.

'And Nakaa said to all of them, "I go on a journey. See that ye turn away from each other when I am gone, the men to north, the women to south." He said again, "This is my word: there shall be no traffic between the men and women when I am gone." He said again, "There is a mark that I shall know when I return, if perchance the men play together with the women." Those three commands spake Nakaa before he went on his journey.

'And when he was gone, the men returned to their tree in the north, and the women returned to their tree in the south, and each company abode with its own thoughts. So it was for a long time. But their hearts were not at ease, for they had looked on each other's bodies. As it were, their hearts were turned over within them.

'And after a long time it was night, and a south wind moved in the trees. Cool was that wind and sweet with the scent of the flowers of the women's tree. And the scent was blown upon the company of the men where they lay sleeping in the north. Behold! the men stirred, they awoke; their hearts were drawn to the women. They arose. They said together, "We will go play with the women, for the scent of their tree is sweet." See them now! They go forth, they are running, they are beneath the tree of the women, they are playing with the women beneath the tree. Alas! the mark of Nakaa is upon them, but as yet they know it not.

'And after that, time was not long ere Nakaa returned. He arrived, he stood in the midst between the trees, he called the people to him, saying, "Come, gather here before me." They heard his word. They came to bow before him, and when they bowed he took their heads between his hands. He lifted the hairs of their heads with his fingers, he searched here, he searched there; and alas! he found his mark upon them; he saw grey hairs among the black, and he knew they had not hearkened to his word. He said, "Ye have played together under the women's tree," and the people answered nothing.

'And Nakaa said again, "Because ye could not hearken to my word, ye shall leave the land of Matang for ever."

'Then the men and the women entreated him, saying, "Drive us not forth. If thou hadst not gathered us together, we should not have looked upon each other's bodies, and our hearts would not have been overturned. This was thy work." So also the spirits of Matang spoke for them.

'And his heart was softened, but only a little; he said, "Sometimes ye shall see Matang in dreams. Yet ye shall not come near it. Think not to land upon its shores." And when the people wept, he said, "Enough! There shall be no return to Matang."

'He said again, "Here be two trees, the men's and the women's. One of them ye shall take with you, the other shall remain. Which tree do ye choose?" And the men answered, "We choose the trees of the women." And Nakaa said, "Ye have chosen the tree of Death. So be it. The tree of Life shall remain in Matang. Ye shall have Death always with you. And because this is my tree that ye take with you, the ghosts of your dead shall find me sitting at the gate between the lands of the living and the dead; and none shall escape my net or my pit whose way has not been straightened according to my word."

'And he gave them the ritual that is called *Te Kaetikawai* (The Straightening of the Way), saying, "Perform this over your dead, that they may escape my net and ye may escape my pit." And he said, "Let no man lie with his sister, or eat the totem of his fathers, or do dishonour to his father's bones if he would escape the stakes of my pit." And he said again, "Ye shall bury your dead in mats plaited by women of the leaves of the tree of Death. That is also my word to you." These were the judgements of Nakaa when the people had chosen their tree; and we have done his will from that day to this, lest the spirits of Matang turn away from us; for the spirits of Matang fear the eye of Nakaa.

'And when the people lifted the tree of the women to take it away, Nakaa plucked leaves from it. And he wrapped up in the leaves all the sicknesses and pains known to mankind – toothrot, and stomach-ache, and rheumatism, and coughing, and fever, and fading away – a multitude of ills; and he pelted the heads of the people with the leaves; and those things have been with us ever since.

'Alas! there is no return to the shores of Matang, no, not even in dreams. But Au of the Rising Sun will return to us one day with his Company of Matang, for this he has promised. And the gate of Nakaa is not shut for us when we die, for if we obey his words it will lie open before us, and the way will be straight to Bouru, and Marira, and Neineaba. And there we shall be happy, for there the ancestors await us, and we shall be gathered with them for ever.'

Cricket in the Blue

The beginnings of cricket in the Pacific were not invariably attended by the spirit of brotherhood that this noble sport was once believed to inspire. Something went wrong from the start in Samoa, for example. A match there was an affair of hundreds, not elevens; no tally of sides was kept, no amiable warnings of visits were issued; one village simply arose on a day and set forth to give battle to another. 'Battle' is the key word. The marching crowd paraded around the village of its chosen enemies with taunts and brandished bats until these emerged to accept the challenge. The bats, which were made of local hardwood and weighed eleven pounds apiece, were carved into shapes suited at once to conditions of war and peace. Competition was so terrific in the field that winning was a hazardous business. The position of the batsman who scored the winning hit was peculiarly trying. His was the heart of oak who, ringed around by a horde of furious fieldsmen, dared slog his side to victory. Those earliest Samoan matches lasted for weeks at a time and often ended in considerable slaughter. It was excellent for courage but poor for the moral score-board. The Missions rather understandably banned the game for the converts as one unsuitable for aspiring Christians, however militant their church. But I think it had been revived on more neighbourly lines by the early nineteen-hundreds.

Cricket was certainly going strong on Ocean Island when I arrived there. In the fair-weather season from late March to early

October, there were a dozen or more native police out for practice every day from 4 p.m. to sundown, and either a pick-up game or a match with the Company's team was billed for every Saturday at 2.30 p.m. The Old Man had notions derived from the very choicest public schools of his epoch about how often an officer and gentleman of the European staff should turn up at the nets. Every day, barring acts of God or the Resident Commissioner, was the rule for a good little cadet. It was lucky for me, in the circumstances, that I dearly loved the game for its own sake.

The cricket field was still very much in the making at that time. Starting with little but a pitch of tamped earth, over which a strip of coconut matting was laid, Methven and his prisoners had gradually cleared and levelled about three acres of stony flat around it on the Residency plateau. He heartily despised cricket, but he wanted a parade ground for his police. The south and west sides commanded a tremendous view of the Pacific, while palms and forest trees screened the north and east boundaries; but a dozen years were yet to run before any kind of grass began to grow cheerfully on that torrid waste of phosphate dust and rock. Every known variety was tried, and practically everything throve in the wet season, but nothing survived more than a month of the dry spell. When the effort was abandoned after many failures, the flat was triumphantly invaded by the tussocky grass of the island. That looked better to the ladies, but the man never lived who could drive a clean ball through more than sixty yards of it. The consequence was, we all became deliberate moonshooters and cowshooters. It was deeply immoral cricket and, for that very reason, highly amusing. Nevertheless, I preferred the stone age, when a batsman could score along the ground and even a wicked fluke off the edge of the bat could roll as sweetly (for me) to the boundary as the most accomplished leg glance.

The Company had an all-Australian team; the Government could put only two or three Europeans in the field; but half a dozen policemen – and especially the Fijian N.C.O.s – batted and bowled well up to the best of an average English club eleven. Despite that, I don't remember our ever winning a Government–Company Test rubber (for of course we played five

Test Matches a season). It struck me then, and I verified it later in other places, how notably higher the performance of average Australian cricketers was, age for age, than that of their English equivalents. But the ale we drank together after five hours of it under the equatorial sun tasted no less sweet for that. Maybe that was because the Australian ale was almost as good as the Australian cricket, and Australian good fellowship even better than either or both.

The Old Man was anxious to spread the gospel of the game more widely among the Gilbertese. He told me one Saturday to give the first lesson to twenty-two of the Company's labourers whom the police had inveigled up to the field. At the end of the practice, which had not proved very enthusiastic, I asked them if they would like another trial some time. 'Sir,' replied their spokesman with courtesy, 'we shall be happy to come, if that is your wish.'

I explained that there was no enforcement, but put it to him that the game was a good game: didn't he think so too? 'Sir,' he said again, 'we do not wish to deceive you. It seems to us a very exhausting game. It makes our hearts die inside us.'

I naturally asked why, in that case, he had said they were willing to have another go. He whispered seriously for a while with his companion. 'We will come back,' he answered at last, 'on account of the overtime pay which the Government, being just, will give us for playing on its ground.'

Those early teaching days provided some pretty problems of umpiring. In one case at least, no decision was ever reached. Ari, a little quick man, and Bobo, a vast and sluggish giant, were in together when Ari hit what he judged to be an easy two. He proceeded to run two, paying, as usual, not the slightest heed to his partner's movements. The gigantic Bobo ran only one, with the result that both players were at Ari's original crease when the ball was thrown in. But it was overthrown; seeing which, Ari hurled himself upon Bobo, started his great mass on a second run, and then himself careered away on his third. Bobo finished his second, but by that time Ari was back at his original crease again, having finished his fourth. He started on his fifth, but collided with Bobo, who was making heavy work of his third, in mid-pitch. Both collapsed there, Ari on top of Bobo, and Ari's original wicket was thrown down. Which of the two was out? In point of fact, it was Bobo whom we sent back to the pavilion, but that was not on an umpire's decision. It was because Ari's head had butted with great force into his diaphragm and left him gasping for medical aid.

Another case was much discussed. One Abakuka (Habakkuk) so played a rising ball that it span up his arm and, by some fluke, lodged inside the yellow and purple shirt with which he was honouring our game. Swiftly the wicket-keeper darted forward and grappled with him, intending to seize the ball and so catch him out. After a severe struggle, Abakuka escaped and fled. The whole field gave chase. The fugitive, hampered by pads donned upside down (to protect his insteps from full-pitchers) was overtaken on the boundary. Even handicapped as he was, he would hardly have been caught had he not tried there, by standing on his head, to decant the ball from his shirt-front; and though held, feet in air, he resisted the interference with such fury that it took all that eleven masses of brown brawn could do to persuade the leather from his bosom. After so gallant a fight, it would have been sad to judge him out. Fortunately, we were saved the pain, as he was carried from the field on a stretcher.

Ten years later, cricket was popular everywhere, and a better grasp of its finer points was abroad, but odd things still happened now and then to keep us alert. When I became, in my turn, the Old Man on Ocean Island, there was a game between two Police teams in which the umpire of the fielding side, for no obvious reason (since nobody had appealed), suddenly bawled 'Ouchi', which is to say, Out. We were interested to hear what he meant, especially the batsman, but all the answer he gave was 'Sirs, you know now how bad that man is. *O, beere!*' The expletive usually denotes disgust at a nasty smell. We decided that a man's personal odour had little to do with the laws of cricket, and that batsman continued his innings. But, an over or two later, there was a legitimate appeal against him. In attempting a leg hit, he had flicked a strap of his pad and it looked from point's angle as if he had been caught at wicket.

'Ouchi!' yelled the umpire with splendid gusto.

'Ouchi?' queried his victim, 'and for what reason, O eater of unclean things, am I ouchi?'

'Rek piffor wikkut!' The decision was rendered to the sky, resonant with triumphant conviction.

We decided again that the batsman had better continue, but he was so shaken by that time that his stumps were pushed back by the very next ball, a deplorable long-hop.

'Ouchi!' gloated the umpire, 'ouchi-ouchi!' and followed his retreat, prancing with glad hoots, to the very pavilion.

We learned later that the complex behaviour of a light-hearted village girl was at the bottom of this regrettable business. But the sequel to the story has a nicer flavour for cricketers. Both men gave up playing for a while; a few weeks later, however, they came to the Residency hand in hand, with garlands on their heads, to say they wanted to be taken into practice games again. By that time, I knew the background of their quarrel, and said something severe about umpires who imported private feuds into their cricket. 'Yes, Old Man, of a truth,' the offender answered, 'our sin was to play this game while we were contending over that female person. It is not expedient for men at variance about women to be making *kirikiti* against each other, for behold! it is a game of brothers. But now we are brothers again, for we have turned away from that female.' As a matter of cold, hard fact, it was *she* who had turned away from *them*. But that aspect of the matter was, after all, beyond the cognizance of the M.C.C. whereas his finding that cricket is a game of brothers was sound beyond all argument.

But I like best of all the dictum of an old man of the Sun clan, who once said to me, 'We old men take joy in watching the kirikiti of our grandsons, because it is a fighting between factions which makes the fighters love each other.' We had not been talking of cricket up to that moment, but of the savage land-feuds in which he had taken a sanguinary part himself before the hoisting of the British flag in 1892. The talk had run mainly on the family loyalties which had held his faction together. His remark, dropping out of a reflective silence at the end, meant that cricket stood, in his esteem, for all the fun of fighting, and all the discipline needed for unity in battle, *plus* a broad fellowship in the field more valuable than anything the old faction wars had ever given his people. I doubt if anyone of more sophisticated culture has ever summed up the spiritual value of cricket in more telling words than his. 'Spiritual' may sound over-sentimental to a modern generation, but I stand by it, as everyone else will who has witnessed the moral teaching-force of the game in malarial jungle, or sandy desolation, or the uttermost islands of the sea.

2

RECRUITING TRIP

A new accountant had arrived early in 1915. His coming did not bring Methven and me instantaneous relief from Treasury preoccupations, as he kept both of us, for the next few months, constantly busy explaining what had happened to his books. But the worst storms were over by the end of June, and then the Resident Commissioner ventured some light humour. According to him, all my local instructors, including himself, were suffering from nervous exhaustion. Would I be kind enough to grant everyone a short vacation? In any case, I had passed my first language-test and he had decided it was time for me to see something of the other islands. I was to do a trip in a recruit-ship, so that I might learn how the Company collected its Gilbertese labour force for Ocean Island. My function would be to act as doggie – that is, clerical assistant and odd-job man – to Charles Workman, the District Officer who was going to supervise recruiting operations. 'The chief duty of a doggie,' observed the Old Man in despatching me, 'is to behave as little as possible like a pup.'

The company recruited its Gilbert and Ellice workers under indenture for two years' service, in drafts of two or three hundred at a time. One-third of every draft was made up of married men, who were allowed to bring their wives and children with them; the rest were *roronga*, or bachelors. Living conditions on Ocean Island were excellent for married and single workers alike. The recruit-ships were handsome vessels of 6,000 tons or more with covered decks and spacious 'tween-decks admirably fitted for their purpose. The young men flocked to the recruiting tables.

The Company, which became the British Phosphate Commissioners, a nationalized industry, in 1915, was justly proud of its record as a thoughtful employer; I do not suppose its care for the welfare of native labourers has been often equalled or ever bettered in any other part of the British Empire. One way or another, the Gilbert and Ellice Islanders had to be prepared, in a world from which they could not remain forever segregated, for the shock of new ideas and disturbing influences from outside. Fate could not have given them a kindlier or more profitable teacher. Missionaries had brought them schools, the British administration had assured them protection in their homes, and they had learned from trading ships something about the value of their goods to the white man; but it remained for the phosphate industry alone to endow them as a nation, from 1900 onwards, with a sense of their own personal value to the world at large. From Ocean Island they got a working knowledge of Europeans in the mass, a standard of the manual skills needed to compete with the demands of civilization, and real opportunities of learning and exploiting such skills. What the Company and later the Commissioners gave them was, in effect, a kind of university where in a happy indigenous environment, they could graduate from the state of neolithic fisherfolk into beings with a technique and a morale sufficient for their survival under the inevitably increasing pressure of modern cultures. If the Gilbertese have outlived today, without loss of their national *élan vital*, the disintegrating effects of the Japanese invasion of 1941 followed by the American occupation of 1943, this miracle is greatly due to the new interest values, standing for a bridge of hope into the future, which the phosphate enterprise built up in them over the first forty years of the century.

*

Our big ship came up to the entrance of Tarawa lagoon a little before sunset. 'So this is a coral island,' said Olivia, who was coming round with us: 'Where's the lagoon? And is that all the land there is? I thought it was going to be a circle.' We were creeping up dead slow over coral heads, on a bearing by a beacon on a sandbank five miles east of us. The land was three miles to southward – a low, straight line of palms that tapered away to nothing over the horizon behind the beacon. There was a smudge on the horizon to north-east; it looked like a separate island about ten miles off. Running away due north was a reef drowned under surf, and beyond it emptiness. Save that the water ahead was calm, there was little to show that it was a lagoon enclosed by land on all sides but the west.

The picture in our dictionary showed an atoll as a small ring of sand and coconut-palms around a dead flat lagoon kept fresh by the ebb and flow of ocean tides through breaks here and there in the land. Marakei in the Northern Gilberts is indeed rather like that – a ribbon of palm-green not more than twelve miles round; the regular golden circle of its beaches, closed save for one tidal passage, encompasses a sapphire lake forever exquisitely at rest. But five of the other atolls are straight, lagoonless strips open on every side to the big Pacific rollers, and, though the remaining ten have lagoons, they are very far from circular. Their twisted shapes, cut into short lengths by tidal passages, appear from the height of the soaring frigate birds like clasped necklaces of narrow green beads flung down at random on the deep azure of the ocean. But it is as if the western side of each necklace had failed to float, for there, instead of land, is a sinuous line of half-submerged beads – the barrier reef which, broken at intervals by deep-water channels, divides the ocean's darkness from the burning colours of the lagoon.

Olivia's difficulty as a sightseer in Tarawa lagoon was its size. Though it had less than the area of Butaritari, Nonouti or Tabiteuea, more than the half of Middlesex could be dropped into it with room to spare. Afloat on one of those big inland seas, where the containing land never rises as much as ten feet above high water, not much of your island is visible at a time. It is the twenty-mile atoll curved in a deep and regular bow – like

Abaiang and Abemama, whose names mean Land-in-the-Wind and Land-of-Moonlight – that fills the eye with most delight. There, nothing is out of sight, yet everything seen carries vision outwards to infinity . . .

Your canoe is racing in mid-lagoon to the clip of the joyous trade-wind. Away to eastward beyond turquoise waves, the beaches of the near mainland flame golden above their emerald shallows. Waterside villages glow homely golden-brown against shadows of violet within the forest of palms. Beach and village and forest are fused in a single purple blur as they dwindle north and south towards the horizon. In the northern and southern bights the land is hull down, but its palms are seen etched tenuous on the sky-line, like the lashes of a great blue eye serenely open to the great blue dome of heaven. Along the bowstring of barrier reef to westward, a few islets vivid as gems float palm-tufted amid the rainbowed tumult of the surf. The blue-black ocean lies limitless beyond them. You shout for the immensity and the friendliness of it all as your lean craft hurls itself, shuddering as if for gladness of the wind's urge, through the singing water . . .

The captain of our ship would not take her into the lagoon before daylight. He lay at anchor in the twenty-fathom water outside the reef while the Company's Recruit Manager and I went ashore by boat to report to the District Officer, Charles Workman. The moon was high when we started. At noonday, the lagoon colours are sheeted flames of cobalt and viridian, agate and emerald so fierce they sear the sight. But under the milk-white glamour of the moon that night, the cobalt was changed to murex, the viridian to green-purple and purple-green; the glare of white-hot light among the sands was muted to an amethystine glimmer; and where blind emerald had flared across the shallows, there was a mother-of-pearl translucence. Light and colour and peace were fused for me in a single rapture that beat like a gentle pulse over the water. The waters themselves were so pellucid, our boat seemed poised on some shining essence of dreams as it glided over coral head and sandy bottom. Scents of flowers grateful for the cool of night beneath the palms came out to meet us as we waded shoreward over the lambent shallows.

My houndmaster for the trip, the famous Charles Workman, was a dashing giant of six feet five inches, idealist, classical scholar, Regency buck, and Elizabethan buccaneer rolled in one, and a man of puckish humour. He loved to face people with situations, and I think my gangling looks always tempted him to peculiar indulgences of his passion. He heartily endorsed the Old Man's view about the puppishness of cadets in general. He did not actually mention mine in particular, but observed that a recruiting trip with the likes of him would do the likes of me a power of good. The first job he gave me to do, however, had no connection with recruiting.

It was nearly midnight when the Recruit Manager and I reached his quarters. There was a small trading steamer (*not* one of Burns, Philp and Company's, I hasten to add) lying in the lagoon, and her captain was ashore with him, sitting hunched up on the verandah floor and groaning as if in great pain. 'The drunken old sailor,' said Mr Workman when we were settled in chairs, 'wants more liquor, which I refuse to allow. That is his immediate cause of complaint. But beyond it, he has another. He was picked up and thrown overboard from his own ship this morning by the second engineer.'

It was difficult to extract details from the captain, but one gathered from his story that the second engineer was the terror of the ship – a man of gigantic size and demoniac temper. Everybody, according to the allegation, thought he was more than a bit mad. After he had flung the captain into the lagoon, the whole ship's company had fled ashore; so there he was now, alone, stamping the deserted decks.

'This,' said Mr Workman, 'cannot be tolerated for a moment . . . not in my District. The fellow must be apprehended; he must be haled before my court. And you, my lad,' he added, 'will effect the arrest.'

'What – me?' was all I could find to say at the moment.

'You,' he confirmed, with a note of unmistakable unction in his voice, '. . . and you alone. A most instructive experience for a cadet! How I wish I were in your shoes! Now, attend to me closely. He is a European. There must be no initial show of force by our rude island police. You will proceed to the ship at 7 a.m. in the station bum-boat, rowed by a single native constable. You will go aboard alone. You will produce the person of the accused in court before me at 8 a.m. precisely.'

We put the captain to bed between us. After a little more talk on the verandah, Mr Workman drew up his towering height of brawn and bone to run a reflective eye over my unimpressive physique. 'It might be as well,' he murmured, 'if you were to avoid any attempt at man-handling the accused while taking him into custody.' Then he and the Recruit Manager retired to their rooms.

The captain was snoring already. I spent the rest of the night wheedling from him a sworn statement to back the warrant of arrest. Every time I woke him up, he called me something different. I disturbed Mr Workman at dawn to get his signature to that warrant. That was not a popular move, either. When I ventured to quote the Pacific Order-in-Council in justification, he replied, 'My good man, I happen to be a Barrister-at-Law. If you ever study the admirable Institutes of Justinian (or was it Gaius?) as I did, you will meet with a maxim to the effect that the Law cares nothing for trifles. However, give me the document.'

He added with a remote smile as he signed, 'Now remember. Leave the policeman in the bum-boat. He will pick you up if you are unfortunate enough to be thrown overboard. Good-bye.'

The so-called bum-boat was in one of the canoe sheds. She was a rickety nine-foot dinghy with rowlocks for a pair of sculls up in the bows. With the policeman and myself aboard, she took in a lot of water amidships. A fresh wind was raising quite a lop in the lagoon, and the going was uncomfortable; but I got a little unexpected relief as we drew near the ship; there were several white men walking about the boat-deck. 'At least,' I thought, 'the crew have returned. I shan't be quite, quite alone with this murderous maniac.'

A giant shape was leaning over the rail by the ship's ladder. He was glowering down straight into my eyes. He had a most frightful walrus moustache; there could be no mistaking the huge, bristling bulk of him, the wild and sullen look; that gorilla was my man. I tried hard to think only of the grand old

British Raj as I went up the ship's side. It afforded me, I regret to say, not a grain of comfort.

'Are you William Clarence W—?' I heard myself asking. He heaved himself upright, to overhang me like a cliff, and replied in a growling bass that he was, and who the blank might I be, if it wasn't too blankly much to ask. I informed him with modesty about myself and added huskily, 'I hold a warrant to arrest you on a charge of criminal assault.'

He stepped back and stood glaring while I recited the usual warnings; then he spoke, as if groping in a haze; 'Well . . . spare me days . . . criminal assault . . . arrested . . . what . . . by *you*? Here, *gimme* that blanky paper.' He snatched the warrant from me. As he finished reading it, he emitted a hoarse bellow, which brought the first mate running. Now for the trouble, I thought; but instead of attacking me he looked down into the dinghy, burst into a howl of laughter, and said, 'All right, I'll come quiet, you poor little pup.' That beastly word again.

The whole ship's complement draped itself over the rail to watch us into the boat. 'Now, you all keep right out of this,' he bawled at them going down. 'You betcha life,' replied the first mate with a guffaw. They all guffawed. Of course, everyone knew perfectly well what would happen with William Clarence's vast weight in that miserable dinghy. It did. A hundred yards from the ship's side, the lagoon lop filled us to the brim and we slowly sank, all sitting.

My prisoner took charge at once. He had it all planned in advance. 'Leave the blanky policeman to rescue the blanky little boat,' he commanded, 'an' I'll look after you. You're not too good in the water, are you, son?' I wasn't at that time; it was only with a lot of help from him that I got through the quarter-mile struggle to the shallows. 'Hold on to yer old uncle,' he said when the going got really bad, and I did; I had begun to like the chap. His arm was round me for support when we walked into the courthouse.

The place was a single-roomed building of native materials, beautifully cool and spacious; but it had no furniture that morning save a kitchen table, two kitchen chairs, a portrait of Queen Victoria, and a floor mat. Mr Workman sat at the middle of the table, under the portrait, a gold half-hunter watch before him; the captain sat at one end. We stood dripping together on the mat. 'You are thirty-seven minutes late with your prisoner, Mr Grimble,' said Mr Workman, taking not the least notice either of our soaked clothes or our affectionate attitude.

I groaned a few reasons, to which he replied 'Ah' non-committally and read the charges.

'Not guilty,' growled the accused, his arm still firmly around me.

'First witness for the prosecution,' called Mr Workman, looking at the captain. But the captain was incapable of speech; it appeared that he had discovered where the bottle was hidden before Mr Workman got up; it appeared further that this was regarded as my fault, as I had woken him up before leaving to make the arrest. He remained mute even when William Clarence called him a something something.

'Other witnesses?' The question was directed at me.

I reported that, as far as I could judge, the entire ship's company was on board, and had never been anywhere else. I seized the occasion to enter upon a fuller story of the morning's events, but Mr Workman cut me short: 'The court is aware of all the circumstances, Mr Grimble. The court observed them through a telescope. The court is now waiting to know if you took any steps whatever to bring witnesses ashore with you.'

'What . . . all of them, or who, sir? . . . what in? . . . in that little . . . that little burn of a boat?' I said, on an upsurge of the stubborn anger of the meek-hearted. William Clarence rewarded me with a hearty laugh.

'All of them, or who?' Mr Workman asked the captain with no sign of emotion on his face: 'Have you any other witnesses to produce or testimony to offer before the verdict is considered?'

The captain raised his head from the table, leered at the Bench, slipped from his seat, and sank paralysed to the floor.

'No witnesses, case dismissed, court adjourned. And now,' Mr Workman turned a genial smile upon William Clarence, 'I have to thank you on behalf of His Majesty's Government for so nobly rescuing my esteemed young colleague from a watery grave. It shall be recorded in the archives of my District and reported in the most exalted quarters. You will leave this court covered with honour. Having said which, may I venture to ask what you actually did, and why you did it, to this drunken old man? Quite off the record, you know.'

'I threw the old blank overboard,' replied the trustful William, 'because he kicked me kitty.'

'Because he kicked your *what*?'

'Me kitty . . . me little cat.'

'And did he hurt her very grievously?'

'It ain't a her, it's a him, it's a little bull-cat.' William's voice rumbled deeply tender on the bull.

'Well, of course, that explains everything,' said Mr Workman: 'Now let's all go and have some breakfast.'

We left the captain under the table. The Recruit Manager was waiting for us at the house. He also had watched my landing with William and was suitably sympathetic about it. I enjoyed my breakfast a lot – much more than I should have done had I known that, within less than three hours, I should be sampling Mr Workman's humour again before an enthralled audience in the Native Government maneaba.

*

Every Gilbertese village of any size had its own maneaba, or speak-house, in those days. The building was the focus of social life, the assembly hall, the dancing lodge, the news-mart of the community. Under that gigantic thatch, every clan had its or-dained sitting-place up against the overhang of the eaves. Every-body's material was pooled to build it, each clan contributed its traditional portion of work to the construction. One manu-factured thatch-pieces for the roof, another lashed them into place; there was a clan to gather the timbers, a clan to dress them, a clan to lay them in place; and so on for the capping of the ridge-pole, the trimming of the eaves, the setting up of the corner-stones, the shingling of the floor, the plaiting of coconut-leaf screens to cover the shingle and hang below the eaves. The ridge soared sixty feet high, overtopping the coconut-palms; the deep eaves fell to less than a man's height from the ground. Within, a man could step fifty full paces clear from end to end, and thirty from side to side. The boles of palm-trees made columned aisles down the middle and sides and the place held the cool gloom of a cathedral that whispered with the voices of sea and wind caught up as in a vast sounding box.

Our recruiting-table was set, with a clear space before it, at one end of the maneaba, looking down the middle aisle. The space was kept open by a cordon of village kaubure, or headmen, seated cross-legged on their mats in uniform of white duck coats and waistcloths of navy-blue serge. Behind their immaculate and statuesque line sat the packed audience, a tumultuous sea of bronze torsos, its waves crested with the white foam of flower-crowned heads and aflame with the orange and scarlet of trade-store prints. Recruiting operations were as popular with the general public everywhere as with the men who rushed to get themselves recruited. There were fifteen hundred villagers there, by my reckoning, that day.

I sat at the right-hand end of the long table, lost in the delight of my first sight of the massed people in the superb setting of their maneaba. Next on my left sat the Native Magistrate; beyond him were the Company's hand-picked recruiting clerks, the Recruit Manager and, at the far end, Mr Workman. I waited dreamily for my chief to open. The multitude of vivid faces had set me longing for the time when my Gilbertese would be good enough for me to talk easily to such a gathering. I was indeed already addressing that very audience with incomparable oratory in my imagination; they were quivering to the passion and the mirth of it when Mr Workman's cool clear voice interrupted:

'And now, Mr Grimble, as you have passed your initial interpreter's test, you will doubtless wish to tell the assembled people how glad you are to be here among them for the first time today.'

My whole being cringed at once, and ignominiously, away from the notion. I pleaded with misery that, unaccustomed as I was to public speaking – especially in Gilbertese – there were reasons in the name of mercy to spare me this honour. I said that every word of the language had now gone out of my head. I said my memory was always like that, tricky; it ran in the family; two of my uncles suffered the same way. I implored him to say the gracious words for me himself.

The only point he troubled to answer was the last one: 'My dear fellow, *I* don't talk Gilbertese in public. It's far too dangerous. I *invariably* speak through my interpreter. And by the way – before you ask – no, you may *not* use my interpreter.'

So I got up amid a great hush and said (the words are burned on my memory), 'People of Tarawa, this is a beautiful island. This is the first time I have seen Tarawa. I think Tarawa is a beautiful island. This is the first time I have seen it. I think it is very beautiful. I have never seen it before. I think it is . . .'

There are no means of estimating exactly how long I should have continued had not Mr Workman's voice cut in: 'Perhaps, Mr Grimble, we might now with profit pass onward to the next thought. Time flies, you know.'

I had no next thought save a wild desire to have done: 'I think it is very, very beautiful,' I reminded the audience. 'This is the first time I have seen Tarawa. I am glad to meet you today and shall always be very, very glad to meet you,' and sat down incontinently.

I was, of course, aware of some difference of quality between this performance and my recently-imagined eloquence, but I did not expect the storm of laughter that rewarded my climax. It swept the maneaba like a hurricane, and lasted for minutes. The shadows of the soaring roof seemed to rock with it. My usually impassive chief himself was twisting on his chair. Everyone else at the table was convulsed. It seemed an ungracious response to my constantly favourable comments about Tarawa, and it made the worm within me turn. I got up amid the din and walked along to Mr Workman: 'You all seem to be having a frightful lot of fun, sir,' I said bitterly: 'I wonder if you could spare time to tell me why, if it isn't too much trouble.'

He pulled himself together, wiped his eyes and explained. My first assurance of happiness at meeting the people had been successfully put across, but not so the more ambitious repetition, it all turned on the wrong use of the word *ma*, which could mean *and*, *with* or *but*, according to context, and a reckless addition of the prefix *ka* to the word for *meeting*. What I had said in effect was, 'I am glad to meet you today, but I shall always be very, very glad to say good-bye to you.'

Fortunately, this struck me too as funny. I will not claim that my smile was enthusiastic, but it was a smile; seeing which, the stately, big old Native Magistrate, in his beautiful white tunic and belt of office, did a thing that my heart is still wrung to remember, so typical it was of the royal tact of his race. He stood up, walked to my side and, putting an arm around my shoulder, laughed in company with me. The crowd responded with re-newed ecstasies. When they were quiet again he said, still shielding me with his arm, 'You people, we have already heard from Baanaba of this Man of Matang. They say he likes our people over there. We know his heart, and we do not laugh at it. We laugh only because we know his tongue refused to say what was in his heart. The day will come when his tongue will obey him, and then, behold! his words shall blow upon us like a strong wind. May the day come soon. Stop laughing now, and say to him, *Ko na mauri* (thou shalt be blest).'

'*Ko na mauri!*' The traditional words of greeting came roaring back from the crowd while I stood, with my face saved whole, thinking how miraculously this old brown man had divined my secret dreams: '*Behold! his words shall blow upon us like a strong wind.*' It came to me blindingly again in that moment that I had fared across the sea of the world to live in no strange land.

'As you will have observed, Grimble,' said my smiling hound-master, 'we dwell among gentlefolk in these parts,' and I thought that he too was not without intuition at times. Thus prosperously passed the hour of my maiden speech in Gil-bertese, and we got along with our recruiting business.

The dialectic high-light of that particular meeting was con-tributed by a madder-brown lady of incredible age and agility dressed in a short *riri*, the old-time skirt of smoke-cured water-weed. She had sat crumpled up in the front row of sightseers, opposite a gap in the cordon of village kaubure, quietly awaiting the appearance of her adopted grandson at the recruiting table. Aware of her talents, everyone, including the kaubure respon-sible for the break in their line, had of course conspired to secure that exact jumping-off place for her. When the young man emerged from the medical inspection-booth into the space before the table, she nipped through the gap and flung herself upon him. 'Alas!' she shrilled, showering slaps upon his brawny buttocks, 'Alas! Good-for-nothing! Alas! Man without shame, dung of a man! Come home with me at once!' and tried to drag him away. Ignoring massed officialdom when he stood his ground, she turned to face the delighted house, and treated it to a superb oration, punctuated by assaults of ever-increasing vigour upon her victim, about the vileness of his crime in running away to dig the excrement of birds on Baanaba. '*Anaia, anaia!* (Go on, go on!)' and '*Katonua!* (Round off the phrase!)' and '*Kanenea!* (Make it blaze!)' roared back the audience whenever she showed signs of flagging. The Gilbertese believe in encouraging sore hearts to talk themselves out. Speech is privileged for the aged, and the stronger the merrier. A thunder of applause burst forth to reward her crescendo finale.

Mr Workman tapped the table for silence at last. His interpreter stepped out into the arena. 'Now,' began Mr Workman, 'let us carefully examine this lady's protest. We may, perhaps, for reasons of law and tact, pass over her more intimate genealogical reflections. This limits our inquiries to the living generation, namely, the father and mother of the young man before us.' He turned to the interpreter: 'Will you ask the complainant if I may take it as correct that the parents of this young candidate are so averse to his being recruited that the father weeps all day and the mother is sick unto death?'

'It is true, Man of Matang!' she answered.

'She says it is true,' clamoured the crowd.

'Alas, it is a lie,' said the young man simply: 'Woman, thou art to be pitied for thou knowest thy lie.' She slapped his face and sprang away from him.

'He says she lies' – the crowd timed it perfectly – 'Woman, what of that?'

'She lies,' suddenly shouted a male and a female voice together: 'I am his father; I am his mother,' and the two stood up from seats a few rows back from the old lady's.

'Behold! His father and his mother!' vociferated everyone together, 'They say she lies! Woman what now?'

'But perhaps she does not lie,' the Native Magistrate intervened, 'perhaps you do not wish your son to go.'

'Do you wish him to go?' bawled voices.

'We wish him to go,' replied the mother, and the father nodded.

'See now, Magistrate! See now, Woman! They wish him to go,' the audience intoned.

'This, then, is the truth of it,' summed up the Magistrate: 'you wish him to go.'

'They certainly wish him to go,' the crowd came in again like a Greek chorus, as if to say 'We knew it all the time,' which, of course, was a fact.

The grandmother had stood arrow-straight throughout, facing them all as fearless as an old eagle. Mr Workman, admiring her pluck and wishing to save her pride in the end, said to the interpreter, 'Tell her, if you please, that we all understand it was for the love she bears her grandson that she laid this protest before us.'

She swept all of us with her arrogant eyes: 'I have laid no complaint before you. I came to talk not to you, but to my grandson,' she said in a low voice; and then, louder, 'I do not love him;' and finally, at the top of her lungs, 'He is a *nikiranibobo*.'

To European ears, the word ripples with the exact lilt of 'Sing-a-song-of-sixpence'. Not its ripple, however, but the ripsnorting shamelessness of it bursting at siren-strength from those aged jaws, was what made the ecstatic climax for everyone. You could translate all that matters of its meaning by the word runt. But there are ways of saying things, and this way shattered even the statuesque line of kaubure: they rolled on their mats, kicking for the perfection of fulfilment in *nikiranibobo*, and the people rolled kicking behind them. The Native Magistrate himself was sobbing, face between arms, on the table. 'I dare not translate this word, sir,' stammered the interpreter when he recovered himself; 'it is a very old and clever word, but it is not official.'

There were gasps of '*Ko raba, ko raba!* (Thanks, thanks!)' from the multitude, as power of speech began to return to it.

69

The old lady stood as haughty as an empress to take her meed of applause; but it must have softened her heart, for, when the tumult died, she turned and took her grandson's hand. 'Thy sin is loosed. Go in peace,' she said, and the audience roared 'Thanks, thanks!' again as she resumed her seat with the dignity of an all-forgiving saint.

3
FIRST DISTRICT

Measure of a Job

The Gilbert and Ellice Islands Protectorate was turned into a Colony in 1915, but this made no difference to our working relationship with the powers that were. Our Resident Commissioner (in company with his opposite numbers in charge of the British Solomon Islands Protectorate and the British New Hebrides) remained still responsible for his administration to the High Commissioner for the Western Pacific in Fiji. But the High Commissioner, as such, was only one-fifth of a chief. The other four-fifths of him were Governor of the Colony of Fiji, a totally separate and distinct personality. The result was that he operated as little more, for us outside Fiji, than a relaying agent for Colonial Office orders relating to our territories and for the replies which such orders extracted from our respective Resident Commisssioners. As for visits of inspection, no High Commissioner was ever seen in the Gilbert Islands for the first thirty-nine years of their life under the British flag.

Things are better today. In this year of grace 1952, the High Commissionership for the Western Pacific stands at last divorced from the Governorship of Fiji. But even at that, and with air transport (a development as yet far from our most sanguine dreams in 1915) now possibly assured, the High Commissioner will still find it hard to penetrate into every corner of his command. The Solomons and New Hebrides, a curving chain of land-masses 1,600 miles long some 1,200 miles to north and east of a theoretical take-off at Townsville in Queensland, Australia, might seem a fairly compact proposition for flying tours of inspection. But the Gilbert and Ellice Islands colony is another kettle of fish. The hop by air from, say, the Solomons to the Northern Gilberts is about 1,000 miles; from Townsville, about 2,200. A flight down the sixteen Gilberts and the eight Ellices makes a fairly easy run of 650 miles for a sea-plane, with sheltered lagoons here and there available for landings. But the Gilbert and Ellice chain does not make the whole of the Colony. There is the Phoenix group too, 500 miles to eastward of the Southern Gilberts; there are Fanning and Washington Islands, worked as government plantations, 1,600 miles to eastward of the Northern Gilberts; and there is Christmas Island, with its hundred mile-round lagoon and great possibilities of development, 100 miles more distant still. A rectangle drawn on the map of the Pacific to frame every scattered speck of the colony where brown men live, and have the right to see justice or aid brought to them, contains within its limits over one-and-a-half million square miles of ocean and less than 250 square miles of land.

*

A new Cadet had arrived at Ocean Island before the end of 1915; a Cashier had been added unto the Accountant; a wireless station had gone up and two Wireless Officers were installed. The place, as the Old Man said, was stinking with officials.

The twenty-four Group islands, on the other hand, were almost devoid of European staff. Charles Workman had been seconded from Tarawa District to act as Administrator of Nauru, Baanaba's sister phosphate-island recently captured from the Germans; Hyne Gibson, District Officer, Butaritari, was away on sick-leave; Geoffrey Smith-Rewse, District Officer, Ellice Islands, had had no leave for six years and was waiting at Tarawa for a chance to get to Australia, Methven, also at Tarawa, had received permission to join up in Australia for service at the front. Failing reinforcements, a single District Officer in the Central and Southern Gilberts, George Murdoch, would be left to cope with the whole 650-mile Gilbert and Ellice chain.

By early 1916 a proposal put up by Charles Workman to take me and a thousand Gilbertese rank and file to the war had been

71

rejected with a swinging snub. I had passed my final language tests some months before. The law examination was still to come, but I was ready for it. The Old Man thought I had better go at once to relieve Methven at Tarawa, if only to leave breathing-space for my betters on Ocean Island. We sailed for the group towards the end of March 1916.

'We' by that time included Joan Ruth, aged eleven months, in addition to Olivia and me. Our transport was a wooden-hulled monster of 110 tons register, originally built for sail but hur-riedly converted to steam because nobody could sail her. She was reported to be the most unweatherly craft and the un-cleanest object afloat between Sydney and the Golden Gate – it took a lot to earn a name for dirt in that ocean of squalid ships. When we climbed aboard, Olivia said she remembered the stink of the old *Moresby* with nostalgia, as it were the breath of some lost rose-garden. She, and the baby, and the Ellice Island nurse-maid, Faasolo, began being sick within the first few minutes of the 80-hour crossing (240 miles at 3 knots an hour in the teeth of a tremendous trade-wind swell) to Tarawa. I was flat out myself not an hour later.

It was the friendly habit of all good sailormen in those times and climes to offer pork-fat to landlubbers suffering from sick-ness. They said there was nothing like it for settling the insides. They told stories of how, as young men before the mast – always in square rig and generally in the neighbourhood of the roaring forties – they had cured themselves of agonies of vomiting which could otherwise have ended only in dissolution by chew-ing gobbets of the grisly stuff from the brine-tub.

'Not the lean; that's too stringy-like; it must be the beautiful soft fat, like this-here,' bellowed the captain in our foetid little cabin, dangling a fearful, sweating ribbon of it before our eyes.

I was collapsed on the floor beside the nursemaid and the baby's basket. Olivia was lying in the single bunk, even more torn with spasms than I, but it was she who found the strength to say the right thing: 'Take the something stuff away, you silly something!' Her voice rang clear as a bugle on two words that girls born in Queen Victoria's reign simply did not know.

The captain goggled at me for a second. 'Cripes!' he said.

'She's a fair bosker, ain't she, son! Called me a silly something, she did. She'll do all right in the Islands,' and left us in high good humour to our misery.

It was not exactly a triumphal approach to a first command, and, when you come to examine it in the dull light of reason, the command itself, compared for land area, population and wealth with a District of tropical Africa, was not much to write home about. For area, the Tarawa and Butaritari districts together comprised half a dozen bent wisps of coral sand and coconut palms, the biggest not forty miles long or much more than half a mile broad anywhere at high tide. For population, outside a handful of missionaries and traders, there were ten or eleven thousand brown folk in their lagoon-side villages of thatch and rustic timber held together by string. For wealth, the total export of copra and shark-fins was worth less than £25,000 a year in those days. For inward shipping, a trading steamer arrived from Sydney every six months or so, and, once each year (if you were lucky) the London Missionary Society's s.s. *John Williams* showed up from Australia and a recruiting vessel from Ocean Island.

This list of official positives concerning my new charge did not make grandiose public arithmetic, even to my romanticism. And then, one had to take into account the list of domestic negatives. There was no doctor within call most of the time, because the one Medical Officer had to be forever on the move. Fresh milk, fresh butter and fresh meat were unobtainable, as there was no grass fit for grazing. Refrigerators, and therefore also chilled foods and drinks, were unknown. In consequence of these conditions, it was dangerous to keep children there after the age of five or six. Yet the Government gave almost no help (a grant of £60 every sixth year of service) to get an officer's family home. It was normal to get no home news for six, or eight, or ten months together, because of the lack of ships.

But there are ways of looking at things. In the fever-soaked Melanesian Islands – the British Solomons and New Hebrides – a thousand miles to west and south, the conditions limiting leave and home passage grants were just as disgraceful, the all-round health conditions infinitely worse. Many years were to pass before the Colonial Office began to show any sign of caring about the fate of its officers' wives and children anywhere in the Pacific. In tropical Africa, the leave and pay conditions were much better, but, jungle for ocean and continent for island, District Officers there lived lives as hard, and lonely, and dangerous as those of their opposite numbers in Melanesia.

We in Micronesia were pampered by comparison. It was hot, but what R.L.S. wrote of Abemama was true of every Gilbert Island; we enjoyed for nine months of the year a 'superb ocean climate, days of blinding sun and bracing wind, nights of a heavenly brightness.' Malaria was unknown. The only sicknesses we had to be really careful about were amoebic dysentery and paratyphoid. There were no head-hunters as in Melanesia, no open or secret racial hates as in Africa. The Gilbertese had their quota of bad individuals and mass madnesses – they were neither more nor less angelic than any European community in that respect – but a District Officer started out among the great bulk of them, in those days at least, as an honoured chief of the Breed of Matang. Barring the more tragic or sardonic twists of circumstances, he had to be a pretty bad fellow or an outright coward to forfeit the friendship of the average villager. However far from home, or ill, or forgotten by the Colonial Office he might be feeling, it was, in the last analysis, impossible for an ordinarily decent European to suffer in the Gilberts the black loneliness of Melanesian bush or African jungle, for he knew himself surrounded by friends, no matter where he went.

What gave extra value to the friendship of a Gilbertese man was his rugged determination to be a person of his own. He remained inveterately an individual even on the islands where paramount chiefs were most firmly established. It is pretty certain that the last migrating swarm to invade the Gilberts (which came from Samoa some six hundred years ago) set up dynasties of *Uea*, or High Chiefs, on every unit. But the people of the southern islands had done away with Uea, and established democracies instead, centuries before the coming of the British flag in 1892, while, in the northern islands, the only royal lines still securely seated at that date were those of Butaritari, Abaiang and Abemama. The Abemama dynasty was of comparatively new

74

creation – not more than two hundred years old – and the event that brought it into being illustrates just how carefully a High Chief of former days had to observe the independence of his subjects. The Uea in question was Tetoka-ni-Matang of Butaritari, a man much loved by his people. Nobody had the least objection against being ruled by him, according to the tradition, but his brother Mangkia was a bad man. Mangkia was forever breaking a law which Tetoka-ni-Matang himself, in *Kabowi* (conclave) with his people, had passed against the drinking of fermented coconut toddy.

The recognition of drunkenness as a social evil by a rustic monarch two centuries before European influences were felt is a historic fact worthy noting by the way. Even more so is the constitutional method of legislation used by Totoka-ni-Matang. 'In Kabowi with his people' means that his law was made in the maneaba, where every man – whether chief, freeholder or villein – had a hereditary sitting-place and freedom to join in debates. There is proof in what followed that the rights of entry and speech meant something real in terms of democracy, for it was the villeins who took action in defence of the law. They went to Mangkia's house as he lay drunk one day and arrested him.

'And they took him to Tetoka-ni-Matang,' runs the tradition, 'and they said, "We are in thy hand, yet allow us to speak." And he answered "Speak." They said, "Thy brother Mangkia over-passes the judgement that was judged in the maneaba, for he drinks fermented toddy."

'Tetoka-ni-Matang answered, "My heart is heavy for him, for he is my brother." They said then, "Our hearts are heavy also for thee, for we love thee. But this is the way of it: Mangkia shall die or thou shalt not be Uea over us."

'Then Tetoka-ni-Matang begged them, saying "Kill him not but send him away from among us." They answered, "We are in thy hand, yet behold! thou hast begged us. It is good. We will not kill him. We will send him away, according to thy wish."

'So they took Mangkia, and set him in his canoe with food, and sent him away. And many chiefs and freeholders went in their canoes with him. And they all sailed to Marakei, but Marakei drove them off. So it was also at Tarawa. But when they came to Amebama, they were able to land; and Mangkia became Uea of Abemama; and his descendants are Uea there today; and the descendants of Tetoka-ni-Matang are Uea over Butaritari and Makin-Meang.'

The ultimate triumph of the exiled drunkard does not make very gracious reading for teetotallers. 'But lay that aside,' said Airam Teeko of Abemama, himself a chief of Mangkia's line, who gave me the story: 'Tetoka-ni-Matang remained Uea over his people because he would not favour his brother above the judgement that was judged in the maneaba. A wise chief he. Our people do not like to be ruled by rulers who allow them no word in the judgements that are judged.'

This undying independence of spirit, which made the friendship of any average villager worth winning for its own sake, also gave the true yardstick for measuring the size of a District Officer's job. By commercial or cadastral standards, his little flakes of territory made less than a drop in the ocean of Empire economy; by human standards, it depends upon how you count. Ten thousand bodies, white or brown, do not amount to much in vital statistics or power politics. But ten thousand cheerfully pugnacious minds, each one vividly aware of its independence and passionately bent on remaining independent, call for quite a lot of individual attention. The District Officer who, outside his purely clerical functions as correspondent, sub-accountant, customs authority, and postmaster-general of his region, kept level with his island tours, his village tours, his countless interviews, his work with the Native Courts, and the queer surprise-packets that his duty as a leader sometimes pushed his way, lived days not less crowded with delight than labour; but he was a pretty tired man by nightfall. Charles Workman used to put it the other way round. His dictum was that, if you weren't tired, you ought to be kicking yourself, because you must have left a hundred things undone; and I dare say he was right.

Domestic Days

Before Ocean Island was included in the Protectorate (which happened in 1900) Tarawa had been the official headquarters of

76

the group, and there, near its southern end, stood the old Residency looking north over the lagoon, with a flagstaff and a sea-wall of dressed coral blocks before it. As one faced the lagoon, a broad road, bordered by crinum lilies and shaded by palms, led away to the right, two hundred yards along the sea-wall, to the boat harbour. A long, low mole of coral blocks stretched from the boat harbour out across the tidal flat of rust-red coral to the edge of blue water, like a thin grey finger pointing into emptiness. On the left of the house, beyond a clump of bitter figs, were the prisons and police lines. The senior Medical Officer lived over by the thunderous ocean beach near the colony's central hospital. A spare bungalow stood there too, waiting for another Medical Officer who (in those days) never appeared.

The busy village of Betio lay curved around the beach-head of its own bay beyond the police lines, at the southernmost extremity of the land. It was very much the same, on a big scale, as Baanaban Uma, with its canoe-sheds and airy lodges, its lily-bordered avenue and the flicker of shadow and sunlight beneath the moving canopy of its palm-crests. Only the hot crimson and vermilion of poinsiana and hibiscus were absent. All the flowers were starry white. It was as if Nature had conspired there to give tired eyes rest from the flames of beach and lagoon. It was form, not colour, that entranced us in the brown villages of the atolls – the grace of trees overleaning water, the rare sensitiveness of pencilled line and shadow, the matchless transparencies of atmosphere.

An ancient Austrian sailorman whom everyone called Old Anton had his trade-store in the village, and a Father of the Sacred Heart Mission was stationed there. Old Anton, the Father and the Senior Medical Officer were all the white company we had in those days, save for the aged Roman Catholic Bishop and two other Fathers who came to see us sometimes from up-lagoon. But we were not particularly looking for white company, and we were delighted with our lagoonside home. The old Residency was a handsome wooden house, a big one for that part of the world, built on two floors with deep verandahs shaded all round by louvred shutters. Upstairs were two large bedrooms west and middle, but, instead of a third room under the eastern gable, an open loggia of forty by twenty feet. With its shutters wide to the trade-wind, the loggia was divinely cool for sleeping, so Olivia and the baby and I had our beds there.

We loved to walk down to Betio village half an hour before sunset with our nursemaid Faasolo pushing Joan in her pram between us. The trade-wind often dropped its wings (as the lovely Gilbertese idiom put it) when the expectation of dusk was falling on sea and forest. There was a pearly mist over the lagoon, infinitely fine-drawn and tender. A heavenly coolness, as of dewfall, pervaded the village. Shadows were purpling under the high vault of palm-leaves. People sang and children shouted. The canoes of the fishermen were home with the day's catch and the evening meal was cooking. The noise of life and laughter was stabbed randomly by the staccato of snapping sticks and the joyous crackle of embers. The babble of talking groups rose and fell like the beat of a pulse of happiness on the lily-scented air.

No white baby had ever been seen before on Tarawa. The villagers seemed never tired of looking at Joan's blue eyes and golden hair. One evening, a small naked girl in the crowd mustered at gaze around the pram piped aloud, '*Ai bia arau arante tei-n-aine aei* (I would that this girl-child's name could be my name!)'

They hushed her and shushed her as if she had uttered an infamy. But, creeping to Olivia's side, she clung to her hand and gazed up into her eyes repeating in an urgent whisper, 'I would that her name could be mine!' Olivia drew her close and I protested, 'What's all the fuss about? Why shouldn't she take the name of Joan if she wants to? Would her parents mind?'

The crowd was silent. Then someone shouted, 'Here is her mother!' and they all fell back a step or two.

The mother stood forward in the ring, a tiny, vivid creature dressed only in a tight waistcloth of gay print. 'Sir, is this true?' she cried, taking both my hands in hers. 'Will the woman of Matang allow it? May my child take the name of her child?'

I turned to Olivia: 'Of course she may,' she said: 'What's to stop it if the mother likes it?'

There was a shout of pleasure from the audience. The mother, looking her thanks, led her small girl to the side of the pram and, bending over it, addressed our sleeping Joan with a smile of tender courtesy: '*Neiko* (Woman), I have thrown away the name of this my girl-child and taken your name for her instead. Your mother says I may. See, here is your name-sister and servant for evermore, Joan of Betio, who shall obey your word in all things.'

And the new Joan, leaning in her turn over the pram, whispered, 'Joan-o-o, Joan-o-o, my name-sister and my *toka* (chief), I will love and serve you for evermore and obey your word in all things.' Then, turning to Olivia, she added with clear-eyed candour, 'Neiko, look you! I must go to school every day, or the Father will be angry. But after school every day, I will be ready to come to my sister, no matter when you call me.' And ready she always was, never intruding, never in the way, but infallibly on the spot with love and service for Joan or any one of us, for as long as we stayed on Tarawa.

On our walks through the village, we often turned into Old Anton's trade-store to pass the time of day. All our main shopping was, of course, done in the trading ships, whose supercargoes took our orders for bulk supplies to Australia and brought the goods back on their return, half a year or more later. But catering for six or eight months at a time is a tricky business. There were always odds and ends that we found we needed by the way. Anton kept a marvellous assortment of these beyond the ordinary run of prints and tobacco, sailcloth and fishing gear, sheath-knives and tools, sewing-cotton and kerosene that ranked as village necessities. He was particularly strong on Chinese silks, mouth organs and perfumery. The two last made very acceptable presents for village friends.

It was pleasant to take small gifts to friends at the happy hour before sunset. The polite approach was to walk up to the side of a mwenga and stand there silent, with one hand resting on the edge of the raised floor as if begging leave to enter, until someone said the right welcoming words.

Usually, a grandfather or grandmother sitting inside spoke first: 'Sir and Woman, you shall be blest. Whence come you at the sunset hour?'

'You shall be blest. We come from our house over there in the east.'

'And you will do what in this place?'

'We will visit this mwenga and those who dwell in it.'

'*Aia!* It is well. You wish to gossip with us?'

'We wish to gossip a little. That is the way of it.'

'*Ai-i-i-a!*' – on a long, indrawn breath of deepest pleasure – 'So it is well. Blessings and peace. Mount! Mount!'

On the last words, the young women of the household would dart forward to spread fine mats on the edge of the floor next to us. We would take our seats there with legs dangling over the side, saying as we mounted, 'We pray this mwenga may be blest with all of you within.'

'You shall be blest,' answered everyone together, and after that the gossip was free for all.

The gifts we brought would be given only just before leaving. We had a working agreement about how they must be given: Olivia did all the presentations to females, I to males, except where very old people were concerned. This arrangement seemed to guarantee us freedom from the least breath of scandal. Scandalous talk was, as a matter of fact, a thing much more to be guarded against on my side than on Olivia's. The attitude of Gilbertese men to white women was the perfection of reverent chivalry, wherever one went. The attitude of the laughing, golden girls towards white men was perhaps on the average, a little profane, for the simple reason that, on the average, the white men seldom qualified to be reverenced by them as saints. The idea of my never making a personal gift to a lady was absolutely sound. But there was just one case that our careful technique failed to provide against.

The thing happened when Olivia was expecting another baby early in the New Year, and the whole of Tarawa was agog with delight at the prospect. The new arrival would be the first child of the Breed of Matang ever to be born on their own soil of Tarawa. It was an epoch-making event for all the eighteen villages, but most of all for the people of Betio, who talked with Olivia every day and claimed the right to reckon themselves her private bodyguard.

They treated her like a beloved goddess wherever we went, and hung upon her every word, seeking to find in even the littlest things she said some guide to how they might help and protect her. They noticed me only as her husband, at most to ask how I thought they might ease the feet of Missis – as they were calling her by then – along the road to her great hour. That protective spirit, that eagerness to interpret her every need, was really the key to what followed – not forgetting, of course, the subtleties of custom in connection with gifts of perfumery.

Olivia and I had just finished tea one afternoon when a very sweet village girl, crowned with a wreath of white flowers, came up the front steps and stood with bowed head on the verandah waiting to be invited farther in.

'Why, hullo, Voice-of-the-Tide!' said Olivia. 'Do you want to talk to us? Come in and sit down.'

Voice-of-the-Tide crept forward, her head still deeply bowed, and sat on the mat before our feet. 'Yes, I come to speak . . . I come to say . . .' she murmured and fell silent, nervously clasping and unclasping her beautiful hands.

"Well, don't be afraid of us. We won't bite your head off' – Olivia and she had always been great friends – 'What's on your mind?'

'I come to thank you for yesterday evening. I am very proud . . . I come to say . . .' Speech failed her again. She had not yet lifted her eyes to ours.

'*Te raoi* (Don't mention it),' Olivia answered her word of thanks. We thought we knew what that referred to. We had visited her people's mwenga the evening before, and Olivia had given her a small bottle of scent. But why should a casual gift have left her so constrained?

It was only after a long, long silence that she raised her head and whispered, looking me in the eyes, 'The gift of love that Misses gave me . . . I am very proud to be chosen . . . I am ready . . . when shall I come to the Man of Matang?' and burst into bitter tears. 'But my sweetheart will never forgive me!' she wailed. 'Alas! Alas! The miserable girl I am!'

The ghastly truth took half an hour to piece together between her tempest of sobbing.

It was the custom for a Gilbertese lady of high birth to choose, during her last months of pregnancy, some young unmarried friend of hers for the nightly comfort of her husband. 'For look you,' said Voice-of-the-Tide's father to me later, 'it secures the safety of the child. And not that alone. It secures also for the mother the continual loving-kindness of her husband and that other woman.'

But the matter was one of such delicacy for all concerned that no preliminary words about it might ever pass between them. The husband and the not-impossible-shes simply waited for the expectant mother to give the customary sign of her choice. The sign was the handing of a gift of anything sweet-scented – a wreath of flowers, a bottle of perfume – to the chosen girl in the presence of the husband. So high was the compliment, so deeply felt the obligation of kindness to the pregnant, that no girl of good breeding could possibly refuse the charge thus laid upon her.

Nobody in the village doubted for an instant what Olivia had meant by her gift. The place was buzzing for joy at the delicate correctitude of it. Everyone was pleased, in fact, except Voice-of-the-Tide and her sweetheart. I felt that Olivia was a little malicious about that when Voice-of-the-Tide, most earnestly reassured by myself as to the purity of my own intentions towards her, dried her tears and smiled again: 'Tell me,' said Olivia, 'if you had not had a sweetheart, would you have felt differently about it?'

'*I aki* (Not I),' replied Voice-of-the-Tide without a moment's courteous hesitation.

'And why not?' Olivia's tone simply egged her on.

She eyed me up and down gravely before she answered: 'This chief of Matang is very kind . . . but' – she rippled into giggles.

Nothing, I am glad to say, would induce her to say more. I left them to their laughter. I had a few words to say in the village – alone.

The crux of the fresh-food problem for Europeans in the Gilberts was that humus just would not stay put on top of the pure, white coral sand. Coconuts and pandanus trees loved it; it kept their roots aerated; but it was not good for beans or tomatoes. One dug a trench, filled it with painfully prepared compost; the rains came; the compost disappeared underground. Or perhaps no rains came – because, every few years, there was a drought that might last as long as eighteen months. We could spare no water then for plants, seeing that our parched household was limited to two buckets a day for all purposes. The compost stayed on top, but we got no vegetables.

Sometimes – though not often – we were able to get breadfruit or pumpkins from the villages. There was also an enormous tuber of the arum family called *babai*, cultivated by the villagers in muddy pits. This could be eaten mashed with butter or in cheesy, steamed slabs and was incredibly indigestible either way. No other vegetable foods except coconuts grew locally, and the only sort outside tins that ships brought us every six months or so was potatoes. These always arrived looking depressed after their long, hot trip from Australia; but, with luck, half the weight we bought would be found good when picked over and, with care, we could reckon on enjoying fifty per cent of the good ones before the lot went bad on us. On the average, we were able to make beasts of ourselves on potatoes for two thrilling gastronomic periods of three weeks each a year except between 1918 and 1920, when we went to live at Beru and had none at all for seventeen months.

Some years were yet to pass before any type of refrigerator within the reach of £400 a year became known in the Gilbert group. Olivia never had the comfort of one as a District Officer's wife. And so, whatever oranges or apples the ships might get through to us in their primitive ice-boxes had to be consumed within a week of their arrival. But, as Olivia observed, we were saved from too much heartburning on this score, because the fruit hardly ever survived as far as the lagoon islands. By and large, therefore, no fresh fruit except a very occasional locally grown pawpaw figured in our dietary at Tarawa, and, save for our six sumptuous potato-weeks per annum, the only fresh vegetables Olivia could always count upon for the exercise of her virtuosity in the kitchen were coconuts and that gross tuber I have mentioned – babai – whose unhallowed starchiness no treatment under heaven was ever known to exorcise.

The answer to all this was, of course, contained in tins. It sounds simple enough. Tinned goods in these synthetic days are often made to taste rather like the commodities so brightly pictured on their labels. But that was not so thirty years ago – not, at least, in the Pacific. With the honourable exceptions of asparagus and beetroot, which always seemed to retain faint memories of their better selves, the vegetables doomed to canning in 1916 entered their iron cells bleakly determined to betray every sweetness of their early promise. When they emerged, the eye dared hardly dwell upon their livid looks, and the taste of one and all – celery or onion, pea, cabbage, cauliflower, bean or potato – was as the taste of iron filings boiled in dishwater.

Nevertheless, with tinned asparagus and beetroot as sure standbys, babai at least always with us, potatoes, pumpkins, breadfruit and pawpaws now and then available (and, by the way, pawpaws cooked green made a reasonable substitute for vegetable marrow) we did not do so badly on the whole. Our goats, unfortunately, conspired among themselves to live a life of embittered chastity, which kept them forever fruitless and ourselves without the fresh milk we had dreamed of; but we found the tinned milk palatable enough. Our imported fowls refused to lay and died of gapes; but bush eggs were always to be had from the villages at the rate of three for a stick of trade tobacco, and these yielded sometimes as many as three or four to the dozen that did not explode like stink-bombs in the housewife's hands. The bush fowls at sixpence each gave decent broth; there was plenty of rice in the trade-stores; the jelly-like flesh of green coconuts made a good vegetable food for infants; the sweet sap of the coconut blossom called toddy fed us with vitamins; the supply of fish from the lagoon was unlimited.

But it was difficult to get good cooks. Cooking for white folk was for some reason always regarded as a man's job, and the men, born of a race of fighters, brought up to wage an endless war of survival against the terrors of the deep and the stern soil of their homeland, never found the happiest expression of their virtues in terms of culinary art. Their strong hands were ill at ease among the puny tools of the kitchen. But as Olivia rhetorically asked, how could one grouse at that when they came to work crowned as for a dance with garlands of white flowers and made up for what they lacked of measurable cooking skills with measureless daily gifts of gentleness and humour? The kitchen rang with their laughter and song most of the time, and, if we found the things that came out of it sometimes a little wanting in sensuous appeal, we knew that they came garnished at least with the sauce of a friendship beyond valuation.

We couldn't help noticing now and then that spiritual sauces, however rich, left the gross flesh craving still for solid food; but this raised few problems when we were alone; if the fish course looked disastrous, a mere wave of the family tin-opener was enough to produce some kind of substitute. It was when we were *not* left alone that embarrassments assailed us. Our trouble with visitors was that they always came ashore fed to the teeth with the tinned provisions of their ships and filled with dreams of getting down to a lovely home-cooked meal or two before returning to their misery. Though they bore their disillusionments with courageous courtesy, we thought they failed in average cheerfulness. We never entertained one whose face brightened perceptibly when bullimacow and beetroot were placed before him in compensation for charred pumpkin and incinerated mullet.

The Resident Commissioner was gloomier still. He said once that he envied our casual guests the standing advantage they had over himself. They could always refuse a second venture at our table, and go far away and forget at last the things we had done to them. He was not in the same happy boat; it was his duty to tour the Gilbert and Ellice groups at least once a year, and he was forced to include Tarawa in the schedule of his visits; yet, as he bitterly concluded, landing there inevitably meant staying with us, because the Medical Officer's quarters had no spare bedroom, and the spare bungalow was unfurnished. We felt his way of putting things over-invidious. Heaven knows we had not planned the series of events that led up to his outburst.

It all began with a quarrel in the back premises. About three hours before dinner on the day of his arrival from Ocean Island, our nursemaid Faasolo had discovered Sila, our cook, talking alone behind the kitchen with a lady from the village. Sila was her husband; the lady was one whom she had long suspected of having designs upon him.

Faasolo was a gentle, smiling person most days of the year, and Sila had always seemed to us an exemplary husband. I am still quite sure he was. But they were childless, and the reproach of her barrenness was never very far from poor Faasolo's thought. The sorrow and frustration of it turned sometimes to despairing fury when she saw the soft glances that other women threw at her kindly, handsome Sila. She had his lady visitor by the hair and was flogging her horribly with a broom-handle when we intervened. Fortunately, our formidable Chief was not there to hear her deep-chested roars of rage or the rending screams of her victim. He had taken a stroll round the hospital with the Medical Officer. By the time he returned, the unwelcome girl was gone and Sila was doing his best to placate Faasolo in their dwelling near the police lines.

But we could not leave them together for long. Dinner had to be cooked – and what a dinner too! Our Chief had most kindly brought with him from Ocean Island an exquisite little shoulder of frozen lamb, *and* some onions, *and* potatoes, AND a tin of real French petits pois. We ourselves could put up such things as mint sauce or redcurrant jelly, as well as olives, salted almonds and the rest; beyond which, to crown perfection with beauty's ultimate grace, there was our plum pudding, tinned but delicious. It was so delicious, in fact, that we had decided to hoard this last of six trial tins for Christmas. I grudged the premature sacrifice of it at first, but Olivia was more generous. The Old Man liked a good sweet, she said; and anyhow, her argument ran on, what sort of a main course were we going to get at Christmas comparable to roast lamb? Why not decide to look on this night's feast as our Christmas dinner in advance and make an artist's job of it, soup, joint and pudding in one sweet symphony. I thought of the *allegretto* of the soup, the pastoral *andante* of the lamb and little peas, the *scherzo* of almonds and wittily stuffed olives running into the rollicking *rondo* of the pudding. My mouth watered. I withdrew my niggardly objections.

The joint was popped into the oven about an hour and a half before dinner, with Sila on guard. Faasolo was quiet now, he said. Last instructions were given. We bathed, changed, had a final look at the dinner-table, saw that it looked nice with our best glass and rose candleshades, felt young and adult and proud, passed out to the cool downstairs loggia, were presently joined there by our Chief, and relaxed a while with pleasant drinks beside us.

The hour after sunset was always the Old Man's best. That evening, he was mellower than I had ever seen him. He began to talk quietly about the rewards of living in the tropics, the relief of darkness after the day's glare, the night breeze, the whisper of palms, and, best of all – a gift that Ocean Island never gave him – the hushed lap-lapping of high tide upon our beach. His sincerity and the loveliness of the night touched and emboldened me so much that I dared to recite the octave of a sonnet I was writing at the time:

> No more the torrid sands beat back the sun
>> Nor sun-drenched breakers shatter into gems
>> To crown the reef with poising diadems.
> The sunset leapt, blazed, shuddered once, was gone;
> And now night drops her blessings one by one
>> From star-cool hands – the fragile scent of seas,
>> The merciful darkness, and the long heart-ease
> Of knowing that the jaded day is done.

'Yes, Grimble,' he said, 'yes . . . you must finish that. Finish it with something about never wanting to go back to civilization again . . . something about the false values of it . . . something about all these big simplicities being enough for anyone. I believe you could manage it – you've got the right spirit, my boy, you've got the right spirit.'

It was marvellous, coming from him. I was stirred to the deep heart's core. As we took our seats at the rose-lit dining-table, I felt that we were all one together for always in this land that was no strange land now for any of us. And the soup, when it appeared, looked a creamy dream to me. Olivia always could do heavenly things with chicken stock, asparagus and tinned milk. Sila, too, had become an adept at it.

But Sila's unhappy Faasolo had crept into the kitchen while we were at drinks and asked him to refill her hurricane lamp. I, for my part, never did much mind a *soupçon* of kerosene in any food except fish, so I went on with my helping. Olivia and the Old Man chose to abandon theirs in favour of sherry, toast and *jeux d'esprit*. That seemed rather a pity, but neither said a word about the soup. What was there to worry about, anyhow, with lamb and plum pudding still in prospect?

I was lapping up the last spoonfuls when Sila appeared at the door naked to the waist, in a not very clean state. He made no apology for intruding like that, but spoke in English, presumably in honour of our guest: 'Missus, come quick!' he cried urgently. 'Gravy, no bloody good!' and bolted back to the kitchen.

Olivia rushed wildly after him. The Old Man lit a cigarette and sat mum. I became aware of tension in his silence. I was tense myself. Gravy is important.

Looking back from now to then, I realize that Sila's report did little justice to himself. For gravy to be good or bad there must *be* some of it, and in this case there was none at all. That was his real problem, and it was one that no cook on earth could have solved in the circumstances. As for blaming anyone else, I can see that if he was innocent so also was poor Faasolo. She like him was, in the last analysis, but the driven puppet of calamity. She had come to the kitchen at seven o'clock intending to leave as soon as he filled her lamp. But she was a woman, and what woman in her place could have resisted the temptation that assailed her then? Her heart was bursting with heavy new thoughts about his lady visitor. She stayed to confide them to him. He paused in his work to reply. One thing led to the next; she went on, he went on. They lost themselves in each other, oblivious to all else until disaster fell upon them. It was the ooze of greasy fumes from the oven that told them what had happened. The shoulder of our little lamb was burned to a cinder. One cannot make gravy with ashes.

If this had been fiction, my story would have ended with the walkout of our furious Chief when cold bullimacow and beetroot were laid before him. But real life has small regard for climax and anticlimax; it just goes on, as that meal went on. We finished our gross substitutes for lamb and petits pois with little gaiety. He did indeed rise at the end and say he thought that would be about enough for that evening. Olivia, I could see, was keen to let him go, and be damned to the plum pudding. But something in me rebelled at the total waste of that one remaining treasure. So I told him the history of it, despite her reproachful glances. In the end, I was glad I had done so, because he consented with visible softening of temper to stay on. We all sat down again.

There was a longish wait before the pudding arrived. Sila came along at last himself to explain the delay. His first attempt at sauce had gone wrong, so he had made another just as good.

'Well, well, better later than never!' observed the Old Man brightly when it was uncovered. 'And, my word! what have we here? The sauce looks very handsome, I must say.' And so it did swimming crimson-red around the pudding's foot.

'Yes, he good Sah,' volunteered Sila, 'I makem myself. I boilem with plenty sugar.'

'Some kind of wine sauce, eh?' The Old Man had recaptured his benevolence with extraordinary decency. I could see Olivia was glad now that I had got him to stay.

'No, Sah,' replied Sila, 'he not wine – he juice. He beetroot juice outem tin.'

It was then that the Old Man walked out, and Olivia wept.

*

A few days after he had left Tarawa, I finished the sestet of my sonnet. I tried hard to make it say something about not wanting to return to civilization and all that; but every thought of what the Old Man had said was bound up with memories of lost lamb and little peas. The thing just wouldn't work itself out on his lines. What I actually wrote was:

But I would back to England once again,
    Where lush things grow, where even summer ends,
      To firelit books, to all the clean, dear things
Whose memory keeps us always English men,
    And haunts us as the quiet eyes of friends
      Haunt us, and clings as old-time perfume clings.

The Spell on the Oven

When our houseboy Biribo married, it was only natural that
Mareve, the lady of his choice, should take charge of his kitchen.
The main job of a Gilbertese woman is to cook for her man, and
Mareve's skill with the native earth-oven was a byword in the
villages of Tarawa. The earth-oven is a bowl-shaped pit paved
with hot stones on which food is left to cook covered over with a
roof of matting. It is a tricky thing to manage, especially for the
baking of those complicated puddings of babai and coconut
called buatoro which so easily go sad at the centre. Mareve was
famous in particular for her buatoro. But for this, I doubt if our
kindly and laughter-loving Biribo would ever have married her,
for she was a heavy, shrewish creature; and beyond that, she
had made a point of bullying his sister-housekeeper Tanoata
ever since the two had been children together at their village
mission-school.

Tanoata, at nineteen, was everything Mareve, at twenty-two,
was not – light-hearted, swift and very comely in the sleekness
of her apricot-satin skin. But, as Biribo told me, her cooking was
more than an orphaned bachelor could properly tolerate. He was
quite tired of beating her for the undutiful messes she served up
to him. So Tanoata was displaced; Mareve came to rule the
hearth-place, and from then on nobody was at peace from her
scourging tongue in Biribo's house by the lagoonside. We did
not see much of Tanoata after that. She spent most of the time
away in a village with her adoptive grandmother. Whenever she
returned, there was furious squabbling in the back premises.
The climax came when Biribo, at his wits' end one day, drove
her out with blows, whereas, by rights, he should have given
Mareve the beating.

I was pottering round Biribo's quarters after lunch a day or two later, when I heard someone muttering and moaning very quietly in Mareve's cooking-hut. It was strangely alarming. Everyone was supposed to be asleep in the dwelling-house at that sweltering hour. As I tiptoed to investigate, the idea came to me that someone wrung with pain had crept out to hide himself in that murky little den. What I saw there only increased my anxiety. On the floor squatted Tanoata, naked, with an ugly grin on her face, stabbing with a stick at the ashes of her sister-in-law's earth-oven. As she stabbed, she alternately muttered at the ashes and was torn by gusts of strangled laughter. Real horror gripped me when, with a deep groan, she flung herself backwards on the floor, her legs and arms jerking wildly, as in a fit. With every jerk she hissed a word – always the same word '*Tuki!*' – meaning tense or tight-drawn, as if in piteous complaint at the spasms that racked her. I started forward: 'Oh, Tanoata!' Her legs and arms slumped to the floor. She lay for a moment all limp, staring up at me. Then with a shriek, she snatched a loincloth from beside her and bolted out along into the beach. I managed to catch her as she tried to double back into the bush. She made no struggle, but collapsed there, face to ground, writhing and groaning. It was quite a time before I grasped that the cause of her distress was neither epilepsy nor any form of pain, but a storm of laughter.

But I didn't find it funny. Tarawa women made little enough of clothes, but they were ferociously modest about entire naked-ness. There was something very wrong about the girl's laugh-ter. In any case, there was hysteria in it, I thought, so I gave her a good hard smack, of which I have never yet been ashamed. She stood up, immediately silent, put on her loincloth without haste, looked at me unsmilingly, and breathed: 'I want Biribo to thrash that woman Mareve. I want him to thrash her! Do you see?' I did not see at all. She suddenly wept then, and explained. When Biribo had driven her out, she had gone crying to her adoptive grandmother. The old woman had agreed with her that the only medicine for a woman like Mareve was the father and mother of a hiding. The difficulty was, Biribo was much too soft, but that could be changed. The solution was to put a spell on Mareve's earth-oven. The right ritual would infect with black anger everything she cooked in it and within three days of the third performance Biribo would be making the house-place ring with her yells of anguish.

So Tanoata had learned an age-old spell called 'The Spoiling of the Oven'. She had been finishing the third performance when I stumbled upon her. Here is a translation of the words she muttered:

> I stab them north, I stab them west,
> I stab them south, I stab them east,
> The ashes of the oven of Mareve.
> Spirits of fire, spirits of stone,
> I stab, I confuse, I overturn.
> Bring stinking, bring anger.
> Be sick at the stomach, you Biribo, Biribo! Be enraged!
> For the food of Mareve stinks and stinks:
> It is *tiiki – tiki – tiki*

Tiiki and *tiki*, meaning in this context 'soggy and full of lumps', was the word I had heard her hiss as she lay twitching on her back. Her grandmother had told her to stiffen every muscle each time she repeated it. She must actually be in her own person, at that moment, a pudding refusing to rise. Otherwise, although the spell could be counted upon in any case to make Mareve's food nauseous to all comers, it could not succeed in sending Biribo fighting-mad. Hence the contortions I had taken for an epileptic fit.

If I had believed that anything could possibly come of this childish mummery, I should certainly have intervened on Mareve's behalf. But I did not believe, and did nothing except reprimand Tanoata and threaten to report her to her Mission authorities. Anyhow, the third day after her performance passed without the least outburst of conflict in the back premises; so also did the fourth day, a Sunday. But on Monday something queer did happen. Biribo said a word – a very vile word indeed – over the noon-day meal about Mareve's cooking. It was the first time he had done anything of the kind since his marriage. Tanoata, who happened to be there, crowed with delight, and that was more than enough for Mareve. She hurled the criticized food – a buatoro pudding – into Biribo's face and thrashed him disastrously with a stick while he was plucking the hot mess out of his eyes. She then turned and beat the paralysed Tanoata with equal soundness. I had to run out and stop the appalling noise. Biribo was completely cowed. Tanoata, strangely enough, apologized to Mareve that evening, and stayed on in the house.

I got Biribo to change the site of his cooking-hut the same day. The move proved welcome to Mareve. She came especially to thank me. She felt her old hearth had somehow become unlucky. She said she had been having bad dreams about it. That struck me as rather queer. For four days after that, her puddings resumed their former mastery. I took care to inquire from Biribo himself. He lavished the most servile praise on them, and so did Tanoata. I was idiot enough to believe that everyone would now live happily ever after. But on the fourth evening, the comfortable dream was broken. As we sat at our sundown drink, there burst on our ears a tearing shriek from the back premises. It was the shriek of a woman in the extremity of pain and fear. I hurled myself off the verandah. As I ran, I heard a man's voice savagely rumbling, and the sick thuds of a stick on flesh, and newer, wilder shrieks with every thud. It was Biribo thrashing Mareve. He was mad; he hurled me aside when I tried to stop him; he would have beaten her to death if Tanoata had not helped me to drag him off. Even when we pinned him down, he struggled, gnashing his teeth, to get back at her. He raved all the time about her food; he kept shouting 'Tiiki! Tiiki!' It may have been pure chance – the word is common enough – but it gave me gooseflesh. I had to put two friendly policemen on guard over him all through the night.

Tanoata had disappeared when I returned from the police lines, but she crawled into our room and woke me at daybreak. She was too terrified at her own thoughts to excuse herself for breaking in at that hour. She began talking as soon as I sat up. I must change Biribo's cooking-hut again. Please, please, would I do it at once. Her confession poured itself out. She had been wicked; she had wanted her revenge; that was why she had stayed on after Mareve had thrashed her – to have her revenge. She had cursed the second oven. She had done everything properly this time. She had not laughed, for one thing: real anger had driven her. For another thing, she had been able to throw herself into the mad-making 'Tiiki-tiiki' convulsions without interruption from me. It was not cheerful hearing. I could think of nothing better to do than dress and hurry her to the Mission station for immediate advice. She followed me eagerly. I returned and got the station police to move the beastly cooking-hut to another place within the next hour. Biribo was sane again by then.

The most probable explanation of all these happenings is, of course, that Tanoata's grandmother gave her something to bury in the bottom of the earth-oven – something or other that tainted the food as it cooked – maybe a fish-poison. Tanoata denied it, and I found no suspicious remains in either oven, but these two negatives might mean very little. The question that puzzled Olivia and me was: why did the poison (assuming there was some) leave Biribo meek enough to take a beating from his wife the first time, yet drive him killing mad the second time? Or if, for argument's sake, my intrusion the first time prevented Tanoata from putting the poison in place, what was it that suddenly made Mareve's cooking bad enough to wring that vile word out of him? And if there was no poison in either oven, then why did Mareve's hand resume its cunning only when she cooked somewhere else? I cannot pretend to know. The only thing that cheers me about this story is that the thrashing Mareve got did her a lot of good. It sounds all wrong, but it is a fact. She never resumed her nagging of Biribo: she was scared stiff of him; and from that time on there was shining peace in the back premises.

It is worth adding that Tanoata got herself married from Biribo's house a few months later. The wedding feast that Mareve put up for her was reckoned by all comers as the most delicious in human memory.

4

NATIVE COURTS

The chief business of a District Officer was to supervise the work of the island Kabowi, or Native Courts. A Kabowi was an assembly of village kaubure or headmen, presided over by a Native Magistrate. The assembly sat every month, in the Native Government maneaba, to deal with the current administrative and judicial business of its community. Its powers were derived from a code of native laws which adapted the application of British forms to local usage. On the judicial side, the code allowed the District Officer nothing but advisory status in the Kabowi, and did not oblige him to be present at any proceedings save trials for homicide or for offences against English law not specially mentioned in the code; but it required him to review every conviction made in his absence, and gave him power to quash illegal sentences or reduce any that he found excessive. Beyond the District Officer, appeals against convictions lay to the Resident Commissioner, and no sentence of death could be carried out except after review of the written evidence by the High Commissioner in Fiji.

On the executive side, the Kabowi had power to make, subject to the Resident Commissioner's approval, regulations for the cleanliness and good order of the villages. The village kaubure, who were unpaid, assisted by village policemen, who earned the princely salary of £6 a year, or less on the smaller islands, saw to the maintenance of these regulations, looked after the general welfare of their parishioners and either voiced their grievances at the monthly sessions or introduced their delegated spokesmen to the Kabowi. A Chief Kaubure and a Chief of Police (at £12 each a year, or less) both resident on the Native Government station, were directed by the law to visit every village at least once between monthly meetings, so as to keep things on the move and give people the latest news from Head-quarters. An Island Scribe (£12 a year or less) was charged with the registration of births, deaths, and marriages, the reporting of defaulters, the keeping of a cash book, and the duties of Island Postmaster.

In any matter of debate which demanded a *moti*, or judge-ment, by the Native Magistrate, a division of the assembled kaubure was taken. The kaubure, in effect, performed parliamentary functions as representatives of their people in conclave with regard to administrative affairs, and operated as

95

jurymen in all judicial cases. The Chief Kaubure sat with the Native Magistrate as an assessor at the table of justice, while the Chief of Police conducted prosecutions. There was no such thing as a secret session of the Kabowi for either judicial or administrative purposes, and the public followed the proceedings at every meeting with intense interest. On a big island, there would be an audience of fifteen hundred or more to watch an important trial or listen to the oratory of petitioners, counter-petitioners (and, if heaven was bountiful, cross-petitioners also) before the Court. The silence and orderliness of those great crowds during judicial proceedings could not have been bettered in any English court-room; nor could their liberty of utterance during debates on matters of general concern have been less fettered anywhere else in the world.

The method of electing village kaubure for office was democratic, though the ballot was an open one all along the line. The villagers assembled first in their own maneaba under the chairmanship of the Chief Kaubure and, by a show of hands, nominated two or three candidates, whose names were laid before the Kabowi at its next meeting. The majority vote of the Kabowi decided the final choice, and the new member took his seat at once. A small village had only one kaubure; the larger ones, where the population might run up to 1,000 or more souls, had sometimes as many as five. On the fifty-mile island of Tabiteuea, with twenty-odd villages and a total population of about 5,000, there were over thirty representatives of the people in the Kabowi. There was no preliminary training for the work. The young members learned their business from the older ones; the gifts of commonsense and eloquence natural to the Gilbertese, allied with their phenomenal memories, made them very quick learners. I have met in the Western Hemisphere no oratory in high debate that could compare, for average pithiness of content, beauty of diction and ease of delivery, with that of those rugged brown fishermen working for no reward in the cause of their village communities.

The salaried heads of the system – the Native Magistrate and Chief Kaubure – were men who had qualified for appointment by many years of service as village Kaubure. In the early days, most of them could neither read nor write. Some of the old sort were still in office when I got to the group, and I was in a state of continual astonishment at their powers of memory. They were word-perfect in the native laws and regulations, and two readings aloud by the Island Scribe of any letter or record in Gilbertese were enough to store the whole text of it in their minds forever. The spread of Mission education brought with it in the long run a natural demand for literacy, even among the village kaubure. That was all to the good as time marched on, for it widened horizons; yet, excellent as it was, it certainly produced no finer breed of justices or administrators than those unlettered and, more often than not, pagan Native Magistrates of old.

The effect of the truly remarkable initiative wielded by the native courts and the representative nature of their constitution was to keep alive among them (quite independently of European supervision) a high sense of responsibility for their decisions, and to maintain among the people at large a vivid and critical interest in the conduct of their own affairs. The Kabowi system was established by an extraordinarily wise dispensation of the eighteen-nineties. 'Wise' is not to imply that the penal code was entirely devoid of flaws; for example, it forced monogamy, under pain of imprisonment, upon a historically polygynous people and made criminal offences of certain sex-relationships that were basic to the old moralities. That was itself a moral and anthropological crime of the first magnitude, which no British missionary body or government would have dared to attempt, even in those days, against a more powerful community. But, for all that, the Kabowi system as a whole stood for an almost unique effort, in the heyday of Imperialism and thirty years before the publication of Lord Lugard's *Dual Mandate*, to engage the genius of a subject race on a really big scale in the vital business of self-rule.

*

One of the Kabowi's most important annual tasks was the assessment of native taxation. Though nine-tenths of the colonial revenue spent on the maintenance of services in the two groups was drawn from the mining industry of Ocean Island, the villagers of the lagoon islands also contributed their quota. This was collected by way of a land tax which was paid not in money, but in copra. The copra tax could not be assessed on acreage, for a boundary survey of the thousands of smallholdings was far beyond anybody's financial reach in those days; nor could it be based upon an overall average of productivity, for the yield of copra varied enormously from atoll to atoll and from year to year, according to rainfall. The only possible method of assessment was to name a tonnage figure for each island's total contribution, based on its average annual export, and ask the local Kabowi to consider at the beginning of every year, first of all, whether the average quota could be fairly insisted upon or not, and, second, how much each separate landowner, according to the size and fertility of his holdings, should justly contribute towards the agreed total.

The task of allotting out individual proportions was never a simple one. The Gilbertese man in the street was no more in love with his copra tax than the Englishman with his income tax, and he had many more chances than an Englishman enjoys of arguing special pleas before his local authorities. Also, he was a humorist, a dramatist, and an orator in his bones, and the magnificent setting of the maneaba packed with listeners was a temptation that his artistry could never resist. The staging of an elaborate petition was pure joy for him. A man would begin to think over his piece and coach his witnesses for their parts months before the date of his great production. The rejection of his plea, *qua* plea, was of course a foregone conclusion; but it was neither here nor there that nobody but an idiot could be expected to take it seriously. He was a weaver of dreams, a creator. The delight of the crowd at his glorious flights of humour and fancy was all he needed to soothe the aching of his wistful heart.

'Sirs,' the Native Magistrate would say to his kaubure when the plaudits and the laughter died, 'what think you of the crying of this man? Does he speak truth or lies?'

'*Ekeve* (he lies),' the kaubure would answer, single-voiced save for those who preferred '*E banga ni keve* (he is stuffed with lies).'

'*Ai e aera* (How about that)!' someone in the crowd would shout, and '*Ai ngaia naba anne* (There's the truth of it)!' the rest would roar, while the petitioner stood with unruffled serenity awaiting the Magistrate's last word:

'Sir, thou hast heard the voice of the people. They think thou liest. So it is also with me, and that is my judgement. Thy wish cannot be granted. Yet calm thy heart and go in peace, for the crying of thy voice has been heard from beginning to end, and it was a good crying.' Wafted from the maneaba on the wings of that last compliment, the petitioner would go happily home to think up an even better piece for next year's production.

But invariably in cases of genuine hardship the petitioner presented his plea without rhetoric and unaided by witnesses of his own choosing. Every man's poverty or wealth was known to the last pound of copra by everyone else in his village. Nobody with the truth behind him needed to worry about the evidence; the kaubure would look after that. The crowd, with its acute sensitiveness to the truth, would show its sympathy by silence. In my eleven years as a District Officer I never met a case in which a taxpayer with a *bona-fide* hardship to present had been turned away without proper relief by his Kabowi.

*

The only real trouble about the copra tax that ever happened my way was a very grim business indeed. It began one April when the people of Onotoa Island (who were 96 per cent Protestant, the rest being Roman Catholic) heard that the London Missionary Society's steamship *John Williams* was coming to visit them in June.

I was Resident Commissioner by then. I had known the Onotoans for sixteen years and counted them among the gentlest and merriest of all Gilbertese populations. But they were torn that April by a mass fury so terrible, I was tempted almost to believe in such a thing as possession by devils. Only Koata and a few strong souls resisted the sweep of it. Koata was the Native Magistrate, and this is the story of how he stood firm.

Halfway through the month, the people of two villages decided to get ready a fine gift of copra against the Mission vessel's arrival. As well as being generous, this was a perfectly legal intent, as the *John Williams* was licensed to trade through the Gilbert Islands. But the problem for Koata, as Native Magistrate, was that the island's copra tax was due to be delivered in June, and the gift proposed for the Mission was so big that he knew it must strip the villagers' trees of every ripe nut during April and May. That would mean the default of hundreds in the payment of their tax, and subsequent trouble for everyone concerned.

Koata was a moderate-minded man. When news of the intended gift came to him, he took a day or two to think things out. The main point was that, if the villagers were to reduce their offering to the Mission by about two-fifths, the balance of copra saved would be enough to cover the tax liability. So he called the native pastors and deacons of the villages to the maneaba and put the figures to them. In the course of his talk, he said he was not asking the people to deny God an offering of love, but only to limit the gift so that Caesar also might also receive his just due. He urged that, as the motive of the gift was religious, they, much better than himself – a Roman Catholic – could first approach their flocks with good counsel, and he asked them to take the initiative.

It was a statesmanlike proposal, as typical of the old pagan courtesies as it was of the Christian charities, but the pastors and deacons would have none of it. They were men driven by the blind zeal of inquisitors. Koata, for them, was not merely a Roman Catholic sinner but one who, baptized a Protestant, had treacherously in his adult years gone over to the Scarlet Woman. It added blasphemy to his wickedness that he had dared to quote to them the Bible text about God's and Caesar's dues. They accused him to his face of a deliberate attack upon their church, and broke off all negotiations there and then.

From that day on, they exhorted their congregations to persist in their gift to God and to welcome for His glory any form of martyrdom that the unjust judge might visit upon them. But though their speech was florid and Koata's name was branded with religious infamy, they preached no sedition at that stage. Their theme was at worst one of active work for God, passive disregard for the tax-law, and God punish the unjust judge. Any liberal could condone it, and Koata was a natural-born liberal. He took not the slightest notice of the anathemas hurled upon him from the village pulpits, because, as he explained later, he did not think a Native Magistrate was paid to take private revenge on anybody.

But he had to take some sort of line as father of his island (that was his own phrase) when, in the middle of May, the gift was handed over to the pastors. The only nuts now left on the villagers' trees were far too young for tax-copra making in June, and it was his duty to be firm about that. At the same time, he thought that the people, having satisfied their own leaders and consciences, might now be willing to take some worldly advice from himself. Everything could be straightened out if the two villages could be persuaded to borrow the copra for their tax from the rest of the island, subject to repayment in July, when their own young nuts would be ripe. So he called the congregations to the maneaba and put the suggestion to them, after warning them that their failure to pay in June could hardly be condoned by the Government. He even offered to negotiate the loan for them.

But an unexpected complication arose to balk him. The congregations had answered his call hoping for punishment, not help, from Caesar. Their teachers had despatched them to court with promises of instant martyrdom. All pathos was in their utter sincerity of purpose; they put their case with heartbreaking simplicity. 'We have sinned against the law,' they pleaded. 'It is now thy duty, Koata, to put us in prison. That is what our pastors have told us, and we wish it so. We beg thee to put us in prison.'

He explained with kindness why he could not grant their plea. Their gift to the London Mission was in itself no breach of the regulations. Nobody wanted to punish them for that. Non-payment of the copra tax was the only sin the law would worry about. But not a man among them could be charged with an offence until he had failed to pay, and no evidence of default could possibly exist against anyone before the very hour of the last day of June had run out. Beyond this too, the law gave even a proved defaulter the option of paying a fine over and above his tax instead of going to prison. He dismissed them on that note, with a final plea that they would return to him after thinking things over.

The missed martyrdom was a crushing disappointment for them. They went back to their villages like children fooled of their reward and taxed their pastors with misleading them. It was a deflating moment. Shepherds and sheep alike might well have come to their senses then, as Koata hoped, but for a single man among them – the senior pastor, whom I shall call Ten Naewa.

Ten Naewa was a middle-aged man, sternly ascetic in his habits, arrogant and ignorant, but of acute political wit. He saw more clearly than most that, among his people, the only cure for a broken dream was the creation of a new wonder, so he pulled one out of the bag on the spot. Leaping to his feet and shouting down the flow of recriminations, he burst into perfervid speech about a message he had that very instant received from Heaven. By God's grace, he said, the chapel in which they were sitting was to become a place of miracles. O, sinful generation, to pollute it now with angry reproaches, for a light was to shine out of it – the light of a New Revelation. God Himself was about to speak to His people in dreams, for their gift had found favour in His sight. They were His Elect from that day forth for ever. In the dreams He was about to send them would lie concealed the key of the Day of His Second Coming, and the clue to all things that must be done before He appeared. But none among them could discover the key save only himself, God's Prophet. Let them therefore bring all their dreams to him so that he might interpret them there in the chapel of dreams.

His superb acting carried the day. They believed him. Koata said afterwards, in defence of him, that he had probably reached total belief in his own words before he rushed out into the forest, as a man possessed, yelling damnation upon the Roman Catholics and the Government.

So the people dreamed dreams and had visions from God, which Ten Naewa interpreted endlessly, between sessions of prayer and hate, in the place of miracles. The two congregations moved *en masse* out of their villages and set up a great encampment of leaf shacks around the chapel.

Almost at once, the habit of dreams became general; people from other villages began to flock into the camp, but not yet fast enough for Ten Naewa; success had set him hungering for more; so he issued a prophecy that the Last Day was but a month ahead, and launched a campaign upon it. God would arrive at high noon, he said. In the eleventh hour He had ordained that a wave should arise to the height of the Government's flagstaff and sweep away the Flag, the Roman Catholics and all traitorous Protestants who refused to be gathered near the chapel.

The threat started a terrified exodus from the villages, but still the Prophet was unsatisfied. To speed things up he embarked upon a course of propaganda that must surely be unique, even in the chequered annals of partisan religion. He began by limiting God's status to that of God the Father, changing his own title of Prophet to that of 'Father-of-God' and appointing his son to be 'God Almighty'. His next moves followed quickly. He organized a body of women, whom he called his Sheep, and charged them to stand around him wherever he went, shuddering or falling into trances at the sound of his voice. He interpreted somebody's vision of a flaming sword on the wall of his chapel as God the Father's direction to form a band of hooligans – The Swords of Gabriel – who marched about the island bringing terror of death to all who stayed at home. He named two women 'Christ-the-Sufferer' and 'Christ-the-Forgiver' to receive and pardon the repentant who turned to him at last. Three weeks after the first scene in the chapel, only aged folk and infants outside the forty or fifty Roman Catholics remained in the villages, while nearly thirteen hundred men, women and children with dogs and pigs complete were gathered in a hugger-mugger of squalor, hunger and hysteria around the Father-of-God, awaiting the Advent of God the Father.

Koata had done all a brave man could to prevent it. Ignoring the threats of the Swords of Gabriel, he followed hard on their heels to every village, trying to allay the terrors they spread. But it was not only physical force that drove the people. They believed, with all their capacity for fear, in the merciless new god of the pastors. The Last Day was at hand. What furies of damnation awaited their souls if they listened to the Scarlet Woman's messenger? They stoned Koata from the villages in their panic of self-salvation.

But there is one good thing to remember of those days. Two Protestant villagers took an open stand from the beginning against the sweeping madness. If ever the courage of a few just men saved the honour of a creed it was theirs. They went together one day to offer Koata their support. 'We are Protestants,' they said, 'but we think those pastors are mistaken. You do well to hold out against them, and you have always been a fair Magistrate. We will stand by you.'

The gesture put new heart in him. He needed it much, for some of his colleagues had deserted the Government Station that very day. Only two other men and five women remained with him. The newcomers with their households raised the moral strength by eight souls. All told, fifteen men and women stayed by his side to abide the day of wrath.

The day arrived. The distraught camp waited with fasting and prayer from sunrise to noon. But no wave from the sea came to destroy the wicked, no God appeared in the chapel.

Mutterings began. A few hundred of the quieter folk returned in sorrow to their villages that afternoon, but others stayed to reproach the man who had called himself God the Father: 'Where is thy wave, and where is thy Salvation now, thou man of many words? And who shall now save any of us from the law?'

He had no answer for them. The turmoil mounted. Not he, but the woman who called herself Christ-the-Forgiver, silenced them this time. It was near sundown when she suddenly shrieked, 'Fools! Fools and Sinners! A new vision has come to me. Listen, lest God strike you dead where you stand.' They stood dumb at the fearful threat.

She was a heavy, wild-haired creature with a voice of brass. She lumbered among them with upflung arms mixing curses with calls upon God to pity their unbelief: 'It is ye who have failed,' she screamed at them, 'ye, who have waited for God to send a wave from the sea. This is the meaning of my vision. God will send no wave; He waits for us; we are the wave that shall arise to make the way clear for His feet; we are the wave that shall destroy Koata and his Roman Catholics. Arise! Make an end of them, that God may forgive our blindness and be with us tonight.'

A great number fled from the camp in instant horror, but several hundreds stood convinced, and almost at once the Sheep and Swords, yelling, 'Kill them, kill them!' set forth from the chapel, Ten Naewa at their head the rest behind, their bodies contorted in an insane kind of dance towards the Government Station.

Men ran to warn Koata of their coming. He begged his friends to go at once and hide among the trees, but not one deserted the Station, and his wife defied him to budge her from the house. He did not argue, but pulled out his best sleeping-mat and spread it on the floor. She knew what that meant; she was to bury his dead body in it. She said, 'Sir, it will be big enough for both of us,' and sat down beside it: He answered (she told me afterwards), 'Woman, it is well,' embraced her and went out.

He stood alone on the edge of the Government Station awaiting the mob. He had put on his navy-blue lava-lava, his white uniform coat and his belt of office with the bright silver crown. He was not a big man; he must have looked very small, standing there alone in the twilight under the tall palms; but there was something about him that gave pause to that mad procession. It halted and fell silent. He walked forward to Ten Naewa, saying, 'Sir, if it is myself thou seekest, here I am.'

The quietude of it seems to have shamed Ten Naewa. He looked down and gave no answer. Koata spoke again: 'Enough. Turn back now. Too much evil has already been done. Let the people return to their villages.'

That started a talk. Ten Naewa began to bargain for a general amnesty for all who had terrorized the villages. But Koata could not promise that; he could only guarantee a fair trial for anyone charged with an offence; the law could not be traded away for his own safety. His firmness, and the sight of their own leader actually pleading with him at last, enraged the crowd anew: 'Kill him, kill him!' they shouted. A dozen Swords of Gabriel leapt forward; Koata was struck down.

It was a terrible head wound, which held him near death for many days, but it did not kill him. He would not have been left alive but for a sudden decency of Ten Naewa's. Perhaps something in his quiet talk had opened a gate of remorse in the Prophet's heart, for, when Swords and Sheep surged in to trample the prone body, their erstwhile leader straddled it and fought them off. They swept on impatiently to the back of the Government Station. He followed in their wake. They had beaten and wounded everyone before he caught up with them, but his new fury prevented them from murder. They scattered into the villages where he could not follow. A hunt for Roman Catholics ensued. Two unfortunates were caught and killed with crowbars and broken bottles. Most of their co-religionists fled at once in canoes, forty miles overseas to the island of Tabiteuea. An edict went out from the Swords of Gabriel that night: if, by noon of the next day but one, the few who remained had not presented themselves at the chapel for conversion to the creed of Ten Naewa, they would be slaughtered. Ten Naewa had no hand in that, but he had created a monster beyond his powers of control.

Guards were set around the Government Station to see that none escaped. It was an idle precaution. Some of the loyal party were, indeed, strong enough to have slipped away before dawn, but they had decided to stand by Koata and the other wounded to the end. It was the real spirit of Onotoa's ancestors that spoke through those few mouths: '*Ti a tia n teirake, ni mate* (We have stood up to die)' was the way they summed it up. The old idiom meant that they had reckoned every chance of death from the beginning, and would not be running away from it now.

'And behold! the day dawned,' said one of them afterwards, 'and it was a day of life.' The Gilbertese tell their tales, whether in court or in private, with a fine sense of drama, and they expect their listeners to play up. A climax is a thing to be savoured. You must drag it out of them.

'How then, Aberamo? A day of life?'

'A day of life. Those others were waiting to kill us on the morrow, yet we died not. No, for death was prevented that day.'

'Prevented, Aberamo?'

'Ay, Sir . . . prevented by the ship.'

'Aberamo! . . . The *ship*?'

'Ay, truly. The ship.'

A long silence. The listeners are artists too. A deep sigh greets his finish, 'The ship of the London Mission – even the *Tom Wiriami*.'

In more prosaic words, the *John Williams* arrived, with a District Officer and the local heads of the London Missionary Society aboard, on that one small day of grace decreed by the Swords of Gabriel.

Though most of the people had deserted the camp overnight on hearing of the murders, a good many still remained, and some of these tried to bluff things through with the white representative of the Mission's local Board. One of their moves was to produce before him a Sheep of Ten Naewa's fold, who was alleged to have fallen into a trance at hearing the Prophet speak. Nothing could wake her, they said. The Missionary's reaction made island history. He was surrounded by fanatics of incalculable temper, to whom the prestige of the Men of Matang meant nothing but a hateful pagan memory. But he did not hesitate.

He looked at the Sheep for a while and then advised gravely, 'This woman is very sick. Nevertheless, I think I can cure her. Go quickly and bring me a bucket of water.'

They raced each other to get it. He took the bucket. 'Yes,' he murmured, 'water's the stuff; the colder, the better,' and emptied the lot over the Sheep. She came out of her trance with a yell, and fled. 'Hysteria,' he finished quietly, 'that's what we call it. Now I've shown you how, go do the same yourselves to anyone else who falls into these trances.'

It was touch and go for him in that moment, I fancy. Had he laughed, anything might have happened to him; had he even allowed the incident to prolong itself in words, their madness might well have worked itself up anew; but he did neither. 'Now, let's get down to business,' he said matter of factly, and held their minds firmly switched to other lines. It was beautifully done. His courage and deftness of touch throughout that day broke the last of the madness before nightfall.

There was a commission of inquiry, and sad things remained to be done when the leaders came to trial. The murderers of the two Roman Catholics were never traced; it is doubtful if anybody except the actual killers ever knew who was guilty – their chiefs among the Swords of Gabriel were certainly not present in the same district that night. But some long sentences for riot, wounding and attempted murder had to be inflicted. A magistrate feels a heavy sense of futility in dealing with such cases. The individual's guilt is so often only the symptom of a disease spread by others; the disseminators themselves so often escape scot-free, through the ignorance or dogged loyalty of their dupes. Most of the teachers escaped serious punishment. The only people I was glad to see put away were Ten Naewa and the evil women called 'Christ-the-Sufferer' and 'Christ-the-Forgiver'. Ten Naewa might have got as much as fourteen years but for witnesses who testified to how, in the end, he had defended Koata from the rioters. The prisoner's friend who brought these witnesses forward to help him was the father of his island, Koata himself.

5

LAGOON DAYS

Sharks

There is a four-fathom bank of Tarawa lagoon where the tiger-shark muster in hundreds for a day or two every month. If you let your canoe drift offshore at rising tide, you can watch their great striped bodies sliding and swooping with arrogant ease not six feet under your keel. They range in length from nine to fourteen feet, with an occasional giant of seventeen or eighteen feet among them. There is nightmare in the contrast between their hideous size and the slack grace of their movements in the glassy water. Their explosions out of quietude into action are even more atrocious. An evil shape comes gliding below you, smoothly, negligently, as if tranced in idleness; the next instant, one monstrous convulsion has flung it hurtling into attack.

In my earliest days at Tarawa, I spent a good deal of time

watching the tigers there. I wanted to find out why, for a couple of days each month, they preferred that particular hunting-ground to a dozen others that seemed as good. Tigers always do cruise around banks where the smaller fish swarm, but not usually in hundreds. Any village fisherman could have told me the whole story in a few seconds, but I was new to the place, and the Gilbertese do not render up their knowledge easily to strangers. It was only by chance that I stumbled on the first clue. I happened to tell my cook-boy that I wanted to go trolling for trevally over the shark-grounds.

He smiled: 'When the *rereba* (trevally) are there, the *tababa* (tiger-shark) also are there. If you hook a rereba you will end with a hot bottom, for the tababa will take it from you.'

I paused to wonder what a hot bottom might be. 'Sir,' he replied, 'it is the fisherman's word for the state of one who sits, and sits, and catches nothing, and behold! as it were, his bottom burns.'

'And say now – if the tababa are there for the rereba, what are the rereba there for?'

'*Kai ngkam*,' he replied, meaning anything from 'I really couldn't say' to 'I'm not sure I ought to tell you that.'

But I had my clue. The inquiry that followed led me right back from the trevally in the four-fathom water, down through a gradually diminishing series of ravenous mouths to the shoreline.

The land in that part of Tarawa is cut by a tidal passage between lagoon and ocean. When the springs flood high through the passage, they bring riding in with them from outside a minute marine organism, which settles along the shallows. The weed, or animalcule, or plankton (I do not know which it is) makes tempting food for millions of tiny soft crabs that live on the water's edge. Great hosts of these, none much bigger than a sequin, are lured by the bait an inch or so deeper into the sea than they usually venture.

The next scene belongs to the teeming sardines. Perhaps they too have mustered in their millions because of the tide-borne food; or perhaps they know that the coming of the food spells crabs in the shallows. Whichever enticed them first, they remain for only one purpose. Their battalions, massed like silver clouds in the two-foot shoals, charge wave upon wave to the lip of the tide bent upon nothing but the massacre of crabs.

But sardines make just the food the grey mullet love best. The mullet have been massing for their own purposes a little farther out. If these again are initially attracted by the floating food, they soon forget it. They plunge in among the sardines, a ravening army of one-pounders. The small fish twist and scatter wildly into open water, the bigger ones after them.

And that is why the vivid, blue backed trevally have come so close inshore. Their meat is mullet. They sweep to landward of their quarry and hunt them out to sea, devouring as they go. But alas for their strength and beauty! Engrossed in their chase, they drive straight for the bank where the tiger-shark are mustered. A sixty-pound trevally is a streak of azure lightning over the shining bottom. He can zig-zag in a flash and leap a man's height sheer from the sea to escape a close pursuer. No heavy-barrelled tiger-shark, hunting alone, is a match for his dazzling tactics. But for all his desperate twists and turns, his breachings and his soundings, he is lost where a hundred rushing jaws are above and below and around him.

Yet, in the last act, it is not the tigers that triumph. The ultimate destroyer in that chain of hungry bellies and ravening jaws is no creature of the sea but man himself, out after shark-flesh in those innocently smiling waters.

Thirty-five years ago, the Gilbertese were beginning to use steel hooks for shark-fishing; but there were many who still claimed that the old-style twelve-inch ironwood hook, trained to the right shape on the living tree, was the only thing for tiger-shark. A twig of the tree (*pemphis acidula*) was bent so that it recurved upon itself, and left to grow lashed in that position for a year or two. When it was rather more than half an inch thick, it was cut and fashioned for service. The outstanding virtue of this gigantic instrument was that it could be grown with magic, trained with magic, cut with magic, and trimmed with magic. Good luck for the fisherman and bad luck for the shark could be poured into it at every stage of its manufacture, whereas a steel hook bought from a trade-store could only be magicked once, as a finished article. According to the old men, nobody but folk ignorant of the proper spells would ever dream of using anything but ironwood.

A three-foot length of plaited hair from the head of the fisher's wife or daughter made the trace for an old-style hook, and the line was a coconut-fibre rope as thick as a man's forefinger. The shark-hunter was not out for sport; he wanted nothing but dead shark. His gaff was not a gaff, but a glorious club with a ten-pound rock for its head. And it was not for simple fun that he did his fishing from a canoe not much longer than a man; the basic reason was that he could not handle the line himself; if he did, the bite of any sizeable shark would snatch him flying into the sea. He had to make the line fast to the middle of his craft; and that spelt a small canoe, because the resistance of a big one to the first furious jerks of his catch would tear the hull apart.

I imagine the broad technique of it is still very much as it used to be in those days. The fisher paddles out in his cockleshell, baits his hook, whether ironwood or steel, with a couple of pounds of almost any kind of offal, lets it hang from amidships on two or three fathoms of line, and drifts waiting for a bite, his club beside him. A big one takes the hook. The quiet canoe gives a sudden lurch and starts careering round in mad little circles; or it bounces insanely up and down; or it zig-zags like a misdirected rocket; or it rushes off in a straight line, forwards or backwards as the case may be, at sizzling speed, the fisherman holding on grimly whatever it does. Half a dozen small craft milling around like that all at the same time, without visible means of propulsion, make a wildly eccentric sight from the shore. But the fury of a tiger-shark's struggles soon exhausts it. It floats limply to the surface and then comes the high moment of the fisherman's day. He hauls the spent brute cautiously alongside and, letting out one piercing howl of pleasure, cracks it on the nose with his trusty club. That is the only part of the business, I think, that affords him anything like the savage thrill that civilized sportsmen get out of killing things.

But although safety first is the rule when tiger-shark are about in numbers, plenty of Gilbertese are ready to fight a lone prowler in its own element. Owing to his great girth, a tiger cannot turn quickly; once launched on its attack, it thunders straight forward like a bull; there lies the hunter's advantage in single combat. Out sailing with a Tarawa friend one day, I pointed out a cruising dorsal fin. 'That's a tababa,' he said, 'watch me kill him.'

We lowered sail and drifted. He slid overboard with his knife and paddled around waiting to be noticed. He soon was. The fin began to circle him, and he knew he was being stalked; he trod water; it closed in gradually, lazily to fifteen yards.

He held his knife right-handed, blade down, the handle just above the water, his crooked right elbow pointed always towards the gliding fin. He would have a split second to act in when the charge came. It came from ten yards' range. There was a frothing swirl; the fin shot forward like an arrow; the head and shoulders of the brute broke surface, rolling as they lunged. My friend flicked aside in the last blink of time and shot his knife into the upswinging belly as it surged by. His enemy's momentum did the rest. I saw the belly rip itself open like a zip-fastener, discharging blood and guts. The tiger disappeared for a while, to float up dead a hundred yards off.

That kind of single combat used to be fairly common. It was rather like a nice score of fifty at cricket in England; the villagers applauded but did not make a great song about it. But the feat of Teriakai, another Tarawa man, became a matter of official record. Teriakai was a guest of His Majesty's at the time, having got himself into trouble for a rather too carefree interpretation of the marriage laws. He was an exceptionally welcome guest; his vital, stocky frame was the equal of a giant's for work, and the bubbling of his unquenchable humour kept his warders as well as his fellow-prisoners laughing and labouring from morning to night. A happy prison is a tremendous asset to any Government Station. Whenever there was a special job to be done, he was the man we always chose to do it. It followed naturally that, when the captain and chief engineer of S.S. *Tokelau* – lying beached for cleaning in Tarawa lagoon – wanted to go out for a sail in weather that threatened to turn nasty, Teriakai went also to look after them.

The south-east trades have their treacheries on the Equator.

Though they breathe steady at twenty-five miles an hour for months on end, you can never afford to forget how suddenly the wind can slam round to the north and blow a forty-mile gale. If the northerly buster brakes your mainsail aback close-hauled to the south-easter you are capsized before you know what has hit you. The Tarawans call that particular wind Nei Bairara, the Long-armed Woman. She caught Teriakai and his friends just after they had put about for the homeward run. They were spilled into the lagoon ten miles from their starting point and eight miles from the nearest land on Tarawa's northern arm.

Two chief dangers threatened them then: tiger-shark were all around them, and they were near enough to the ocean reef to be sucked out to sea when the tide began to fall. Teriakai attended to the sharks first of all. He started by hacking the mainsail adrift with gaff and boom complete (His Majesty's guests are not supposed to carry sheath-knives, but he had one, bless his impertinence). The canvas, buoyed at head and foot by its spars, made a fine bag under water, into which he ushered the captain and engineer: 'Stay inside this,' he said, bridling their refuge by a length of halyard to the upturned boat, 'and the tababa won't smell you.' Then he looked for the anchor. The chain had fortunately been made fast to a thwart, but it took him an hour of diving and groping to get everything unsnarled so that the anchor reached bottom. 'I'll go and get help now,' he said when that was done: 'If I can get past those tababa, we shall perhaps be meeting again.'

He swam straight at the ring of tigers – the captain and engineer watched him – and the devils let him through. I asked him afterwards if he had any notion why. He replied, 'If you stay still in the sea, the tababa will charge you. If you swim away from them in fear, they will smell your fear and chase you. If you swim without fear towards them, they will be afraid and leave you in peace.' So he chose his shark, swam full speed towards it, and lo! the line melted away before him. There was absolutely nothing to it except a courage that passes belief.

He had gone about four miles before anything else happened. I have an idea it need not have happened at all unless he had wanted it to. He said the next tababa just attacked him, but he never could explain for laughing why he trod water and waited for this one instead of trying to shoo it off like the others. It is a good guess that he was overcome by the thrill of wearing a sheath-knife again and the delight of feeling himself, after months of prison, alone and free for a little in his loved lagoon. Then again, the tababa was a male. I do not know how males and females are distinguished from a distance, but the Gilbertese fishermen knew, and they valued the genital organ of a bull-tiger very highly. They said a man who had the right magic could appropriate its virile qualities to his own unspeakable advantage as a squire of dames. Teriakai made a nice job of the tababa, extracted the priceless organ from its ventral slot, tucked it into his belt, and swam on.

The swift night of the equator fell on him in the next half-hour. The moon was not yet up, repeated busters from the north were whipping the water to fury. In the welter of waves about his head, he missed his direction and swam into a maze of reefs off the coast to left of his objective. The breaking seas flung him on cruel edges, rolled him over splintering coral branches, sucked him into clefts bristling with barbs, spewed him out again stabbed and torn until more than a quarter of the skin (so the doctor reported) was flayed from his body. But he got through still conscious, swam a mile to shore, waded and walked two more to a white trader's house, and collapsed on his verandah. The trader brought him round with a tot of rum, but refused to take his boat out to the rescue on a night like that.

Teriakai's answer was better than words. He grabbed the bottle of rum (forbidden by law to natives) from the man's hand and ran with it out into the night. He had another five miles to struggle to the next trader's house; I doubt if even his gay courage could have made it but for the liquor. In any case, it would be pettifogging to carp at the good cheer of his arrival. He awoke Jimmy Anton with a stentorian song about tababa, and himself, and girls, and capsized white men, beating time for himself on the front door with whangs of the thing he had cut from the shark. In his left hand was an empty rum bottle. He streamed blood from head to ankles, but a smile of pure rapture shone through the torn mask of his face.

Jimmy Anton, the son of an Austrian father and a Gilbertese mother, was not the man to refuse a risk either for himself or his boat. He called out his Gilbertese wife, and between the three of them they got the boat launched at once. His wife brought coconut oil for Teriakai's wounds, blankets and brandy for the rescued. They set out together. The moon had risen by then. They found the capsized boat just before dawn. The captain and engineer had been in the water twelve hours, but they were still safe inside their canvas bag. Teriakai was awarded the bronze medal of the Royal Humane Society. Before that arrived he had acquired a uniform to wear it on, for we discharged him from prison at once and made a colony policeman of him. Nobody ever found out what he did with the trophy the shark gave him. It disappeared from official ken the moment we got him into hospital.

*

There is just one kind of shark that really does scare the Gilbertese. They call it the *rokea*. It is a giant as slim as a panther, that doubles on its tracks at full speed. Fortunately, it never haunts lagoons, being a deep-sea hunter, but when the bonito hold their annual swarming over the forty-fathom banks outside some lagoons, the rokea are there too in their scores. The biggest of them run well over twenty feet long. You never see them lurk or prowl, for their dreadful quickness exempts them from any need of stalking. They flash like hurled lances through the water, and they can leap bodily from the sea, using tails as well as jaws to kill.

I had hooked a bonito outside Tarawa one day, when there was a jerk followed by a deadness at the end of the line. I started reeling in, but my canoe-mate jumped forward and without a by-your-leave cut the line. 'A rokea has bitten your fish in half,' he said then, 'give it the rest.' He explained that, if the half-fish had been hauled aboard, the enraged rokea might have attacked the canoe, and that would have been the end of us.

I did not really believe him then. It was only a couple of years later that I saw what he meant. My canoe with a dozen others was trolling for bonito off Nonouti, when we heard a thud and a crack from a craft not sixty yards off.

As we looked up, there came another thud; a vast tail had frothed from the water and slammed the canoe's side. A second later, the whole fish leapt, and there was a third smashing blow. We saw the hull cave in and start sinking. The rokea leapt again, and one of the two fishermen on board was swept off the foundering deck by that frightful tail. We saw him butchered as we raced to rescue the other man. While we hauled the survivor aboard, the sea near us boiled with shark as other rokea, attracted by the victim's blood, fought each other for fragments of his body. The survivor, a boy of seventeen, confessed with tears that he was to blame; he had whipped a bonito aboard as a rokea was after it; the demon's attack followed in the very next instant. There was no more trolling there that day. They said the rokea would now connect every canoe-keel with human flesh, and attack unceasingly. We made off at once for other grounds, sailing bunched together for safety.

I gave up fishing after a few years, because I found my heart aching for the beauty and courage of the things I caught. But there were two terrors of the sea whose death I never could mourn – the octopus and the tiger-shark. These seemed to me as little worth pity as any prowling bully, and I felt no sense of guilt in killing them.

In the early days at Tarawa, I did want just one tababa all my own. I could not get the brutes to take any kind of trolled bait or cast lure, so I had to fall back on the villagers' technique with a one-man canoe, a twelve-inch ironwood hook bought as a curio, and a lovely loaded club. My cook-boy immediately doubled up with laughter when I announced my intention to him. I asked him why all that mirth, but he only clutched at his stomach and staggered some more around the verandah. He found further entertainment in watching me attach the hook to a trace of steel dog-chain, and in putting up an idiotic burlesque of magic-ritual over the finished work. His antics had the other servants hooting with him in the end. They clung to my arms, gurgling, 'O, the Man of Matang . . . the Man of Matang, o-o!' to show no offence was meant. But nobody would tell me exactly what was the great joke behind it all.

The next day, when we got to the sandspit where my little canoe lay waiting, it became clear that the whole village had been warned of the event. The beach was crawling with sight-seers. They were all immensely courteous, but the shining of their beautiful eyes gave them away. I was wafted on to the canoe and pushed off in a silence that throbbed with joyous expecta-tion. I found this more than a little embarrassing, but it was nothing to what followed.

Eighty yards offshore, I dropped the baited hook, made the line fast and, following instructions, set the canoe drifting beachwards with a paddle-stroke or two. I had certainly hoped for a quick bite, if only to save my face, but I was altogether unready for the fulminating success that fell upon me.

I was not yet settled back in my seat when the canoe took a shuddering leap backwards and my nose hit the foredeck. A roar went up from the crowd as I was drawn whizzing away from it on my face. I picked myself up with much care and was in the act of sitting again when the shark reversed direction. The back of my head cracked down on the deck behind me; my legs flew up; my high-riding bottom was presented to the sightseers shooting at incredible speed towards them.

In the next fifteen minutes, without one generous pause, that shark contrived to jerk, twist or bounce from my body for public exhibition every ignoble attitude of which a gangling frame, lost to all self-respect in a wild scrabble for handholds, is cap-able. The climax of its malice was in its last act. It floated belly up and allowed itself to be hauled alongside as if quite dead. I piloted it so into the shallows. There I tottered to my feet to deliver the *coup-de-grâce*. But it flipped as the club swung down; I missed, hit the sea, somersaulted over its body, and stood on my head under water with legs impotently flapping in the air.

This filled the cup of the villagers. As I waded ashore, there was not a soul on his feet. The beach was a sea of rolling brown bodies racked on the extremity of joy, incapable of any sound but a deep and tortured groaning. I crept silently from their presence to the seclusion of my home. When my cook-boy was able to stand, he staggered back and told me the point of it. A

Gilbertese youth is trained to sit a bucking canoe about as carefully as we are taught to ride. It takes him a year or so to master the technique. That was why the villagers had turned up expecting some innocent fun from me, and gone away fulfilled. But they despatched the shark before leaving. Their kaubure brought along the liver that evening as a reward for my cookboy. A few days later, the jaws, beautifully dried and cleaned, were sent to me, the champion of the wooden hook, as a consolation prize.

Assignment with an Octopus

I certainly should have never ventured out alone for pure sport, armed with nothing but a knife, to fight a tiger-shark in its own element. I am as little ashamed of that degree of discretion as the big-game hunter who takes care not to attack a rhinoceros with a shotgun. The fear I had for the larger kinds of octopus was quite different. It was a blind fear, sick with disgust, unreasoned as a child's horror of darkness. Victor Hugo was the man who first brought it up to the level of my conscious thought. I still remember vividly the impression left on me as a boy of fourteen by that account in *Les Travailleurs de la Mer* of Gilliatt's fight with the monster that caught him among the rocks of The Douvres. For years after reading it, I tortured myself with wondering how ever I could behave with decent courage if faced with a giant at once so strong and so loathsome. My commonest nightmare of the period was of an octopus-like Presence poised motionless behind me, towards which I dared not turn, from which my limbs were too frozen to escape. But that phase did pass before I left school, and the Thing lay dormant inside me until a day at Tarawa.

Before I reached Tarawa, however, chance gave me a swift glimpse of what a biggish octopus could do to a man. I was wading at low tide one calm evening on the lip of the reef at Ocean Island when a Baanaban villager, back from fishing, brought his canoe to land within twenty yards of where I stood. There was no more than a show of breaking seas, but the water was only knee deep, and this obliged the fisherman to slide overboard and handle his lightened craft over the jagged edge. But no sooner were his feet upon the reef than he seemed to be tied to where he stood. The canoe was washed shorewards ahead of him; while he stood with legs braced, tugging desperately away from something. I had just time to see a tapering, greyish yellow rope curled around his right wrist before he broke away from it. He fell sprawling into the shallow water; the tapered rope flicked writhing back into the foam at the reef's edge. The fisherman picked himself up and nursed his right arm. I had reached him by then. The octopus had caught him with only the top of one tentacle, but the terrible hold of the few suckers on his wrist had torn the skin whole from it as he wrenched himself adrift.

This is not to say that all the varieties of octopus known to the Gilbertese are dangerous to man. Some of them are mere midgets, and very beautiful. Lying face down on a canoe anchored over rocks and sand in Tarawa lagoon, I sometimes used to watch for the smaller kinds through a water-glass.

The smallest I saw could have been comfortably spread on the lid of a cigarette tin. I noticed that the colours of all the little ones varied very much according to where they were crawling, from the mottled rust-red and brown of coral rock to the clear gold and orange-brown of sunlit sand speckled with seaweed. From the height of my top-window, most of them looked as flat as starfish slithering over the bottom, but there was one minute creature that had a habit of standing on its toes. It would constrict its tentacles into a kind of neck where they joined the head and, with its body so raised, would jig up and down rather like a dancing frog. But what appealed most to my wonder was the way they all swam. A dozen sprawling, lace-like shapes would suddenly gather themselves into stream-lines and shoot upwards, jet-propelled by the marvellous syphon in their heads, like a display of fairy water-rockets. At the top of their flight, they seemed to explode; their tails of trailed tentacles burst outwards into shimmering points around their tiny bodies, and they sank like drifting gossamer stars back to the sea-floor again.

The female octopus anchors her eggs to stalks of weeds and coral under water. It seems to be a moot point whether she broods in their neighbourhood or not, but I once saw what I took to be a mother out for exercise with five babies. She had a body about the size of a tennis ball and tentacles perhaps a foot long. The length of the small ones, streamlined for swimming, was not more than five inches over all. They were cruising around a coral pinnacle in four feet of water. The big one led, the babies followed six inches behind, in what seemed to be an ordered formation: they were grouped, as it were, around the base of a cone whereof she was the forward-pointing apex.

They cruised around the pinnacle for half a minute or more, and then went down to some small rocks at its base. While the little ones sprawled over the bottom, the mother remained poised above them. It looked to my inexpert eye exactly as if she were mounting guard over her young. And at that point a big trevally was obliging enough to become the villain of a family drama for my benefit. He must have been watching the little group from deeper water. As the mother hovered there, he came in at her like a blue streak. But she avoided him somehow; he flashed by and turned to dart in again, only to see a black cloud of squirted ink where the octopus had been. (Incidentally, that was the only time I myself ever saw an octopus discharge its ink-sac.) The trevally swerved aside, fetched a full circle and came very slowly back to the edge of the black cloud, while the mother and her family were escaping towards the shallows on the other side. He loitered around for a while, then seemed to take fright and flicked away at speed into the deep water.

The old navigators of the Gilberts used to talk with fear of a gigantic octopus that inhabited the seas between Samoa and the Ellice Islands. They said its tentacles were three-arm-spans long and thicker at the base than the body of a full-grown man – a scale of measurements not out of keeping with what is known of the atrocious monster called *Octopus Apollyon*. There were some who stated that this foul fiend of the ocean was also to be found in the waters between Onotoa, Tamana and Arorae in the Southern Gilberts. But I never came across a man who had seen one, and the biggest of the octopus breed I ever saw with my own eyes had tentacles only a little over six feet long. It was a member of the clan *Octopus Vulgaris*, which swarms in all the lagoons. An average specimen of this variety is a dwarf beside *Octopus Apollyon*: laid out flat, it has a total spread of no more than nine or ten feet, but it is a wicked-looking piece of work, even in death, with those disgusting suckers studding its arms and those bulging, filmed eyes staring out of the mottled gorgon face.

Possibly, if you can watch objectively, the sight of *Octopus Vulgaris* searching for crabs and crayfish on the floor of the lagoon may move you to something like admiration. You cannot usually see the dreadful eyes from a water-glass straight above its feeding ground, and your feeling for crustaceans is too impersonal for horror at their fate between pouncing suckers and jaws. There is real beauty in the rich change of its colours as it moves from shadow to sunlight, and the gliding ease of its arms as they reach and flicker over the rough rocks fascinates the eye with its deadly grace. You feel that if only the creature would stick to its grubbing on the bottom, the shocking ugliness of its shape might even win your sympathy, as for some poor Caliban in the enchanted garden of the lagoon. But it is no honest grubber in the open. For every one of its kind that you see crawling below you, there are a dozen skulking in recesses of the reef that falls away like a cliff from the edge where you stand watching. When *Octopus Vulgaris* has eaten its fill of the teeming crabs and crayfish, it seeks a dark cleft in the coral face, and anchors itself there with a few of the large suckers nearest to its body. Thus shielded from attack in the rear, with tentacles gathered to pounce, it squats glaring from the shadows, alert for anything alive to swim within striking distance. It can hurl one or all of those whiplashes forward with the speed of dark lightning, and once its scores of suckers, rimmed with hooks for grip on slippery skins, are clamped about their prey, nothing but the brute's death will break their awful hold.

But that very quality of the octopus that most horrifies the imagination, its relentless tenacity, becomes its undoing when hungry man steps into the picture. The Gilbertese happen to value certain parts of it as food, and their method of fighting it is coolly based upon the one fact that its arms never change their grip. They hunt for it in pairs. One man acts as the bait, his partner as the killer. First, they swim eyes-under at low tide just off the reef, and search the crannies of the submarine cliff for sight of any tentacle that may flicker out for a catch. When they have placed their quarry, they land on the reef for the next stage. The human bait starts the real game. He dives and tempts the lurking brute by swimming a few strokes in front of its cranny, at first a little beyond striking range. Then he turns and makes straight for the cranny, to give himself into the embrace of those waiting arms. Sometimes nothing happens. The beast will not always respond to the lure. But usually it strikes.

The partner on the reef above stares down through the pellucid water, waiting for his moment. His teeth are his only weapon. His killing efficiency depends on his avoiding every one of those strangling arms. He must wait until his partner's body has been drawn right up to the entrance of the cleft. The monster inside is groping then with its horny mouth against the victim's flesh, and sees nothing beyond it. That point is reached in a matter of no more than thirty seconds after the decoy has plunged. The killer dives, lays hold of his pinioned friend at arms' length, and jerks him away from the cleft; the octopus is torn from the anchorage of its proximal suckers, and clamps itself the more fiercely to its prey. In the same second, the human bait gives a kick which brings him, with quarry annexed, to the surface. He turns on his back, still holding his breath for better buoyancy, and this exposes the body of the beast for the kill. The killer closes in, grasps the evil head from behind, and wrenches it away from its meal. Turning the face up towards himself, he plunges his teeth between the bulging eyes, and bites down and in with all his strength. That is the end of it. It dies on the instant; the suckers release their hold; the arms fall away; the two fishers paddle with whoops of delighted laughter to the reef, where they string the catch to a pole before going to rout out the next one.

Any two boys of seventeen, any day of the week, will go out and get you half a dozen octopus like that for the mere fun of it. Here lies the whole point of this story. The hunt is, in the most literal sense, nothing but child's play to the Gilbertese.

As I was standing one day at the end of a jetty in Tarawa lagoon, I saw two boys from the near village shouldering a string of octopus slung on a pole between them. I started to wade out in their direction, but before I hailed them they had stopped, planted the carrying-pole upright in a fissure and, leaving it there, swum off the edge for a while with faces submerged evidently searching for something under water. I had been only a few months at Tarawa, and that was my first near view of an octopus-hunt. I watched every stage of it from the dive of the human bait to the landing of the dead catch. When it was over, I went up to them. I could hardly believe that in those few seconds, with no more than a frivolous-looking splash or two on the surface, they could have found, caught and killed the creature they were now stringing up before my eyes. They explained the amusing simplicity of the thing.

'There's only one trick the decoy-man must never forget,' they said, 'and that's not difficult to remember. If he is not wearing the water-spectacles of the Men of Matang, he must cover his eyes with a hand as he comes close to the *kika* (octopus), or the sucker might blind him.' It appeared that the ultimate fate of the eyes was not the thing to worry about; the immediate point was that the sudden pain of a sucker clamping itself to an eyeball might cause the bait to expel his breath and inhale sea-water; that would spoil his buoyancy, and he would fail then to give his friend the best chance of a kill.

Then they began whispering together. I knew in a curdling flash what they were saying to each other. Before they turned to speak to me again, a horrified conviction was upon me. My damnable curiosity had led me into a trap from which there was no escape. They were going to propose that I should take a turn at being the bait myself, just to see how delightfully easy it was. And that is what they did. It did not even occur to them that I might not leap at the offer. I was already known as a young Man of Matang who liked swimming, and fishing, and laughing with the villagers; I had just shown an interest in this particular form of hunting; naturally, I should enjoy the fun of it as much as they did. Without even waiting for my answer, they gleefully ducked off the edge of the reef to look for another octopus – a fine fat one – *mine*. Left standing there alone, I had another of those visions . . .

It was dusk in the village. The fishers were home, I saw the cooking-fires glowing orange-red between the brown lodges. There was laughter and shouted talk as the women prepared the evening meal. But the laughter was hard with scorn. 'What?' they were saying, 'Afraid of a kika? The young Man of Matang? Why, even the boys are not afraid of a kika!' A curtain went down and rose again on the Residency; the Old Man was talking: 'A leader? You? The man who funked a schoolboy game? We don't leave your sort in charge of Districts.' The scene flashed to my uncles: 'Returned empty,' they said. 'We always knew you hadn't got it in you. Returned empty . . .'

Of course it was all overdrawn, but one fact was beyond doubt; the Gilbertese reserved all their most ribald humour for physical cowardice. No man gets himself passed for a leader anywhere by becoming the butt of that kind of wit. I decided I would rather face the octopus.

I was dressed in khaki slacks, canvas shoes and a short-sleeved singlet. I took off the shoes and made up my mind to shed the singlet if told to do so; but I was wildly determined to stick to my trousers throughout. Dead or alive, said a voice within me, an official minus his pants is a preposterous object, and I felt I could not face that extra horror. However, nobody asked me to remove anything.

I hope I did not look as yellow as I felt when I stood to take the plunge; I have never been so sick with funk before or since. 'Remember, one hand for your eyes,' said someone from a thousand miles off, and I dived.

I do not suppose it is really true that the eyes of an octopus shine in the dark; besides, it was clear daylight only six feet down in the limpid water; but I could have sworn the brute's eyes burned at me as I turned in towards his cranny. That dark glow – whatever may have been its origin – was the last thing I saw as I blacked out with my left hand and rose into his clutches. Then, I remember chiefly a dreadful sliminess with a herculean power behind it. Something whipped round my left forearm and the back of my neck, binding the two together. In the same flash, another something slapped itself high on my forehead, and I felt it crawling down inside the back of my singlet. My impulse was to tear at it with my right hand, but I felt the whole of that arm pinioned to my ribs. In most emergencies the mind works with crystal-clear impersonality. This was not even an emergency, for I knew myself perfectly safe. But my boyhood's nightmare was upon me. When I felt the swift constriction of those disgusting arms jerk my head and shoulders in towards the reef, my mind went blank of every thought save the beastliness of contact with that squat head. A mouth began to nuzzle below my throat, at the junction of the collar-bones. I forgot there was anyone to save me. Yet something still directed me to hold my breath.

I was awakened from my cowardly trance by a quick, strong pull on my shoulders, back from the cranny. The cables around me tightened painfully, but I knew I was adrift from the reef. I gave a kick, rose to the surface and turned on my back with the brute sticking out of my chest like a tumour. My mouth was smothered by some flabby moving horror. The suckers felt like hot rings pulling at my skin. It was only two seconds, I suppose, from then to the attack of my deliverer, but it seemed like a century of nausea.

My friend came up between me and the reef. He pounced, pulled, bit down, and the thing was over – for everyone but me. At the sudden relaxation of the tentacles, I let out a great breath, sank, and drew in the next under water. It took the united help of both boys to get me, coughing, heaving and pretending to join in their delighted laughter, back to the reef. I had to submit there to a kind of war-dance round me, in which the dead beast was slung whizzing past my head from one to the other. I had a chance to observe then that it was not by any stretch of fancy a giant, but just plain average. That took the bulge out of my budding self-esteem. I left hurriedly for the cover of the jetty, and was sick.

6

STRANGE INTERLUDE

Introduction in Sorcery

Most Europeans who believe in an after-life draw a clear horizon-line between the worlds of the living and the dead. The pagans of the Gilbert Islands, as I knew them, imagined no such comfortable partition. The seen and the unseen made but one world for them. Their dead were helped overseas to a western paradise, it is true, but no known ritual could bind them there; only the lapse of generations could do that.

The belief was that the more recently departed could and did return. They were jealous. They wanted to see what their descendants were doing. Their skeletons or skulls were preserved in village shrines mainly for them to re-enter as they liked. If skulls at least were not kept, their ghosts would come and scream reproach by night with the voices of crickets from the palm-leaves that overhung the dwellings. And so, whether a man was pious or impious to his fathers, his house was a house forever brooded over by unseen watchers.

Not that the older folk thought of their dead only as threatening ghosts. There was love as well as fear in the ancient cult of the ancestor, and mostly the love predominated. I was looking round the waterfront of a Tarawa village one day when I came upon an old, old man alone in a canoe shed nursing a skull in the crook of his elbow. He was blowing tobacco smoke between its jaws. As he puffed, he chuckled and talking aloud: 'The smoke is sweet, grand-father – ke-e-e?' he was saying. 'We like it – ke-e-e?' He told me he was loving the skull because his grand-father – who was inside it at that moment – had been very good to him in years gone by. 'Is it not suitable,' he asked, 'for me to be good to him in return?' and answered himself at once, '*Aong-koa!* (of course!)' He went on to say he had chosen tobacco as his offering of love because, as far as he knew, there was no supply of that particular luxury in the ancestral paradise. For his homely affection, at least, the skull was no grim reminder of death, but a cheerful token of man's and love's immortality.

The sad thing was that the earliest Christian teachers in the Gilbert Islands gave no honour to the spirit of filial gratitude and fatherly goodness that breathed through the old beliefs. More modern pioneers would have used them, much as gardeners use the rugged stocks of wild rose and bitter orange, for grafts of tenderer yield. I saw one or two later missionaries, both Protestant and Roman Catholic, earnestly trying to do that; but the harm had gone too far by their day to be undone. Cruel, unavenged raids on village skull shrines in the last thirty years of the nineteenth century, and indiscriminate derision poured upon the old ways of thought well into the twentieth, had destroyed almost all veneration for the pagan dead among the rising generation by the time I reached the Gilbert Islands. Affection had made its exit with respect, and only superstition remained. Ancient superstitions are not rooted out as easily as ancient loves. The ghosts of the dead still haunted the villages; the difference was that they had become wholly vindictive now in the belief of everyone but a handful of the dying generation.

Then, too, there was the immanence of Things – Things that were not human. The new religion had not yet banished the fear of these. There was not a single inanimate object but had a Thing lurking inside it. A stick, a stone, a tree, a leaf, or the fragment of a leaf was not only its visible self but also a hidden presence. And every presence was a possible menace; it could be enlisted to destroy you. The more intimately it was attached to you, the more dangerous it could be. The spirit of your fish-hook could be turned by nothing more than the fixed stare of your enemy to bring you luckless fishing. The spirit of your cooking-oven could be made by sorcery to encompass your madness or death, the spirit of a fragment of your dress, or a nail-paring, or a stray hair of your head (especially if you were a woman) to work hideous things upon you. And crowding in at you out of the dark with the ghosts of the dead and the Things that lurked in things were the prowling familiars. Every sorcerer had his familiar. It was usually something alive like a beetle, bird or fish, but it might be some unbodied spirit of disease, or rottenness, or the blackness under the earth. Whatever it was, it could spy on you and bring evil as the sorcerer ordained. Beyond the familiars again were the multitudinous creatures whose death might mean your own, you knew not when – the life-index creatures. If your enemy took a lizard or a dragon-fly and slowly starved the breath out of it, using the right rituals, so would yours fade away, and when it died so would you too.

It seems a marvel that the race remained cheerful under the weight of so many dreads, for it did remain cheerful. I found plenty of evidence in the humorous legends and old burlesque songs and dances of the villagers that laughter never died in the Gilbert Islands. I personally believe that the survival of the people's sense of proportion was due mainly to their religion. 'Be of good heart amid all these dangers,' said the village fathers, 'for your ancestors love you.' I am not quoting at random; the words were said to me by Taakeuta, an elder of Royal Karongoa, the Sun clan into which I was adopted, when he believed me to be threatened by a death-curse. His teaching was that I had only to justify myself before the ancestors and the sun – first, by giving them honour, second, by avoiding incest, third, by abstaining from violence against their sacred creatures – and they would save me alive if I called upon them properly. A system of protective rituals had its roots in this comforting doctrine.

The appeal for protection was made in the form of invocations called *tataro*, which were, in effect, simple prayers. Taakeuta gave me two tataro for personal use. He recommended the first for what he courteously styled my 'bad luck' at fishing. It had to be recited sitting on my canoe, looking up at the sun (when it was at its noonday strength, ideally) with the luckless hook raised breast-high between joined palms:

> Sun-e-e, Sun-o-o, I beg thee, I, Grimble!
> Thou knowest me with my ill-wished hook.
> Ancestors-e-e, Auriaria, Tituaabine-o-o, I beg you, I, Grimble!
> You know me with my ill-fortune.
> I am faint-hearted, you! Help me!
> It is ended. Blessings and Peace are mine. Blessings and Peace.

128

The true characters of prayer appear more convincingly, perhaps, in the next example, for an attitude of supplication is associated there with an oblation and a plea of righteousness. My teacher gave me this one with others, as a sure defence against the death-spell I have mentioned. The instructions ran that, before beginning to eat any meal, I must raise a morsel of food on upturned palm before me and repeat aloud:

This is the lifting up of the portion of the Ancestors.
Here is thy food, Auriaria: I have committed no incest.
Here is thy food Tituaabine: I have not harmed thy creature (the Giant Ray).
I am excellent-e-e! I touch the Sun, I clasp the Moon.
Turn back the spirits of the death-magic; turn them back, for I, Grimble, beg you.
I am not lost. Blessings and Peace are mine. Blessings and Peace.

Taakeuta said the prayer would please the Ancestors best if I could get one or two companions of my adoptive clan to repeat it with me, I speaking in the first person singular for myself, they using the first person plural for all of us. It was disclosed to me later by my servant and dear friend Kirewa – also an adopted member of the sun clan – that tataro of the same shape were used in collective ceremonials for the fructification of the pandanus tree and the eating of first-fruits. One of the fructification prayers Kirewa gave me is of double interest here because it refers to the birth of Karongoa's secret sun-god Au, so many times mentioned already, from the crest of a virgin pandanus tree in the ancestral lands of Abatoa (Aba-the-Great) and Abaiti (Aba-the-Little). Abaiti is, of course, the Gilbertese equivalent of the ancient Maori fatherland Jawaiki. The prayer was intoned by a single officiator sitting with hands upturned at the foot of an emblematic pandanus tree. There was no limit to the number of Karongoa folk, men or women, who might be present, and members of Maerua, the moon-clan, might be invited but all others were strictly excluded. The ceremony took place at noon, the sun's strongest hour for ritual purposes:

This is the planting of our emblem of a tree, Au-forever-rising-o-o!
This is the planting of our emblem of a tree, Au-forever-turning-over-o-o!

129

This is our planting of our emblem of a tree, Au-forever-setting-o-o!
I have spread the branches of our tree of fruitfulness, our tree of the Sun
     and the Moon.
The lightning flashes, the thunder and the rain descend, even the
     fructifiers of the tree,
The virgin tree, the pandanus of Abatoa and Abaiti,
Thy tree, thy mother, Au-of-the-Northern-Solstice, Au-of-the-
     Southern-Solstice!
Spirit of the Crest, son of the tree, Au-forever-rising,
Spirits of Matang, Tituaabine, Tabuariki, Tevenei, Riiki,
I call to you, I call only to you:
Bless us under our tree of fruitfulness, fructify our pandanus trees, I beg
     you.
I beg you-o-o! I, Kirewa.
Blessings and Peace are ours. Blessings and Peace.

And when the first-fruits had been gathered in, sweet puddings
called *karababa* were made of the best of them for an offering to
the sun and moon. The officiator, sitting as before at the foot of
the emblematic tree, with the congregation in a half-circle behind him facing east, lifted a fragment of the sweet stuff on
upturned palms towards the crest, intoning:

This is your food, Sun and Moon,
Even the first-fruits of our pandanus tree.
This is thy food, child of the virgin tree, Au-forever-rising,
Even the first-fruits of our pandanus trees.
This is your food, spirits of Matang, Tituaabine, Tabuariki, Tevenei,
     Riiki,
Even the first-fruits of our pandanus trees.
We are blest under our tree of fruitfulness.
Blessings and Peace are ours. Blessings and Peace.

After which, he threw back his head to look up at the sun and
in that position swallowed the oblation, and the congregation,
with cries of 'Blessings and Peace are ours. Blessings and
Peace,' turned their faces to the sky and joined in the ritual meal.

The Gilbertese word *mauri* which I have here construed 'blessings' might also, in a very general sense, mean 'safety'. It has
compendious connotations of material prosperity, good health
and security from the attacks of evil spirits. In its prayerful

context, I think 'blessings' is the better word, as the state of being mauri was regarded always as a gift from the gods and the basis of all human happiness. I found few tataro, and none of those which appealed for protection from the death-magic, that did not close with the wistful formula – statement of faith and benediction in one – 'Blessings and Peace are ours. Blessings and Peace.' An equally touching and constant feature of all the protective prayers was their total freedom from revengeful motives. 'The Sun and the Ancestors will do what they will to your ill-wishers,' said my old friend to me: 'the tataro is not for anger.' These prayers aimed at security, in fact, not through the malice of the suppliant or his gods, but simply through the faith of a man in the love of his fore-fathers.

But the active charities that went with the cult of the ancestor were confined within the family group. There was no obligation upon a man to abstain from the practice of sorcery against members of clans other than his own, except his mother's and that into which he might have been adopted. The same person could be Dr Jekyll and Mr Hyde – a user of tataro for self-defence and of the death-spells called *wawi* and *wairaakau, maniwairaa* and *terakunene*, for aggression. As a sorcerer he was crudely animistic. He believed that everything in the world had inside it an *anti* – or spirit, that could be called up out of the darkness of its imprisoning stuff. Nothing was needed to evoke it but the use of the right words with the right movements. If every detail of his ritual were correct, the sorcerer became the master of the anti; there was no nonsense about its loving him or wanting his love.

But this is not to say that Gilbertese magic was wholly bent on evil. Its spells covered the entire range of village activities; there was not a cranny of a man's or a woman's life into which it did not penetrate, and great sections of it – especially those which covered childbirth, marriage, prosperity, and death – were untainted by human malice. My aged friend Tabanea, of whose traffic in the 'magic of kindness' I shall have more to say later, gave me some samples of spells meant to comfort, not to kill. One of them was of the family known as *te Kaanangaraoi*, the givers of good direction, i.e., roughly, the bringers of good fortune. It was a father's blessing on his son, but Tabanea said it would do well enough, alternatively, for any of my daughters.

'Lead her to an eastern beach just before sunrise,' he instructed me, 'and seat her on a stone facing the dawn. You may take her to the stone I use for myself, if you like. When she is seated, anoint the crown of her head with a little coconut oil – a drop or two will be enough – and tie a fillet of young coconut-leaf about her brows, making a knot like this. Then let her sit very still, her hands upon her knees, waiting for the sun to rise. And when you see the top rim of the sun appear over the horizon, stand beside her with your right hand resting on her head, saying these words three times:

By this crowning with a fillet, by this anointing with oil,
Thou art beautiful, thou art the first of thy generation.
Thou shalt overturn the hearts of the old men,
Thou shalt overturn the hearts of the warriors;
They shall gaze upon thee and eagerly speak thy name.
Thou art become the child of the sun;
Thy feet shall tread high places;
Thy heart shall burn, thy body shall shine;
Thy face shall be beautiful and terrible;
Thy word shall be a judgement that is judged,
And thy name only, Joan Ruth, shall be in the mouth of all people,
Thine, thine, thine!
The Sun is risen.'

Spells of this benign quality lent themselves very easily as a bridge between paganism and Christianity in the days of groping from belief to belief. The old pagans of my time had seen the emissaries of the new faith working ruthlessly against their loved ancestors in the earlier days of missionary work, and for that reason most of them resisted to the very end every effort to christianize them. But they distinguished with extraordinary sensitiveness between the new God and His human prophets. Their stubborn resistance was directed not against the notion of a foreign deity but against the church organization as such. The Christian God seemed very powerful to them. Had He not saved from the anger of their own spirits the desecrators of their village shrines? They had need of the protection of such a

Power, not His enmity, in their bitter loss. So Katutu, a pagan of about eighty, put it to me at Tarawa. 'And besides, God and Jesus do not belong only to the Protestants and Roman Catholics,' he said to me. 'They belong to pagans also. They are not surrounded by a fence up there in Heaven, and we do not have to run into a mission fence to find them here on earth. They are everywhere, like Auriaria and Tabuariki and Tituaabine. We can take them for our own friends if we want them.' And some of them did precisely that, by the simple expedient of using the names of God and Jesus as names of power in their magic of kindness. I cannot think that there was anger in the courts of Heaven when the following prayer was heard there. It was used by Katutu when he was lost at sea in his fishing-canoe. Lifting a little sea water at arms' length in cupped hands, he called:

This is the lifting of the draught of the sightless:
I am cross-eyed, I am blind! I know not North, I know not South,
I know not heaven or the underworld-o-o!
Lift thyself up my draught – I drink thee;
Let them tell me, let them direct me, for I am cross-eyed, I am blind.
O bu-u-u, ba-a-a, God and Jesus!
Only thou, God, art the land, thou the ocean.
The ill wind blows: destroy it, disperse it,
Return it to its place – the ocean-o-o!

'And when I had said it three times,' said Katutu, 'the ill wind dropped its wings, the sea fell, a fair wind blew, and I came safe home.'

Katutu like Tabenea was a professional sorcerer who dealt only in the magic of kindness. His sort brought nothing but help to villagers nominally Christian yet still far less confident than pagan Katutu of the love of their accepted God. But there were few professionals like him; the majority were sinister beings; curses intended to bring madness, disease and death were their common stock-in-trade, and the terror of their works hung like a black cloud over the villages. Here are the words of a curse upon a cooking-oven. The sorcerer is to be imagined squatting naked in the dark before dawn over his enemy's fireplace and stabbing it with a stick as he mutters –

Spirit of madness, Nei Terang!
Spirit of excrement, Nei Tebutae!
Spirit of eating alive, Nei Mataora!
Spirits of rottenness, Maauere, Maauere-o-o!
I stab the fire of his food, the fire of that man Naewa.
    Strike west of him, you! Strike east of him, you!
    Strike as I stab, strike death!
    Strangle him, madden him, shame him with rottenness!
His liver heaves, it heaves, it is overturned and torn apart.
His bowels heave, they heave, they are torn apart and gnawed.
He is black mad, he is dead.
It is finished: he is dead, dead, dead. He rots.

My old friend of the protective ritual, Taaketa of Marakei, gave
me this spell as an example of the kind of curse that had been
laid upon my shrinking self. Obviously, apart from their obscenity, such curses amounted to nothing more than any other
pack of words. But the trouble was, they often worked. The
sorcerers took care to back their rituals with something more
than words. They knew a good deal about fish-poisons, and also
about the blistering secretion of the cantharides fly, which
swarms among the coconut-blossom. And even when no such
adventitious aid was used, there was always man's fear working
on the side of the sorcerer. It is an eerie thing to know yourself
cursed, even if you are a European. A brown man with sixty
generations of terror-struck belief whispering in his blood, and
no trust any more in the saving love of his ancestors, and not yet
any deep hold on the comforts of his new religion, was easy meat
for the death-magic. The sorcerers had little to learn in practice
about the murderous force of auto-suggestion.

I believe all these dark things are done with in the Gilbert
Islands of today. Education in the mission schools and (if I may
be so sentimental) more comforting emphasis upon the dynam-
ics of love in Christian teaching, had already helped much by
1933 – when I left the Pacific – towards banishing dread of the
death-magic from the villages. Since then, exciting new things
like co-operative marketing, and political progress, and radio
have come into the life of the islands. The long tedium of the
village nights is brightened in 1951 by talk and thought about a

hundred interests that were not there to drive out the spectres of old. But I lived there when fear was still master. The villages, so bright by day, were haunted when night closed down upon them.

I am not suggesting that ghosts returned from the dead, or familiars prowled, or presences lurked in things. I write as a sceptic about that kind of belief. But it is my experience that malice and fear are strong infections. They can taint things and places, just as human love can sweeten them. Generation upon generation of sorcerers who willed evil, and of people who dreaded their power, had lived out their lives in those islands. The piled-up horror of their convictions had achieved, down the ages, a weight and a shadow of its own, an imminence that brooded over everything. It was man's thought, more potent than ghosts, that haunted the habitations of men. One felt that practically anything could happen in that atmosphere.

The Sorcerer's Revenge

I don't mind admitting I felt queer when old Taakeuta said a death-curse had been laid on me. You would have felt the same yourself at that hour of the morning. He crept out of his village between 3 and 4 o'clock and got my servant Kirewa to wake me up. As soon as I stirred, they both began begging me not to light a lamp, in case other eyes should see us. So I had to lie there under the mosquito net, listening to their talk of curses in the dark. They were just voices whispering doom at me out of the unseen, and it gave me the creeps.

White men were supposed to be immune from Gilbertese sorcery, but Taakeuta feared I might not be as safe as others because I had recently been made a member of the Sun clan. That gave me magical powers, but it also opened me to magical attack, he thought: the curse would surely work unless I would agree to do as he asked me. My one safety now lay in the prayers of the clan ancestors for warding off death-spells. They were infallible if used aright – but would I use them? He had come hurrying through the night to teach me how to do so before the next sun rose. His tremulous old voice trailed off into entreaties.

I knew the dark obscenity of the death-curses. Not that I really believed that a hotch-potch of words and gestures, however vile, could harm me. But I was alone on an island impregnated with age-old superstition, and I was young, and the living reality of these two friends' dread was heavy upon me. Then, too, there was the deep sincerity of Taakeuta's purpose. I couldn't just turn the shaky old fellow back into the night uncomforted. Maybe I was a little curious as well. Any how, what with one thing and another, I spent the last hour before sunrise over on the eastern beach, learning those protective prayers from him. All of them ended with the lovely benediction, 'Blessings and Peace are mine. Blessings and Peace.' I am not prepared to deny that it did a lot to calm my twittering nerves.

The innocent cause of all this to-do was a poor, half-witted girl who had been brought before me in the Lands Court. It was a real-life case of a defenceless orphan and the wicked uncle. The uncle had contrived, at the death of her father and mother, to get himself registered by the Native Court as the owner of her whole patrimony, which amounted to nearly twenty acres of good coconut land. That was great wealth for a Gilbert Islander. He had got away with it solely because of his fearsome reputation as a sorcerer. He was credited with many victims, and the terror of his curses paralysed the island. The sick-minded child drifted about the villages for eight years living on charity; she could not fail to find that among those kindly people, but no one dared to complain on her behalf until I arrived to set up a Lands Commission. Then, because I had become a member of his clan, old Taakeuta did tell me about her. It was an act of superhuman courage for an islander. Two others followed his lead, and their evidence eventually enabled me to put things right for her.

It was no part of my court's job to pursue the wicked uncle. I merely recorded the facts about him for the judicial attention of the District Officer and got along with my Lands Commission. So he, on his side, was able to stick around considering how best *he* might pursue *me*. As a matter of fact, I'm sure there was more than a streak of insanity in him, which loss of face had whipped up into a maniac obsession. It was actually he himself who had told Taakeuta about putting the death-curse on me. He was boasting of it all round the place. He said I was going to fall ill within a week and be dead within three weeks. It may sound puerile, but the insolent certainty of it hypnotized the hag-ridden villagers into something like appalled conviction. The meeting-houses of the island buzzed with debates about my safety.

It wasn't merely for me that people were afraid: they feared for themselves even more. No white man had ever yet been known to succumb to Gilbertese magic. The whole confidence of the brown men in the white race rested ultimately on that one fact. We were queer, often unmannerly creatures, but we were always above being corrupted or constrained by secret sorceries. Yet that terrible man seemed so sure of his powers. Could I resist him? If I could not, what white man was to be leaned on for protection any more? This was not a rhetorical question that I imagined for myself: it was the way my servant and loving friend Kirewa put things to me, and I knew that the stark simplicity of his view stood for the whole island's feeling. It was no good, discounting it as mere hysteria: the hysteria itself was the fact that had to be faced. In that atmosphere of panic, the wicked uncle didn't even have to bring about my death to win a smashing victory. Any real illness that happened my way would be seen as a triumph of his sorcery. And, apart from the white man's prestige in general, there was the special matter of my work on the Lands Commission. Once I was made to appear even a little susceptible to spells, every spark of public faith in my judgements would be snuffed out, for every man would be asking his neighbour whose magic had swayed me. The immediate answer to all this was, of course, that I mustn't fall ill or, better still, mustn't let anyone see it even if I did. There wasn't a doctor within a hundred miles, anyhow, to fuss around ordering me to bed; but the hair-trigger situation did make me a bit nervous, because I was subject to fulminating attacks of dysentery.

As things fell out, however, I needn't have worried about dysentery. The pains that woke me up just before dawn two days later were not like that. I felt as if an ice-cold hand with red-hot fingernails was tearing out a hollow space between my kidneys and my solar plexus. I suppose it was natural for me to dream, as I struggled up out of my sleep, that the clawing hand was the wicked uncle's and that his face was mouthing at me a piece of a death-curse I had learned from old Taakeuta:

> His liver heaves, it heaves, it is overturned and torn apart;
> His bowels heave, they heave, they are torn apart and gnawed.

At that, it might have been only a severe attack of renal colic, but there were other symptoms too. They don't matter here, except that they told me beyond doubt what had hit me. I had had a mild sample of the same thing before, and it hadn't been caused by magic. The all-too-obvious fact was that I had swallowed before going to bed a considerable swig of the blistering stuff known to science as cantharidine. It was easy to make that particular mistake in the Gilbert Islands if you were a toddy-drinker. Cantharides flies (which we called toddy-bugs) crawled in hundreds wherever the sweet sap of the coconut blossom was being tapped. We had to take care to keep them out of our collecting-vessels. No more than three of them drowned in a pint of liquor were quite enough to put a man to bed for a week. The squeezed-out juice of a dozen or so, secretly dropped into a man's drink, was as sure a thing as any sorcerer knew of to make his death-curses work, and horribly.

The only coconut toddy ever allowed near me was that gathered by Kirewa. He was a martinet about that. I got none at all if he found even a single fly drowned in my liquor. But my toddy-tree was well out in the bush: anyone could have climbed it and doctored my drink unseen in the sleepy hours after noonday. There wasn't a mite of evidence to show who had done it; but if nobody had, in fact, given me a dose of cantharidine, the inference was that nothing save the wicked uncle's curse was blistering my insides. Though this made satisfactory nonsense for me, it didn't for Kirewa. He thought the death curse was come upon me, and told me so with tears. It was not comforting. All the same, I did know I could count on his silence outside. He said himself he didn't care who or what was to blame, only one thing mattered now, and that was how to keep the sorcerer's victory dark.

Apart from the pains of my condition, its initial calls for attention were so importunate that they could not possibly have been kept dark without the help of luck – an accident of time, you might call it, unless you preferred just Providence. My trouble happened to begin on a Saturday and Saturday was a day of rest as far as my court work went. So I started off with the merciful gift of a clear week-end of seclusion. Nevertheless, when Sunday night came, I could not even sit up. There wasn't the remotest hope of my being able to open the Lands Court as usual at six o'clock on Monday morning. I lay torn in half with pain wondering what message I should send to the packed meeting-house. Should I say outright that I was ill, but ill, of course, only because somebody unspecified had poisoned me? My mind replied: if my Kirewa didn't believe in the poisoning theory, why should a single other soul in those spell-haunted villages? So, alternatively, should I without a word of explanation suspend court sessions until further notice? The answer to that one was that it would simply bring a swarm of fearful folk, driven by the gibes of the sorcerer himself, rushing round to confirm his triumph. There was absolutely nothing I could do to avoid disaster. Yet I must do something. My mind went on and on; rigors began to seize my body; by four o'clock, I was semi-delirious. And then, in the same dark hour of Taakeuta's warning visit and the first onset of my sickness, more help came. You can call it an accident out of space this time, unless you still prefer Providence. A roaring westerly gale blew up, unprecedentedly late in the season, and pushed over half the dwellings on the island. Nobody was hurt, but it took the villagers a full week of intensive communal work to get their homes standing again. Until the following Monday, not a mother's son wanted to be bothered with me or my Lands Commission.

So I had nine grace-days in all for secret running repairs. Kirewa easily kept the odd caller at a distance by saying I was buried in my writing work. My difficult temper when interrupted at that was well known. The searing flame inside me pretty nearly cooked my goose on Monday and Tuesday, I imagine, for there were sloughings and haemorrhages too. But rest, with an exclusive diet of tinned milk, olive oil and bicarbonate of soda worked something like a miracle in the next few days. I was not to be wholly well again for over three years, but I was able to stand up early on Sunday morning. That night, I staggered without help as far as Kirewa's house in the back yard while he hopped around for rapture under the quiet stars. He made a triumphal song as well as a dance about it; the words were very simple but they meant a lot to both of us: 'O, the white man, the brown man – o – o!' he chanted. 'Blessings and Peace are ours. Blessings and Peace!' But there was still the Lands Court to face.

I got to the meeting-house steadily enough next morning, on a bicycle: there are no hills in the Gilbert Islands. Kirewa was waiting there to hold the machine as I got off: it was quite a usual courtesy in those days, and it helped a lot. There were only eight paces to take from there, and I managed a good, strong walk-on. It was needed. Over a thousand people were waiting under the vast thatch. According to the forecast, I should have fallen ill by now, and they were there to check up. The wicked uncle was squatting on his mat straight opposite my table, in the first row of spectators. He was staring at me. Everybody was staring at me. A sigh moaned through the place like a wind as I took my seat. I don't know why, but that very nearly bowled me out. Maybe it was weakness, maybe relief. To be precise, I desperately wanted to lay my head on the table and cry. But I did have enough sense not to burst into tears, and in the next flash I knew that the only thing to carry me through that moment was a joke – any old joke, as long as it was topical enough. The topic was there, throwing itself at me, a million years young everywhere in the world – the weather. So I stared back at the wicked uncle and said the island would be a lot freer of these westerly gales if the local sorcerers wasted less time on death-curses and put in a lot more on spells for good weather. Everyone knew that good-weather-making was the speciality of my own Sun clan.

There followed what seemed an age of stunned silence. I thought my feeble effort had failed disastrously. As a matter of fact, I never have been sure that it would have caught on at all, but for Kirewa. He suddenly gave a great hoot of mirth from behind me. It was so near my ear, it scared the wits out of me. I whipped round and nearly slipped from my seat. That and the braying noise he made seemed to pull a trigger that released all the sinister tension in one vast explosion of laughter. The house kicked and twisted with it for ten minutes. The Gilbertese are princely laughers, and they have no nonsensical rules about a man not laughing at his own joke: I howled unnoticed with them, and, incidentally, got my chance to shed a few tears then. I knew with certainty that safety (if not exactly blessings) and peace were upon me. When eyes were dried and order restored, the wicked uncle had vanished. He never put his nose back in the Lands Court, and nothing was ever heard again of his curse.

Six weeks later, I finished my work on that island. The evening before I left, Taakeuta took both my hands in his old gnarled ones: 'Sir,' he said, 'what might have happened but for the prayers of the ancestors?' He knew nothing of my illness. I could not bring myself to tell him that I had not used his prayers. In any case, a blank denial would have amounted to an evasion. My rehearsal with him on the ocean beach had left me haunted with a thought. I felt that the ancestors had stumbled on something considerable when they put that phrase about blessings and peace in the form of an affirmation. It seemed to me then that blessings and peace truly were, in the last analysis, entities within a man for him to lean upon at need. Perhaps that was merely wishful thinking, but I found it a very comforting bed-companion in my sickness.

The Calling of the Porpoise

It was common rumour in the Gilbert Islands that certain local clans had the power of porpoise-calling; but it was rather like the Indian rope-trick; you never met anyone who had actually witnessed the thing. If I had been a reasonably plump young man, I might never have come to see what I did see on the beach of Butaritari lagoon. But I was skinny. It was out of sheer pity for my poor thin frame that old Kitiona set his family porpoise-caller working. We were sitting together one evening in his canoe-shed by the beach, and he was delivering a kind of discourse on the beauty of human fatness.

'A chief of chiefs,' he said, 'is recognized by his shape. He is fleshy from head to foot. But his greatest flesh is his middle; when he sits, he is based like a mountain upon his sitting place; when he stands, he swells out in the midst, before and behind, like a porpoise.' It seemed that in order to maintain that noble bulge a high chief simply must have a regular diet of porpoise-meat; if he didn't, he would soon become lean and bony like a commoner or a white man. The white man was doubtless of chiefly race, thought Kitiona, but his figure could hardly be called beautiful. 'And you,' he added, looking me up and down with affectionate realism, 'are in truth the skinniest white man ever seen in these islands. You sit upon approximately no base at all.'

I laughed (heartily I hope) and asked what he thought could be done about that. 'You should eat porpoise-flesh,' he said simply, 'then you too would swell in the proper places.' That led me to inquire how I might come by a regular supply of the rare meat. The long and the short of his reply was that his own kinsmen in Kuma village, seventeen miles up-lagoon, were the hereditary porpoise-callers of the High Chiefs of Butaritari and Makin-Meang. His first cousin was a leading expert at the game; he could put himself into the right kind of dream on demand. His spirit went out of his body in such a dream; it sought out the porpoise-folk in their home under the western horizon and invited them to a dance, with feasting, in Kuma village. If he spoke the words of the invitation aright (and very few had the secret of them) the porpoise would follow him with cries of joy to the surface.

Having led them to the lagoon entrance, he would fly forward to rejoin his body and warn the people of their coming. It was quite easy for one who knew the way of it. The porpoise never failed to arrive. Would I like some called for me? After some rather idle shilly-shallying, I admitted that I would; but did he think I should be allowed to see them coming? Yes, he replied, that could probably be arranged. He would talk to his kinsmen about it. Let me choose a date for the calling and, if the Kuma folk agreed, his canoe would take me to the village. We fixed on a day early in January, some weeks ahead, before I left him.

No further word came from Kitiona until his big canoe arrived one morning to collect me. There was not a breath of wind, so sailing was out of the question. The sun was white-hot. It took over six hours of grim paddling to reach our destination. By the time we got there, I was cooked like a prawn and wrapped in gloom. When the fat, friendly man who styled himself the High Chief's hereditary porpoise-caller came waddling down the beach to greet me, I asked irritably when the porpoise would arrive. He said he would have to go into his dream first, but thought he could have them there for me by three or four o'clock. Please, though, he added firmly, would I be careful to call them, from now on, *only* 'our friends from the west'. The other name was tabu. They might not come at all if I said it aloud. He led me as he spoke to a little hut screened with newly plaited coconut leaves, which stood beside his ordinary dwelling. Alone in there, he explained, he would do his part of the business. Would I honour his house by resting in it while he dreamed? 'Wait in peace now,' he said when I was installed, 'I go on my journey,' and disappeared into the screened hut.

Kuma was a big village in those days: its houses stretched for half a mile or more above the lagoon beach. The dreamer's hut lay somewhere near the centre of the line. The place was dead quiet that afternoon under its swooning palms. The children had been gathered in under the thatches. The women were absorbed in plaiting garlands and wreaths of flowers. The men were silently polishing their ceremonial ornaments of shell. Their friends from the west were being invited to a dance, and everything they did in the village that day was done to maintain the illusion.

Even the makings of a feast lay ready piled in baskets beside the houses. I could not bring myself to believe that the people expected just nothing to come of all this careful business.

But the hours dragged by, and nothing happened. Four o' clock passed. My faith was beginning to sag under the strain when a strangled howl burst from the dreamer's hut. I jumped round to see his cumbrous body come hurtling head first through the torn screens. He sprawled on his face, struggled up, and staggered into the open, a slobber of saliva shining on his chin. He stood awhile clawing at the air and whining on a queer high note like a puppy's. Then words came gulping out of him: '*Teirake! Teirake!* (Arise! Arise! . . . They come! Let us go . . . Our friends from the west . . . They come! . . . Let us go down and greet them.' He started at a lumbering gallop down the beach.

A roar went up from the village, 'They come, they come!' I found myself rushing helter-skelter with a thousand others into the shallows, bawling at the top of my voice that our friends from the west were coming. I ran behind the dreamer; the rest converged on him from north and south. We strung ourselves out, line abreast, as we stormed through the shallows. Everyone was wearing the garlands woven that afternoon. The farther out we got, the less the clamour grew. When we stopped, breast deep, fifty yards from the reef's edge, a deep silence was upon us; and so we waited.

I had just dipped my head to cool it when a man near me yelped and stood pointing; others took up his cry, but I could make out nothing for myself at first in the splintering glare of the sun on the water. When at last I did see them, everyone was screaming hard; they were pretty near by then, gambolling towards us at a fine clip. When they came to the edge of the blue water by the reef, they slackened speed, spread themselves out and started cruising back and forth in front of our line. Then, suddenly, there was no more of them.

In the strained silence that followed, I thought they were gone. The disappointment was so sharp, I did not stop to think then that, even so, I had seen a very strange thing. I was in the act of touching the dreamer's shoulder to take my leave when he turned his still face to me: 'The king out of the west comes to meet me,' he murmured, pointing downwards. My eyes followed his hand. There, not ten yards away, was the great shape of a porpoise poised like a glimmering shadow in the glass-green water. Behind it followed a whole dusky flotilla of them.

They were moving towards us in extended order with spaces

of two or three yards between them, as far as my eye could reach. So slowly they came, they seemed to be hung in a trance. Their leader drifted in hard by the dreamer's leg. He turned without a word to walk beside it as it idled towards the shallows. I followed a foot or two behind its almost motionless tail. I saw other groups to right and left of us turn shorewards one by one, arms lifted, faces bent upon the water.

A babble of quiet talk sprang up; I dropped behind to take in the whole scene. The villagers were welcoming their guests ashore with crooning words. Only men were walking beside them; the women and children followed in their wake, clapping their hands softly in the rhythm of a dance. As we approached the emerald shallows, the keels of the creatures began to take the sand; they flapped gently as if asking for help. The men leaned down to throw their arms around the great barrels and ease them over the ridges. They showed no least sign of alarm. It was as if their single wish was to get to the beach.

When the water stood only thigh deep, the dreamer flung his arms high and called. Men from either flank came crowding in to surround the visitors, ten or more to each beast. Then, 'Lift!' shouted the dreamer, and the ponderous black shapes were half-dragged, half-carried, unresisting, to the lip of the tide. There they settled down, those beautiful, dignified shapes, utterly at peace, while all hell broke loose around them. Men, women and children, leaping and posturing with shrieks that tore the sky, stripped off their garlands and flung them around the still bodies, in a sudden dreadful fury of boastfulness and derision. My mind still shrinks from the last scene – the raving humans, the beasts so triumphantly at rest.

We left them garlanded where they lay and returned to our houses. Later, when the falling tide had stranded them high and dry, men went down with knives to cut them up. There was feasting and dancing in Kuma that night. A chief's portion of the meat was set aside for me. I was expected to have it cured as a diet for my thinness. It was duly salted, but I could not bring myself to eat it. I never did grow fat in the Gilbert Islands.

7

LISTENING AND LEARNING

Happy Old Lady and Sad Old Man

The Gilbertese had few waterside villages before the British Protectorate. The only buildings ordinarily near the sea then were the canoe-sheds. Every household had its home-place on its own land, and the aim beyond that was to scatter the dwellings of a group settlement to the best tactical advantage across the breadth of the coconut forest from lagoon to ocean beach. The siting of each house in relation to its neighbours was as carefully planned as the siting of a pill-box in modern warfare. Every home-place was, in fact, a strong point. The whole idea was to secure defence-in-depth against the infiltration of enemy forces from up or down the length of the land. The muddy pits which were dug for the cultivation of the arum tuber known as babai (which science calls *Alocasia Indica*) were also placed so as to impede the movements of invaders between the strong points. In the savage land-wars that forever racked the islands, every major activity of the private household had to be thus subordinated to the defence of the settlement. The darkness of the times was reflected in the family homes. The lodges were not the companionable mwenga of today, but *uma-toro* – literally, squatting roofs – which is to say thatches resting on the ground, closed at both gables, under whose eaves no spying eye could penetrate.

Except on the islands where dynasties of High Chiefs had managed to remain paramount, a state of faction warfare was the normal condition of Gilbertese life of old. There were wars that involved only two or three villages at a time, and wars that split whole islands into opposing camps. The feuds, on whatever scale, were deathless. In Tarawa, the struggle for supremacy between two factions that called themselves The House of

Teabike and the House of Auatabu kept nine generations of the people almost continually fighting or preparing to fight again to the coming of the Flag in 1892. A dramatic end was put to the conflict then by the arrival of Captain H. M. Davis, R.N. in H.M.S. *Royalist*, to proclaim the British Protectorate on the very morning when the forces of Auatabu, badly beaten in battle the day before, were awaiting extermination at the hands of Teabike.

Pax-Britannica was a phrase perhaps too often used by Imperialists to cover a multitude of sins, but it really did mean the dawn of a newer, richer life for the Gilbertese, as the old folk of my day were never tired of acknowledging. Exactly twenty-five years after the House of Auatabu's escape from annihilation, I was talking about the outcome to a vivid old lady of perhaps ninety-five, who had been one of the survivors.

We were in her village house. Besides myself, sitting around her on their floor-mats, were her son, hale and active still in his late seventies, a grandson of fifty-five or so, a great-grandson of twenty-four, and several great-great-grandchildren of ages up to ten. All the grown-ups were busy at some kind of handiwork as we listened to her story. Her son and grandsons were fashioning the shanks of pearl-shell hooks, as beautiful as gems, for bonito-fishing; she herself, still quick-fingered and keen-eyed for all her years, was plaiting the multitudinous strands of a new sleeping-mat across her knees. The murmur of contented talk drifted in from other houses. The peace of it all seemed to stab her with sudden happiness: 'Listen to the voices of the people in their lodges!' she broke off her tale of fighting to exclaim. 'We work in peace, we talk in peace, for the days of anger are done.'

She resumed an account of her husband's death in battle the day before H.M.S. *Royalist* appeared, and held soberly to that theme until one of her great-grand-daughters arrived home from a visit to the next village. The interruption loosed the floodgates of a new surge of happiness from within her: 'See that!' she cried triumphantly, 'see that! This woman arrives from walking in the north, yet no man has molested her, for we walk in peace.'

She herself, up to the coming of the Flag – when she must

have been about seventy – had never known what it was, maid or wife, to stray outside the village settlement of her men-folk.

'In those days,' she continued, 'death was on the right hand and on the left. If we wandered north, we were killed or raped. If we wandered south, we were killed or raped. If we returned alive from walking abroad, our husbands themselves killed us, for they said we had gone forth seeking to be raped. That was indeed just, for a woman who disobeys her husband is a woman of no account, and it matters not how she dies. Yet how beautiful is life in our villages, now that there is no killing and war is no more.'

She told me of how she had found the body of her husband eyeless after the battle. It was the Gilbertese warrior's ultimate gesture of triumph in the field to pluck out the eyes of a stricken foeman and bite them in two while straddling his corpse. As she spoke, I had a picture of generations of grieving women before her, searching the floor of the forest for the eyes of their dead, lest the departing souls go blind into the Land of Shades. But she was just to her husband's killer: '*Bon te katei* (It was the custom),' she said, 'and I found his eyes beside him.' And it was on her theme of triumphant serenity that she finished: 'Behold, my son and my grandson! These would have died with me that day at Nea if the warship had not arrived. And these' – she pointed to her great- and great-great-grandchildren – 'would never have been born. We live because the Government of Kuini Kabitoria (Queen Victoria) brought peace to us, and here I sit plaiting this mat to be buried in because of the kindness of that woman, with all my generations around me to wrap me in it when I die.'

*

It was the Christian missionaries, not the Government, who gave schools to the villages, and the schools taught rudiments that the villagers had to master if they were to survive the alien pressures which, sooner or later, were bound to drive in upon them. The Gilbert Islands owe much to Protestants and Roman Catholics alike. But the intolerance of some of the earlier teachers of both churches too often frustrated the kind work of their fellows. Their indiscriminate hate of everything pagan rooted by the way much that was beautiful and useful in native custom, and in doing so destroyed agencies that could have been enlisted not only to illumine the message of Christianity, but also to ease the difficult passage of the race from unsophistication to knowledge.

When I had been only a few months on Tarawa, I heard from an aged pagan why he had always resisted conversion to Christianity. It would be purposeless to reveal the denomination of the missionary responsible for the stand the old man took, for both Protestants and Roman Catholics had their iconoclasts – not many, but some, and the hate of a few may often betray the love of many. The pagan was a gentle old fellow, recognized in his village for *te akoi*, which means, broadly, loving-kindness, and I was curious to know his reasons for remaining pagan.

He pointed to a rectangle of coral slabs planted edgewise beside his dwelling. 'See there!' he said. 'That was the *baangota* (shrine) of my ancestors. My father's skull was buried there, and his father's, and his father's fathers' to five generations. I buried them so that their crowns stood forth above the sand. I saw them near me as I lay down to sleep; every evening I went down and anointed them with oil; and I spoke to them, and they answered me, and I was happy with them. Thus it was until those men came and took them away from me.'

'Those men' were a white missionary and a rabble of native teachers whom he had trained to his ways.

'It began in this manner,' the old man went on. 'The white missionary sent a teacher to me one day, and the teacher said to me, "Thou shalt root up the skulls of thy baangota and throw them away."

'And this was my word to the teacher: "These are the skulls of my fathers. They hurt no man and I love them. Why should I root them up and throw them away?"

'The teacher answered, "Thy baangota is an offence to the Christians who dwell in this village, for it is a sin in the eyes of our God, the only true God."

'But I said to him, "I beg thee, let each man turn away content with his own spirits. I am content with mine. Leave me alone with them."

149

'He answered, "Other men have obeyed the voice of the white missionary and thrown away their skulls. Thou alone in this village hast refused."

'I said, "The voices of my fathers are more precious to me than the voice of the white missionary. They are my roots and my trunk. I die without them. I beg thee, leave me alone with them."

'But he arose in anger, saying, "If thou art stiff-necked, our God will come to this village and destroy it because of thee."

'And the people of the village heard him and were afraid. They said to me, "We beg thee to throw away the skulls, lest we be destroyed because of thee."

'But I answered, "Fear not. My spirits will protect all of us from the anger of that cruel God. What kind of God is he who will not let me love my fathers? Is he a slave without ancestry?"

'They said, "He is the God of Wrath. We do not know his origins, only we fear to offend him." But none laid hand upon my baangota, for they feared to offend my spirits also.

'And the teacher himself was afraid, so he said, "We will all return with the white man tomorrow, and he will destroy thy baangota." And all the people answered him, "Yes, return, we beg thee, and destroy it."

'So that night, I anointed the heads of my fathers and spoke to them, and I knew in my heart that it was the last time.

'And on the morrow, the white man, and his teachers, and his company – a great crowd – came with shouting and singing into the village. They gathered by my baangota here. All the village came to behold. I sat in my house. My heart was dead within me. There was nothing I could do save only sit.

'Then the white man told them to be silent. And when they were silent, he walked to the side of the baangota, saying, "Where are now the spirits of this place? Ho there, you spirits! Come and strike me dead if you can! You answer not? Fie! Are you afraid?"

'And alas! he trampled upon the heads of my fathers, and they were crushed under his feet. And he danced upon them.

'And when he was tired of dancing, he took the broken bones in his hands, and made as if to spit upon them, and scattered

150

them among the trees, shouting "Here I am, you spirits of the shrine! Strike me dead if you can." He was not struck dead. He laughed, and all who were there laughed with him.

'So no one was any more afraid of my spirits. They all fell together upon my baangota. They laughed, they danced, they pelted the trees with the bones of my fathers, shouting. "See here! Another piece of dung. Throw it away!" And the white man danced with them, as if he were a madman or a slave. And when the bones were all gone, they spat upon my baangota and left.'

I wish I could have added that that day's wickedness did not go unpunished. But it did, and the noble game of shrine-ragging in the name of Christianity flourished well into the time of the Protectorate. There was, to be sure, a clause in the Pacific Order-in-Council of 1892 which forbade such sacrilege under pain of deportation. But the villagers feared the malice of those white savages and their atrocious deity too much to go reporting them to the Government. Not a single criminal was ever brought to book, and that was Christianity's great loss.

But a few skull shrines still survived in and around the villages of the Central and Northern Gilberts as late as 1916. I found them, though not exactly approved by mission authorties, at least humanely respected for what they meant to the few old pagans left. 'The baangota represents ancient family love,' said a young missionary to me twelve years later. 'We do not wish to destroy that spiritual foundation, but to build upon it, so that our converts may not come as strangers into the new house we give them.' He was speaking in terms of religious teaching, but I thought his phrase summed up the whole of anthropological and administrative wisdom too. A simple folk is strengthened to abide the ferment of alien ideas not by the destruction but by the affectionate husbanding of its age-old loyalties. A tree without roots dies, but new grafts thrive on a trunk that stands deep-rooted in the soil of its homeland.

Warning to Fiddlers

The worst of interfering with the customs of simple peoples, all for their own good, is that it can end by leaving them bereft of their national will to live. The fiddler is a killer on a grand scale. There have been in the past some grim cases of depopulation – especially in Melanesia – due to the premature blotting out of interests that kept people alive in their environment. But from Melanesia also comes the classic example of how fundamental changes of custom, if unavoidable, should be brought about. Sir Hubert Murray, Administrator of Australian Papua, wanted to rid his territory of the bane of head-hunting. A lesser man might have thought himself justified in using force to suppress so murderous a habit; but not he. He took the trouble to inquire first what head-hunting really meant to the people. He found that a great structure of sane and beneficial social practices was based upon the cult of skulls, and would collapse if head-hunting were to be summarily abolished. His problem was therefore to keep the cult alive while doing away with the customary means of maintaining the supply of skulls. He discovered his solution in the fact that pigs, for a number of reasons, enjoyed among the Papuans a personal importance almost equal to that of human beings, Starting from that point, he set out to persuade the folk who lived nearest his capital to adopt pigs' heads instead of human heads for their skull-rituals. He succeeded. The new practice spread to neighbouring districts. There is today a large area of Australian Papua where human head-hunting has been eliminated not only without the use of force but also without damage to the delicately poised social fabric of which it was once the main foundation.

*

During my salad days as a District Officer, my closest friend Mautake-Maeke, Chief Kaubure of Tarawa and a member of the moon clan called Maerua, read me a sound lesson in what you might call the doctrine of compensating values or, alternatively, the anthropological approach to changes of native custom.

Walking one day on the ocean shore of Tarawa, I had chanced on a box-shaped arrangement of coral slabs about eighteen inches square half-buried in the tussocky grass at the beach-head. It looked, with its flat top, like the kind of seat the old pagans were fond of building in such lonely, treeless places for their various rituals to the rising sun. But, though it was three miles from any village, it might just possibly have been a shrine for an ancestral skull, so I lifted the lid to make sure before venturing to sit on it myself.

No skull was inside, but a heap of two-shilling pieces – perhaps thirty or forty of them. The coins lay within a circle of pebbles on the sandy floor. On top of them was a piece of knotted coconut leaf, obviously a *rabu*, or cover against pilfering. Thus protected, the money was indeed pretty safe from thieves, for Christian and pagans alike had a hearty dread of the curses that actuated these magical spring-guns. The rabu spells were not nicely worded:

> Spirit of my rabu, Matakaakang (Eater-of-Eyes),
> Spirit of my rabu, Mataoraora (Eater-alive-of-Eyes),
> Thou shalt eat the man who steals my property.
> What shalt thou eat of him? His hands, his feet.
> What shalt thou eat of him? His head, his eyes.
> Kill him – he is dead!
> He is dead-o-o-dead!

Yet a solitary, exposed beach-head seemed a strange place for the owner to leave his money, guarded only by spirits. I felt, as I closed the lid again, that the man was simply asking for trouble. 'He must be warned,' I thought, 'that people aren't as credulous nowadays as they used to be,' and returned to the Native Government station simmering with excellent urges.

But when I spoke to Mautake-Maeke about it, he quickly disabused me of the notion that anyone needed my advice. 'The thing out there is not what you think,' he said. 'It is a thing made by the villagers for a certain old man named Tabanea. The rabu was put there by the people themselves to prevent anyone but him from taking the money.'

It appeared that Tabanea was a professional wizard famed

throughout the Gilbert Islands for 'the magic of kindness'. He dealt exclusively in spells, amulets and potions that brought good luck and protection against enemy sorcerers. His love-potions in particular brought him clients from end to end of the group, but what Tarawa most valued him for was the singular efficacy of his protective spells. Whole villages at a time sought his services as a warder-off of the dreaded death-magic called *te wawi*.

'And so,' said Mautake, 'Tabanea sends a message before him when he is about to pass through a village: and the people bring gifts or money to the place you saw today; then Tabanea renews his bonota (protective spell) over their village, and everyone is happy.'

'But, Mautake,' I exclaimed, the young fiddler within me suddenly aroused at all this talk of trading in sorcery, 'this thing must be stopped at once.'

He looked at me blankly: 'How?' he said, 'I don't understand.'

'The thing must be stopped,' I repeated.

'Why?'

'Because the man's levying a kind of tax on the villagers.'

'He levies no tax,' Mautake replied firmly. 'The people want his help, and pay for it in advance. What he does makes them happy.'

'But do you believe that they are any the safer for his spells?'

'What I believe or you believe is of no account,' was his notable reply: 'They believe. Only that matters. They believe and so they are happy, and because they are happy they are safe.'

'But,' I protested, 'most of the villagers are baptized Protestants or Roman Catholics. Why should so great a majority be forced to pay Tabanea a tribute just because a few pagans still fear the wawi?'

He smiled: 'The Christians want Tabanea's protection as much as the pagans. Nobody is obliged to pay anything; nor is it known who pays or who refuses; yet the money of Christians is always in that box. The Christians say that their own prayers cannot save them from wawi. They as well as the pagans will die of fear if you take Tabanea's bonota away from the villages.'

'I don't want to do away with the bonota,' I said fretfully: 'That's no affair of mine; but the money part of the business is, and it has to be straightened out somehow. Tabanea is, in the end of things, levying a toll on the villages.'

'And the missionaries?' Mautake questioned, and paused.

'Well? What about them?'

'Only this. The missionaries bring us their prayers and their schools, and they ask for gifts in return. We think that is just; we are happy to have them among us; so we give them much money. And then? Does the Government step in to prevent us? Does the Government measure the gifts we give? Does the Government accuse the missionaries of levying a tax upon us?'

While I was still digesting that one, he continued, 'Tabanea brings comfort to the villages which the missionaries cannot bring. What is his sin in this? Is it that he is a pagan and not a Christian? And will you say to the people, "You are not being taxed when you club together to make gifts to the missionaries; but you are indeed being taxed when you club together to make gifts for protection against the wawi?" If you say this, they will answer, "Alas! are we no longer free to buy comfort and peace as we will?" and if you punish Tabanea for accepting their gifts, they will say, "Where shall we any more find safety from the sorcerers who work in the dark," and they will die of fear in their villages.'

And then, without waiting for my reply, he turned to the general question. The Christians, he claimed, stood even more in need than the pagans of the professionals who dealt in the magic of kindness. Every pagan still had his own private spells for good luck, long life and so forth, inherited from the lore of his fathers. But the children and grandchildren of Christians had no such cheerful heritage, because the actual practice of magic rituals, whether cruel or kind, had been abandoned in all good faith by the earliest converts.

'And so,' he continued, 'if you punish those who are willing to sell *tabunea* (spells) for good luck, what must the Christians do then? Where will they go to find magic for good eating and good sleeping, for excellent fishing and success in love, for being favoured by their masters or their friends, for happiness in their dwellings and their work, for blessings upon their canoes and land and cooking ovens, for finding out their lucky days and their unlucky days, for making their wives fruitful and their children strong, for all the comforts between dawn that the magic of kindness brings them?'

His words meant in effect that the magic of kindness filled the life of his people, Christians and pagans alike, with a mass of daily interests for the sudden loss of which nothing that the white man gave or sold could properly compensate them. He was specific on the point of compensating values: 'If the government or missionaries could give them something to keep their hearts alive night and day even as the magic of kindness does, perhaps they could be happy without Tabanea and his like,' he said. 'But if you cannot give them an equal thing in return, you will kill their hearts by robbing them of their loved wizards.'

Of course he was right. His wisdom saved me from an error I should never have ceased to rue. I did nothing whatever about Tabanea except to seek his acquaintance. He was a fine, kindly old gentleman, whose contribution to the easier passage of his people through the psychological darkness between paganism and Christianity I learned to appreciate deeply. Some years after Mautake-Maeke had given me his 'Hands off!' warning, I returned to England and sat for a while at the feet of that colossus among anthropologists, W. H. R. Rivers, who told me out of the modesty of his greatness that his school of thought was only just catching up with Mautake's private theory of compensating values.

The Limping Man of Makin-Meang

It is clearly up to a District Officer to be listening and learning all the time. But there is a mortal difference of spirit between genuine research and prying. The danger is, the genuine thing can deteriorate by such subtle and unconscious stages into mere over-curiosity that a *bona-fide* student may find himself poised on the very brink of fiddling before he wakes up to the horrid change that has gone on inside him. That was what happened to me on Makin-Meang.

Perhaps the eeriness of the island's reputation for ghosts, added to the odd taciturnity of its villagers, had something to do with my ineptitude. But I base no defence on that. The District

Officer's job is to find ways through to his people, not to leave them groping for ways through to himself.

I had heard of the ghosts of Makin-Meang before I got there. The people of Tarawa and Maiana and Abaiang were full of tales about them. They told me that the whole Gilbertese race, for over thirty generations by their count (it was sixty or so by mine), had looked on that most northerly island of the group as their halfway house between the lands of the living and the dead.

The story went that, when anyone died, his shade must first travel up the line of islands to Makin-Meang. Going ashore there on a southern beach, it must tread the length of the land to a sand-spit at the northern tip called the Place of Dread. This was not an actual place-name, but simply a term of fearful reference to the locality – for there sat Nakaa, the Watcher at the Gate, waiting to strangle all dead folk in his terrible net. The ghost had no hope of winning through to paradise except by way of the Gate, and no skill or cunning of its own could save it from the Net. Only the anxious family rituals, done over its dead body, could avail for that; and even these might fail if any outsider were to break in upon their course.

The reasonableness or not of these beliefs is of no concern. It was the age and intensity of them that weighed on Makin-Meang. Every yard of the island was loaded with the terrors and hopes that sixty generations of the living, and the dying, and the long-dead, from end to end of the Gilbert group, had focused upon it. The impress of man's thought was as heavy as footfalls on its paths. I wondered if that was why those silent villagers always seemed to be listening inside their ears for some sound I could never hear.

They were courteous and gentle, but they would not talk to me about the place where Nakaa sat; they did not even try to change the subject when I raised it; they simply dropped their eyes and removed themselves into abysses of reserve. It was not from them but from my orderly, a Tarawa man, that I learned how best to avoid the horror of meeting a ghost face to face. He lived in such open fear of doing so himself that the Native Magistrate had let him know out of pity.

He told me that the shades of all the folk who died on the other fifteen islands found their way to Nakaa by the road above the western beach, whereas only those of local people used the eastern path. There were therefore many more chances of meeting ghosts on the west side than on the east. Not that it mattered greatly which way you chose going north, because you were travelling with the stream anyhow, and the only thing you had to remember was never, never to look behind you. But coming back against the northbound traffic, you must take no road save the eastern one. You could find out in advance when that was safe or not by asking if any local death was expected the day you planned to use it.

When I had finished my routine work on the island, I naturally wanted to see the Place of Dread, so I called the Native Magistrate along one morning and asked him to find me a guide.

I have never seen a face change and darken as swiftly as his did at my simple request. He stood dumb for a while with downcast eyes; then, still looking at the ground, 'Do not go to that place,' he exclaimed, and again, on a higher note, passionately, 'Do not go!' The edge on his voice made it seem almost as if he had said, 'I order you not to go.'

'But why?' I said irritably. 'What's all this nonsense about Nakaa's place? What's all the mystery? Shall I offend anyone by going?'

'Nobody will be offended,' he replied, 'but do not go. The place is perilous.'

'But why perilous for me, a Man of Matang?'

His only reply was to wrap himself away in a cloak of silence. So I tried another line: 'You're a member of a Christian church. You surely can't believe still that souls go that way to Heaven or Hell. Or do you?'

He lifted his eyes to mine, crossing himself. 'Not Christian souls,' he whispered, 'but pagan ones . . . to Hell . . . they still walk the island . . . and Nakaa stays there . . . and there is fear . . .' His voice trailed off into mumbles; I got no more out of him.

I should of course have made up my mind in all decency then to find the place for myself. The island is a straight, lagoonless ribbon, and I could not possibly have missed its tapering northern end. But I was cussed: 'Please find a village constable who isn't afraid to be my guide,' I said, 'and send him to me here.'

He looked at me mutely, spread his hands in a hopeless little gesture, and left. The constable, a giant of a man with bushy eyebrows and a grimly smileless face, appeared within the next half-hour. He said before we started that, as I was a stranger, I must take the western path going northward, just as the ghosts of strangers did, and that I must be careful not to look back.

'And if I do look back?' I said.

'If you look back and see a ghost,' he replied, 'you will be dead within a year,' and marched off ahead of me without another word.

I followed him in silence, eyes front, for perhaps half an hour, when he stepped suddenly into the coconut forest on our right. 'Come in among the trees,' he called without turning his head: 'This is my land. There is a thing you must carry to Nakaa.'

The thing was a seed-coconut. It appeared that every stranger, on his first visit to the Place of Dread, must bring with him a sprouting nut to plant in Nakaa's grove. I thought well of the idea until he told me I must carry it myself. It had an enormous sprout. I am inclined to believe he chose that particular one with deliberate malice, seeing that the only correct way to carry it (or so he said) was upright in my cupped hands with elbows well in against my ribs. I felt a complete ass sweating meekly behind him in that ridiculous attitude for the next five or six miles with my aspidistra-like trophy fluttering in the wind.

I planted the nut at his order where the trees petered out in a sandy desolation at the island's tip. When it was done to his liking, he just walked away into the forest.

'Here!' I called. 'Where are you going now?'

'I will wait here,' he replied. 'There in the north is the place you seek,' and was lost among the trees.

There was nothing in that empty waste to distinguish it from fifty other such promontories in the Gilbert group. It was merely a blazing acre or two of coral rock shaken by bellowing surf and strident with the shrieks of swarming sea-birds. I walked to the point where the meeting tide-rips boiled. It was from there that happy ghosts, the Net of Nakaa passed, fared forth across the sea to be gathered at last with their fathers. I knew that in that very flash of time, from somewhere down the chain of islands, the thoughts of dying folk might be winging their way in wistfulness and fear to the spot where I was standing. But somehow, my mind only played with the idea. There was no sense of reality. The place itself put me utterly out of tune with the old beliefs. Perhaps it was the noise. Death is so quiet, and there was nothing in Nakaa's domain but that din of birds and shattered waters and the trade wind's diapason booming in my ears.

Nevertheless, the brazen heat of rocks and sand that drove me out at last did have its importance, because it gave me the thirst that led to what followed. I went straight back to my guide among the trees and asked him in all innocence to pick me a drinking nut.

He sprang back as if I had struck him: 'I cannot do that,' he almost barked, 'I cannot do that. These trees are Nakaa's.' Fear oozed out of him, almost as tangible as sweat.

I could not press him to violate his belief; nor had I learned yet to scale a forty-foot tree for myself; so I had to sit down there in Nakaa's grove to a sickeningly dry lunch of bully-beef and biscuit. I remember muttering to myself, 'This is how the old devil strangles foreign ghosts, anyhow,' as I gulped the stuff down.

It was past two o'clock when we started for home down the eastern path. My friend told me that his proper place going south was in the rear, and dropped forty paces behind. Perhaps he just wanted to keep out of my sight as well as the sound of my voice; anyway, it was I who led the way against the traffic-stream of local ghosts.

After ten minutes' walking, with thirst at concert pitch, I stopped and croaked back at him (he would not come near), 'Are we out of Nakaa's grove yet?'

Not yet, he shouted back, there was still a mile or more of it. It was then that an unpleasant little worm within me turned. I made up my mind to disregard his scruples and ask anyone we met, anywhere, to pick me a nut. And there, in the midst of that peevish thought was suddenly a man coming along the track to help me.

Across the arc of a curving beach, I saw him appear round a point. I could follow every yard of his course as he came nearer. My eyes never left him, because my intent was pinned on his getting me that drink. He walked with a strong limp (I thought that might make it hard for him to climb a tree). He was a stocky, grizzled man of about fifty, clad rather ceremoniously in a fine mat belted about his middle (a poor kit for climbing, commented my mind). As he came up on my left, I noticed that his left cheek was scored by a scar from jawbone to temple, and that his limp came from a twisted left foot and ankle. I can see the man still in memory.

But the question is – did he see me? He totally ignored the greeting I gave him. He did not even turn his eyes towards me. He went by as if I didn't exist. If anyone was a ghost on that pathway, I was – for him. He left me standing with one futile hand flapping in the air to stay him. I watched his dogged back receding towards my on-coming guide. I was shocked speechless. It was so grossly unlike the infallible courtesy of the islanders.

He was just about to pass the constable when I found voice again: 'Ask that chief to stop,' I called back, 'he may need some help from us.' It had struck me he might be a lunatic at large: possibly harmless, but we ought to make sure of that. But the din of the surf may have smothered my voice, for the constable didn't seem to hear. He passed the newcomer twenty yards from where I stood, without a sign of recognition.

I ran back to him. 'Who is that man?' I asked.

He stopped in his tracks, gazing at my pointed finger. 'How?' he murmured hesitantly, using the Gilbertese equivalent for, 'Say it again.'

I said it again, sharply, still pointing. As we stood dumbly looking at each other, I saw swift beads of sweat – big, fat ones – start out of his forehead and lose themselves in his eyebrows.

Then it was as if something suddenly collapsed inside him. It was horrible. 'I am afraid in this place!' he screamed high in his head, like a woman, and, without another word, he bolted out on the beach with an arm guarding his eyes. He disappeared at a run round the point, and I didn't see him again until I got back to my quarters.

But there he was when I arrived, on the verandah with the Native Magistrate. I saw the two of them absorbed in talk, the constable violently gesturing now and then as I approached the house. But they stepped apart as soon as they heard my foot-steps, and stood gravely collected when I entered, waiting for me to speak.

I plunged head-first into my petulant story. The sum of it was that the constable had witnessed the discourtesy of the man with the limp, and was now trying his silly best to shield him from censure. It might be very loyal, but did he take me for a fish-headed fool? To pretend he hadn't seen the fellow . . . well . . . really! And so on. I was very young.

The native Magistrate waited with calm good manners for me to run down, and then asked what the man was like.

I told him of the twisted foot, and the belted mat, and the scar.

He turned to exchange nods with the constable: 'That was indeed Na Biria,' he murmured, and they nodded at each other again.

'Na Biria?' I echoed. 'Is he a lunatic?'

He dropped his eyelids, meaning, 'No.'

'Then bring him to me this evening.'

He looked me straight in the eyes: 'I cannot do that.'

'Cannot? What word is this . . . cannot? Is everybody here dotty today? Why cannot you bring him?'

'He is dead,' said the Magistrate, and added as I stood dumb, 'He died this afternoon, soon before three o'clock.'

They were both so remote; the whole place was so secretive; my mind was as fagged as my body; everything in that moment conspired to weaken its resistance against the improbable. Perhaps I was being bluffed; I don't know; but I suddenly had the picture of Na Biria in the article of death projecting his dying thought, with sixty generations of fear behind it, along that path through Nakaa's grove to the Place of Dread beyond. Had I received the impact of his thought as it passed my way? Or if not, what was it I had seen?

I knew it was not only thirst that made my mouth so dry, and that angered me. 'If he only died at three, he is not yet buried, and I can see his body,' I exclaimed.

'His body lies in the village,' replied the Magistrate.

'And I can see it?' I insisted.

He paused a long time before bowing his head in assent. But brusquely then the constable interrupted: 'No! The Man of Matang is a stranger! They are straightening the way of the dead. No stranger must break in . . . No! . . . No!'

The Magistrate silenced him with a gesture. 'I am a Christian,' he said solemnly to me: 'I will take you. Let us go at once.'

I followed him out of the house.

We heard the mourners wailing from a hundred yards off. I saw a dozen of them flogging the purlieus of the open-sided house with staves, to frighten away strange ghosts. I went near enough to see people sitting with raised arms at the head and feet of a body. But I halted outside the circle of beaters. It was finding them so earnestly at work that brought me back to the decencies. These folk believed utterly in what they were doing. For them, the dead man's whole eternity depended on their ritual. For them, the intrusion of me, a stranger, would send him to certain strangulation in Nakaa's net. What earthly or heaven-born right had I, for a moment's peevishness, to condemn them for the rest of their days to that hideous conviction? I suddenly felt as small as I was. I could go no farther. I turned away from the house. The Native Magistrate followed me in silence.

In No Strange Land

There are between twenty and thirty clans scattered up and down the Gilbert Islands, and most of them have members on every atoll. In the old days, a deep sense of brotherhood united and dispersed fragments. A villager of one island could set out for another a total stranger, yet sure that, once he had established kinship there with the people of his own group, he would find a home among them for as long as he cared to stay. He had only to go to the maneaba of the village where he hoped to be accepted as brother, son or grandson and wait there in the *boti*, or sitting-place, of his ancestors. His local kin could not ignore the challenge of that gesture. It was now theirs to come and question him.

My friend Mautake-Maeke once put me through the maneaba ceremonial as if I were a stranger claiming kinship with the clan of Royal Karongoas. So that everything should be right from the beginning, he took me out in his canoe and made me land on the beach by the village maneaba. That was the ancient way of it; all other paths to the communal clearing-house were closed to the newcomer.

We beached our canoe, passed straight into the great building from its seaward side, spread our mats by Karongoa's sun-stone, and waited there for the elders of the clan to come and question me. I was supposed for argument's sake to have arrived from the island of Beru. I had brought with me, according to usage, a stranger's gift (in this case, five pounds of stick-tobacco) to soften hearts and tongues for the encounter.

Nearly a hundred keen-eyed old men came to take part, but they were not all of Karongoa; representatives of Bakoa, the shark clan, and of Keaki, the tropic-bird people, were among them. These went to sit in their own boti as an audience; the examination of a stranger was something the whole village was entitled to hear if it liked. All were dressed in their ceremonial waist-mats of fine mesh girt about the middle with belts of their womenfolk's hair. Most had thrust ornaments of rolled wild-almond leaf, flaming with summer tints of gold and scarlet, through the pierced lobes of their ears. Some carried their pipes slung in that convenient rack. The white-headed senior of Karongoa wore the sun-clan's ceremonial fillet of coconut leaf knotted about his brows. He was the question-master.

His grandson spread a mat for him, and he took his seat facing me across the gift of tobacco, which lay before my crossed legs. There was deep silence in the maneaba save for the echoed hiss-hiss of the wind in the coconut crests outside. I was to be adopted as a member of the Karongoa clan a little later and everybody knew it. This was the real thing acted in earnest by old men to whom the history and customs of their folk were still a treasured inheritance. I was their potential son. Maybe I was too fanciful, but the generations of their fathers seemed to stretch hands out of the past, to gather me back among them, as I sat waiting for the Karongoa chief to speak.

'*Nao, ko ma mauri* (Sir, thou shalt be blest),' he began quietly.

'And thou also, thou shalt be blest.' It was right in answering to push the gift with a gesture of offering towards his feet.

He touched the small pile with his right hand. No word was spoken, but there was a sibilance of insucked breath from among the elders grouped behind him. The gift had been kindly accepted. After a long pause he began again:

'Sir, I have a question.'

'I listen, for I am in thy hand.'

'Whence comest thou?'

'I come from the south.' Pause. 'I come from that island there in the south.' Pause. 'I come from Beru.'

The elder turned back to his companions. They had of course heard for themselves, but it was for him to speak first: 'This man says he comes from the south,' he informed them; 'he comes from Beru.'

'*Ai-i-a!*' they answered in chorus. 'He comes from Beru,' and the news was shouted to the clans of Bakoa and Keaki: 'This man says he comes from Beru.'

'We hear,' answered Bakoa and Keaki; 'He comes from Beru. And what then?'

The filleted elder addressed me anew: 'Thou art a man of Beru. But where sittest thou now?'

'I sit in the boti of my ancestors – my ancestors of Beru and Tarawa.'

'And what is the name of that boti?'

'It is the boti of Karongoa-n-Uea.'

The news was passed back again as before: 'He says he sits in the boti of Karongoa-n-Uea. He says it is the boti of his ancestors.'

'We hear,' replied Bakoa and Keaki, 'he sits in Karongoa-n-Uea. Yet perhaps it is not the boti of his ancestors.'

The elders of Karongoa reported to their leaders: 'The men of

Bakoa and Keaki have replied that perhaps it is not the boti of his ancestors.'

'How, then, shall the stranger answer?' he asked them.

'He shall establish his generations of Karongoa, so that the truth may appear.'

'*Ai-i-a*' echoed Keaki and Bakoa. 'Let him establish his generations.'

'Sir,' the old man turned to me once more, 'we say thou shalt establish thy generations of Karongoa.'

So Mautake traced my descent, with masses of impromptu detail by the way, back to Taane-the-Hero, an old-time Karongoa Uea of Beru. Taane was born a Tarawa man, for his fathers were Beia and Tekai, the famous twins who ruled the island between twenty and thirty generations ago, sharing the throne and their wives in common. Beyond Beia and Tekai, the Tarawa line stretched back through a succession of local Uea, all named Kirata, into a fabulous haze of heroes who had come as conquerors from Samoa in the south or as immigrants from Onouna and Tebongiroro, Ruanuna and Nabanana in the west. Beyond those again were kings of the Breed of Matang in Samoa; and before these, the spirits of the Tree of Samoa; and before the Tree of Samoa, the Tree of Abatoa, which grew in primeval darkness upon the First Land: and before the First Land, the Darkness and Cleaving Together out of which earth, and sea, and sky were fashioned by Naareau the Creator.

The telling took nearly two hours. The sun had set before it ended. In the long stillness that followed, the soaring shadows of the maneaba were peopled for all of us with ghosts of the men of old. Some dividing veil between past and present had been pulled away. There was no longer any time as the dead yet living generations crowded down upon us. The old men sat mute, as if listening to voices; I felt the darkness tense with listening; I was so lost in fantasy myself that my heart missed a beat when the elder of Karongoa suddenly snapped the silence:

'It is enough.'

The old men stirred; there were coughs and murmurs. Memories hung still in the vaulted gloom, but the ghosts were gone and time was upon us again. Not much remained to be said. The elder turned to his clan: 'What think ye, men of Karongoa? Do the words of this man fit well together?'

'They fit,' answered all but one, but he had a point to raise. I think he spoke only to show me how important even the smallest detail of history was to his people: 'This man has said that Beia and Tekai had a slave of old called Noubwebwe. But this was not so. Noubwebwe was the slave of the first Kirata, not Beia and Tekai.'

There were arguments about that, but the chief cut them short. 'This is a little thing,' he said, 'lay it aside. What think ye of this man's telling of the generations? Does it stand firm?'

'It stands firm,' they answered all together, and shouted their finding to Bakoa and Keaki.

'And what is the judgement of Karongoa?' the clans called back. 'Shall the stranger dwell among us?'

'He shall dwell among us as our son.'

'Sir,' the elder finished addressing me, 'thou shalt dwell among us as our son. Our children are thy brothers and sisters, our grandchildren are thy children, our possessions are thy possessions.'

'The judgement is judged,' intoned Karongoa. 'He shall dwell among us as our son,' and at their word the men of Bakoa and Keaki, with cries of approval and friendship, arose and trooped out of the maneaba, leaving the stranger, no longer strange, alone with his kinsmen.

*

Over the next three months, I had to learn by heart the genealogy of my prospective adopter, old Tekirei, who traced his descent down through twenty-three local generations in the male line from the sacred twin kings, Beia and Tekai. That took us back perhaps five hundred years to what he called the age of *toa*, or heroes.

Beia and Tekai were the last of the toa. Their dynasty had been established on Tarawa by invading hordes which, between the twelfth and fourteenth centuries, had swept wave after wave up the Gilberts in their great seventy-foot ocean-going canoes from Samoa, a thousand miles to southward.

Those invaders from Samoa did not come as entire strangers to the place. They and the people whom they found in the Gilberts were descended from a single original stock. Many hundreds of years earlier – say, in the second or third century of the Christian era – the common ancestors, a vast migrating swarm, had burst into the far Western Pacific through the gates of the Molucca Straits by New Guinea. The migrants felt their way ever eastwards for two thousand miles along the Caroline Islands as far as the Marshall group. Thence, they turned southwards down the Gilbert and Ellice chain, leaving colonies behind them as they went, and their main swarm, sailing on close-hauled to the south-east trades when the Ellice group was left astern, eventually reached Samoa and settled there.

The colonists who stayed in the Gilbert Islands remained undisturbed for perhaps thirty generations. Their rustic peace would never had been broken but for a disaster that fell upon their kinsmen in distant Samoa. These, after the better part of a millennium of settlement on Savai'i and Upolu, were driven forth by the indigenous people from whom their forefathers had won a foothold. Fragments of their fleeing race found new homes in other South Pacific islands. At least one contingent reached New Zealand. Another fraction came swarming northwards, back along the original migration-track of the ancestors, to the Gilbert group.

They had to fight for a landing on many islands. But according to Tekirei, there was no fighting at Tarawa, because the newcomers were led by the sacred clan – our clan – Karongoa of the Kings. The reigning dynasty of the day on Tarawa was also of Karongoa. It was not meet that king-priests of the sun should be fighting each other: 'For behold!' explained Tekirei, 'Karongoa ruled by love, not war. Its word was always "Blessings and Peace" to those who came as brother.' The immigrants were welcomed as long-lost kinsmen. And so, round about the time when Edward III became King of England, the Tarawan and Samoan branches of that far-voyaging race, after a thousand years of separation by a thousand miles of ocean, were re-united under Karongoa's peace on that small speck of sand in the central recesses of the Pacific.

There ensued a line of hero-kings named Kirata, which culminated in the twins Beia and Takai. All of these married wives from places far away in the west – from Nabanaba, the land of skulls and bones; from Onouna, the land of bird-men; from Ruanuna, which might have been Liueniua by the Solomons; from Kiroro and Mwaiku, which were possibly Gilolo and Waigeu, 2,500 miles off in the Moluccas.

I was deemed ready for adoption only when I could not be caught out in the details of those marriages or the travel-stories and collateral pedigrees that belonged to them, or about the doings of what Tekirei called his twenty-three 'human' generations and their marriages and adoption outside the Karongoa clan to the third degree of cousinship.

Tekirei said that, by rights, he should confirm his adoption of me by a gift of land, which custom called 'the land of the adopted'. I had a hard time convincing him that he could not do so. He did not see why the law which forbade every European from holding land in the Gilberts, except under short leases, should apply to my particular case. 'We have made thee our son,' he protested; 'we wish thee and thy children and their children and all their generations for ever to inherit a piece of our soil. It shall be written in the Book of the Government. So shall the name of Kurimbo (Grimble) never die among us.'

I managed to persuade him at last that King George would never dream of allowing it, because, in any case, it was more fitting that I should always remember him, my adoptive father, than that he and his family should load themselves with permanent obligations to me and mine. 'Have you not in your gift,' I asked him, 'some token of yourself that I can carry with me and look upon wherever I be, saying, "This thing Tekirei gave me"?'

He looked at me doubtfully. 'I have indeed a token . . . a mark . . . but would the Man of Matang accept it?'

'What mark is this that a Man of Matang might not accept, Tekirei?'

'It is the mark of the serpent . . . this mark, Kurimbo,' he replied, thrusting both arms forward, palms up, to display on each two straight lines of tattooing, a quarter of an inch apart, drawn from where the palm joined the wrist, through the crook of the elbow, to a point above the bulge of the biceps. The lines were crossed at the top to form a fork that he called the tongue of the serpent. 'This is a secret Karongoa that I disclose to you,' he said impressively.

I knew he meant that I must not repeat what he said except in whispers and among members of our clan.

'*Ngkoa-ngkoa-ngkoa* (long, long ago),' he went on, 'perhaps in the Land of Matang before the children were driven forth, the sun loved a serpent. Others will tell you that the sun is a woman, but we of Karongoa know that he is a man, and that he begot children upon the serpent, even the burning twins, Bue and Rirongo.

'And the sun appeared to the kings of Karongoa in their maneaba, a great light up against the sun-stone. He said to them, "I love the serpent and I have made her my wife."

'They answered, "We hear. What shall we do?"

'He said, "You shall make the mark of the serpent on your arms, so that, when you lift your arms sitting before my stone, I shall see there the body of my wife."

'They answered, "We hear. What else shall we do?"

'He said, "You shall teach your children to dance sitting before my stone, thus and thus, so that their arms move this way and that. And to those who are most skilled in the sitting dance, you shall give the mark of the serpent, so that, when their arms move, the body of my wife may move before my eyes."

'And the kings of Karongoa did even as the sun said. They have carried the mark of the serpent on their arms ever since. And they taught the people how to lift their arms thus and thus in the sitting dance before the sun-stone; and to those who were most skilled they gave the mark of the serpent, so that the sun might behold the body of his wife and be happy.'

I thought as I listened to the old man's story, that there was as much of history in it as of myth. I have believed ever since that the bino, as the Gilbertese sitting dance is called, had its origin long ago in a series of ritual gestures performed with sacred song before an altar of the sun in a temple dedicated, perhaps, to the union of the sun-god with his spouse, a serpent. My inference may be impertinent. It rests upon no more evidence than this one tale. But I like it, because it fits well with so many things about the bino that hinted at a religious origin – with the grandiose dignity of its whole-tone chants; with the statuesque and solemn movements of the dancers; with the mask-like gravity of their faces throughout; with the austere, the overwhelming restraint that held the sweep and surge of swaying arms and torsos, hundreds together, to a rhythmic unison that was somehow almost terrible in its perfection. But this is a digression . . .

I went to Tekirei's mwenga on a day appointed, just before noon. Only he and Mautake-Maeke with two girls of fifteen or sixteen, dressed in minute kilts of leaf, were there to receive me. The girls ranged themselves on either side of me as soon as Tekirei brought them forward, and stood silent, holding my arms against their small bosoms.

'Thus it is right,' said Tekirei; 'these are Sea-Wind and King's-Bundle-of-Mats, granddaughters of mine, therefore daughters now of thine, chosen because they are virgins. They are called the companions of thy pain, for their duty is to comfort thy arms against the sore stab of the tattooing comb. No woman who has known a man has power to do this thing, for the comfort is gone out of her. Nor would any not a virgin dare to offer herself for the task. If she did, the sun would pierce her navel with all the pain of the tattooing, and she would die.'

He addressed the children sternly: 'Women, you have heard my warning. What say you now? Are you safe from the sun's anger?'

'We are safe,' they said together, 'we are not afraid,' and smiled serenely back at him.

As we stood so, Tekirei showed me the tattooing comb. It was a flat splinter of bone a quarter of an inch broad and an inch and a half long, beautifully fashioned at one end into a row of five needle-sharp teeth. 'I made this,' he said, 'from the shin-bone of my grandfather. How happy he will be to feel his bone entering the flesh of my adopted son!'

He went on to explain how the comb was to be mounted for use, in the position of an adze-blade, at the end of a little wooden handle: 'First I dip it in the dye, then I set it in this handle. I can hold it firmly so, down upon the flesh that is to be tattooed. And then, so that the teeth may be driven quickly into the flesh, I say, "Strike!" and Mautake strikes down upon the back of the handle with this thing.'

'This thing' was the ivory-like, eighteen-inch spear of a spear-fish, the thick end of which was to serve as a mallet-head. All the courage of the dead brute was concentrated in the thick end, and would pass into my blood with every stroke.

Big Sea-Wind and small King's-Bundle-of-Mats took my shirt from me and drew me by the hands into the coconut grove behind the mwenga, to where a flat block of coral between two higher ones stood hidden from public view by a great uri-tree, myriad-starred with tiny wax-white blossoms. It was in that shady and perfumed seclusion that I received the sign of the serpent. The low, middle block was my seat, the outside ones were for my comforters. As we three sat, my outstretched arms lay comfortably across the girls' knees, palms up, in the proper position for tattooing.

Tekirei and Mautake first drew guide-lines on my arms with stretched strings, which they dipped in their tattooing dye and pressed down on the skin to leave transfer marks. The dye was made of soot mixed with a bright yellow juice wrung from the roots of a Malay custard-apple bush (*morinda citrifolia*).

They began on my right arm. It was high noon, the sun's strong hour for protection, when Tekirei laid the charged comb at its starting-point on my wrist, saying, 'Strike!'

Mautake struck. The teeth bit deep. Tekirei pulled them out, dipped them afresh in the dye, laid them in place again immediately above their first five punctures, called, 'Strike!' and Mautake struck once more.

So it went on – dip, strike, dip, strike – creeping up my arm quarter-inch by quarter-inch, in sets of five punctures at a time, until they reached the top. They worked quickly and deftly. Half an hour saw the first line finished. Then they returned to the bottom and began on the second line. As soon as that was done, they went over to the left arm and dealt with that. The once-over for both arms took rather less than two hours to complete.

Custom dictated that it was my duty to Tekirei to show no shameful sign of suffering under this treatment. If there were groans to be groaned, the tender companions of my pain were there to emit them on my behalf, which they did at exactly the right moments. They had been told in advance that I should hardly feel the stab of the comb during the first pricking-in except at certain points – the wrist, the elbow crook, the shoulder – and it was only around those soft spots that their voices were raised in piteous whimpers. But, as the two men returned to my right arm for the second round, Mautake whispered to Sea-Wind, who was in charge of it, 'Woman, it is fitting that thou shouldst wail all the time now.'

As soon as the crack of the mallet drove the ancestor's shin-bone down into the raw holes left by the first round, I saw what he meant. The synchronized stings of five hornets could not have improved upon the smart of it. Fortunately, I managed to stifle a yelp of surprised anguish and produce a sick smile instead. Happily too, custom allowed me to indicate my true emotions to Sea-Wind by way of contrary statements. 'There is no pain whatever in this thing,' I said: 'How delicate is the bone of the ancestor!'

Sea-Wind, knowing perfectly well that what I meant was 'It hurts like hell,' responded with a scream of mortal agony. King's-Bundle-of-Mats, who was holding my left hand in hers, followed suit rendingly, her right arm around my neck her cheek pressed down upon the crown of my head. They kept it up so in the manner of a fugue, shriek for shriek and comfort for comfort, right-left, left-right, for every remorseless crack of the mallet up either arm, throughout the whole two hours of the second round.

It was even more so for all parties in the third and last round. The twice-harrowed traces up my arms had become continuous lines of raging rawness. 'How delicate is the bone of the an-cestor!' I repeated explosively, as no longer five but fifty hornets at a time now began to stab me, 'How delicate, how persuasive!' and burst into a hooting giggle to conceal a craven grunt. This way of transposing an exclamation of pain into the wild key of a banshee's laugh was another of the personal reliefs allowed by custom. My sally excited the girls to newer and louder efforts. Their screams for me were syncopated by gusts of delirious sobbing as the fiery comb crawled its merciless way to a finish. My ear-drums were racked with the clamour of their grief, my neck half-wrung with the consolation of their strong young arms. The hair on the crown of my head was wet at the end with the tears that their beautiful, innocent eyes had flooded down upon it.

No further ritual attended my adoption. Tekirei simply asked me one evening to go alone with him to the maneaba. Seated there by the sun-stone at the fall of night he asked me to recite in a whisper, close to his ear, the whole tale of his generations, but not backwards into the past as Mautake-Maeke had recited mine three months before – forwards instead, from the creation of the First Land and the First Men down to himself and his scores of collaterals.

When it was done, he took my hands in his. 'Thou hast made no mistake,' he said.

We sat silent, secluded together in the velvet darkness. But the busy village life lapped close around the shores of our aloneness. Cooking-fires made globes of misty-golden light up and down the lines of mwenga outside. Bronze arms and faces glowed happy and kind where people bent over the flames. Friendly voices and scents of food came wafting in under the eaves in rising, falling waves, as if moved by the winnowing of fans in the night to ebb and flow within the confines of our silence and draw us, for all our absorption in the bygone generations, close back again to the warm, the living present.

I think the old man must have divined the hidden urges of my thought – my upwelling gratitude to him and the way I was longing to use the things he had taught me, if only I could, as stepping-stones deeper into the heart of his people – for the first words he threw into the pool of our silence were, 'Yes . . . our roots are the generations of old. Know the roots and thou shalt know the tree. Know the tree and behold! it shall answer to thy cultivation.'

There was another long pause until he said, rising as he spoke, 'Enough! The judgement is judged. I give thee my generations. My forefathers are thy forefathers. Thou art a son of Karongoa, and this shall be the token of it for all men to see: thy table of justice in the maneaba shall be set always up against the sun-stone of our clan, and the sun shall not smite thee for it, for thou art become a child of the sun.'

That was a rare privilege. The customary place for the magistracy, whether Native or European, was in the boti of Strangers at the north end of the Karongoa maneaba. It had always struck me that, thus segregated in the sitting-place of aliens, the table of justice was made to appear, in the last analysis, rather as the symbol of an imported authority never to be wholly admitted to the freedom of the land than as the emblem of a working partnership sealed with the people's own domestic seal. It was not I, but the decay of custom, that eventually made nothing of the discrimination. Within the next fifteen or twenty years, most people had forgotten the entire system of sitting-places in the maneaba. But I dare say my promotion to Karongoa's boti was useful in its day. It certainly is a fact that the villagers who had business with the court began to reveal their intimate griefs and happiness to me more freely than they had ever ventured to do before, as soon as I moved my table into the shadow of the sun-stone.

8

CREATION MYTH

Taakeuta of Marakei, the teller of histories, was an elder of Royal Karongoa. This meant that nobody dared contradict him when he sat in the maneaba talking about the creation story. The sun had a habit of piercing the navels of people who questioned the truths uttered from Karongoa's seat. Cross-legged under the shadow of the sun-stone, he discoursed as irrefutably as a High Priest or Oracle, and he loved it.

The urge to tell stories used to seize him every month anew, round about the full moon. That was his vigorous season, because of the prayer he never failed to make to the young moon on its first or second day's setting. His ritual was a very simple one. He went to stand on the western beach, in silence first of all, with hands outstretched palms-up towards the shining crescent. There was no other right way to begin, he told me once, for this was a tataro (a supplication) not a magic spell. The moon was above all constraint of sorcery's mumbo-jumbo; so he always stood mutely pleading at the start. Then, with statuesque gestures of the standing dance, he broke into a low-voiced chant:

Moon-o! Moon-o-o! Uphold my age, I beg thee.
Moon-o! Moon-o-o! Give me my months, I beg thee.
　　　　　　　　A month, two months, three months,
　　　　　　　　　ten-e-e!
Moon-o! Moon-o-o! Give me my seasons I beg thee.
　　　　　　　　A season, two seasons, three seasons,
　　　　　　　　　a hundred-e-e!
Moon-o! Moon-o-o! Give me my years, I beg thee.
　　　　　　　　A year, two years, three years, a
　　　　　　　　　thousand-e-e!

And, as the moon waxed bigger, he felt the virtue of his prayer surging up like a great wave within him; so that, on the eleventh or twelfth day, the weight of his eighty years was as nothing upon his shoulders, and all the generations of his fathers began to shout in his blood, saying, 'Arise! Gird on thy most beautiful waist mat. Take thy staff and thy pipe. Go forth to the maneaba and tell of the wonderful things of old.'

You would find him sitting in the seat of the sun at any time between forenoon and dusk, a big-boned, gaunt old man with the torso of a time-worn Achilles and the head of a saint, surrounded by listeners as massive and venerable as himself. His adopted grandson would be lying at his feet, ready to fill his pipe or bring him food at command. If you were wise, you would carry a small offering with you, for then he might tell you a story of your own choosing. It depended on what you asked for. Karongoa-of-the-Kings had its own peculiar versions of the basic traditions, which were not for the ears of outsiders. The Karongoa cosmogony was wrapped up in the myth of the sun-hero Au, the Lord of Heaven, who had risen from the depths into the sky on the crest of a pandanus tree. The other clans were allowed to know nothing of Au except under the name and style of Auriaria, a simple clan ancestor.

And so, whatever rendering of the creation-story you heard from Taakeuta in public, you could be quite sure that it was not Karongoa's private version. Indeed, his own navel would have been in danger of impalement by a sun-ray had he ventured to throw that one away on outsiders. The Creators of whom he spoke under the sun-stone were called Naareau the Elder and Naareau the Younger. These, you might say, were the popular First Causes as opposed to Au, the priestly one.

If, as I have supposed, Royal Karongoa was once, in days and lands but darkly remembered, a caste of royal priests who dictated the articles of popular belief from a temple of the sun, it must have been a very wise priestcraft. The heritage of doctrinal tolerance that it handed down through the ages to old Taakeuta and his rustic peers was, at all events, a liberal one. The elders of Karongoa, as I knew them, insisted publicly upon nothing but the barest essentials of dogma about Naareau the Elder and Naareau the Younger. That allowed scope for a stimulating variety of orthodoxies.

A man was free to think, if he liked, that Naareau the Elder was a being evolved from the void through a genealogical series of abstractions and things; or he could begin with an absolute Naareau seated alone in the void from all eternity. Original matter could be a chaos of stuff timelessly coexistent with the god in the void; or, alternatively, a mixture of elemental things directly created by him; or, alternatively again, the result of an evolution totally distinct from him. Naareau the Younger could be the son of the Elder, born of his sweat, or his finger-tips, or a tear of his right eye; or he could be the descendant of a genea-logical series beginning with a woman and a man created by the First of All. And so on, multitudinously. All along the line, the conflicting notions of a unique creating power and a creation self-evolved out of the void were found overlapping each other in the popular cosmogonies.

Every elder of every clan claimed outside the maneaba that his particular rendering of the story was the one and only truth. They argued together about their pet cosmogonies as earnestly at least as the physicists of civilization about their cosmologies. But when they took their differences to Taakeuta sitting by his sun-stone, he never failed to send them away friends. He would listen to each side's story in total silence and whisper at the end (Karongoa always whispered its judgements), 'Sirs, there was Naareau the First of All and there was Naareau the Younger. They did what they did. No man knows all their works. Enough! let each family turn away content with its own knowledge.' Having said which, he would treat them to an account radically different from either of theirs and, usually, quite unlike the last I had heard from him. But I found in the course of years that he never mixed his versions. He handed out each one intact, as it had come to him down the generations.

I pass on now the first rendering he ever gave me.

Dusk was falling as he told his story. All his audience save only myself had straggled away to the evening meal. Odours of cooking mixed with sea-scents and the eternal perfume of lilies hung poised in the maneaba's sanctuaried gloom. The rumour of a chanted song came drifting in from far away.

Taakeuta began, as he always began, 'Sir, I remember the voices of my fathers. Hearken to the words of Karongoa . . .

'Naareau the Elder was the First of All. Not a man, not a beast, not a fish, not a thing was before him. He slept not, for there was no sleep; he ate not, for there was no hunger. He was in the Void. There was only Naareau sitting in the Void. Long he sat, and there was only he.

'Then Naareau said in his heart, "I will make a woman." Behold! a woman grew out of the Void: Nei Teakea. He said again, "I will make a man." Behold! a man grew out of his thought: Na Atibu, the Rock. And Na Atibu lay with Nei Teakea. Behold! their child – even Naareau the Younger.

'And Naareau the Elder said to Naareau the Younger, "All knowledge is whole in thee. I will make a thing for thee to work upon." So he made that thing in the Void. It was called the Darkness and the Cleaving Together; the sky and the earth and the sea were within it; but the sky and the earth clove together, and darkness was between them, for as yet there was no separation.

'And when his work was done, Naareau the Elder said, "Enough! It is ready. I go, never to return." So he went, never to return, and no man knows where he abides now.

'But Naareau the Younger walked on the overside of the sky that lay on the land. The sky was rock, and in some places it was rooted in the land, but in other places there were hollows between. A thought came into Naareau's heart; he said, "I will enter beneath it." He searched for a cleft wherein he might creep, but there was no cleft. He said again, "How then shall I enter? I will do it with a spell." That was the First Spell. He knelt on the sky and began to tap it with his fingers, saying:

> Tap . . . tap, on heaven and its dwelling places.
> It is stone. What becomes of it? It echoes!
> It is rock. What becomes of it? It echoes!
> Open, Sir Stone! Open, Sir Rock!
> It is open-o-o-o!

'And at the third striking, the sky opened under his fingers. He said, "It is ready," and he looked down into the hollow place. It was black dark, and his ears heard the noise of breathing and snoring in the darkness. So he stood up and rubbed his finger-tips together. Behold! the First Creature came out of them – even the Bat that he called Tiku-tiku-toumouma. And he said to the Bat, "Thou canst see in the darkness. Go before me and find what thou findest."

'The Bat said, "I see people lying in this place." Naareau answered, "What are they like?" and the Bat said, "They move not; they say no word; they are all asleep." Naareau answered again, "It is the Company of Fools and Deaf Mutes. They are a Breed of Slaves. Tell me their names." Then the Bat settled on the forehead of each one as he lay in the darkness and called his name to Naareau: "This man is Uka the Blower. Here lies Naawabawe the Sweeper. Behold, Karitoro the Roller-up. Now Kotekateka the Sitter. Kotei the Stander now" – a great multitude.

'And when they were all named, Naareau said, "Enough. I will go in." So he crawled through the cleft and walked on the underside of the sky; and the Bat was his guide in the darkness. He stood among the Fools and Deaf Mutes and shouted, "Sirs, what are you doing?" None answered; only his voice came back out of the hollowness, "Sirs, what are you doing?" He said in his heart, "They are not yet in their right minds, but wait."

'He went to a place in their midst; he shouted to them "Move!" and they moved. He said again "Move!" They set their hands against the underside of the sky. He said again, "Move!" They sat up; the sky was lifted a little. He said again "Move! Stand!" They stood. He said again "Higher!" But they answered, "How shall we lift it higher?" He made a beam of wood, saying, "Lift it on this." They did so. He said again, "Higher! Higher!" But they answered, "We can no more, we can no more, for the sky has roots in the land." So Naareau lifted up his voice and shouted, "Where are the Eel and the Turtle, the Octopus and the Great Ray?" The Fools and Deaf Mutes answered, "Alas! they are hidden away from the work." So he said, "Rest," and they rested; and he said to that one among them named Naabawe, "Go, call Riiki, the conger eel."

'When Naabawe came to Riiki, he was coiled asleep with his wife, the short-tailed eel. Naabawe called him; he answered not, but lifted his head and bit him. Naabawe went back to Naareau, crying, "Alas! the conger eel bit me." So Naareau made a stick with a slip-noose, saying "We shall take him with this, if there is a bait to lure him." Then he called the Octopus from his hiding place; and the Octopus had ten arms. He struck off two arms and hung them on the stick as bait; therefore the octopus has only eight arms to this day. They took the lure to Riiki, and as they offered it to him Naareau sang:

Riiki of old, Riiki of old!
Come hither Riiki, thou mighty one;
Leave thy wife, the short-tailed eel,
For thou shalt uproot the sky, thou shalt press down the depths.
Heave thyself up, Riiki, mighty and long,
Kingpost of the roof, prop up the sky and have done.
Have done, for the judgement is judged.

'When Riiki heard the spell, he lifted up his head and the sleep went out of him. See him now! He puts forth his snout. He seizes the bait. Alas! they tighten the noose; he is fast caught. They haul him! he is dragged away from his wife the short-tailed eel, and Naareau is roaring and dancing. Yet pity him not, for the sky is ready to be lifted. The day of sundering has come.

'Riiki said to Naareau, "What shall I do?" Naareau answered, "Lift up the sky on thy snout; press down the earth under thy tail." But when Riiki began to lift, the sky and the land groaned, and he said, "Perhaps they do not wish to be sundered." So Naareau lifted up his voice and sang.

Hark, hark how it groans, the Cleaving Together of old!
Speed between, Great Ray, slice it apart.
Hump thy back, Turtle, burst it apart.
Fling out thy arms, Octopus, tear it apart.
West, East, cut them away!
North, South, cut them away!
Lift, Riiki, lift, kingpost of the roof, prop of the sky.
It roars, it rumbles! Not yet, not yet is the Cleaving Together sundered.

'When the Great Ray and the Turtle and the Octopus heard the words of Naareau, they began to tear at the roots of the sky that clung to the land. The Company of Fools and Deaf Mutes stood in the midst. They laughed; they shouted, "It moves! See how it moves!" And all that while Naareau was singing and Riiki pushing. He pushed up with his snout, he pushed down with his tail; the roots of the sky were torn from the earth; they snapped! the Cleaving Together was split asunder. Enough! Riiki straightened out his body; the sky stood high, the land sank, the Company of Fools and Deaf Mutes was left swimming in the sea.

'But Naareau looked up at the sky and saw that there were no sides to it. He said, "Only I, Naareau, can pull down the sides of the sky." And he sang:

Behold, I am seen in the west, it is west!
There is never a ghost, nor a land, nor a man;
There is only the Breed of the First Mother, and the First Father and the
    First Beginning;

181

There is only the First Naming of Names and the First Lying Together
  in the Void;
There is only the lying together of Na Atibu and Nei Teakea,
And we are flung down in the waters of the western sea.
It is west!

'So also he sang in the east, and the north, and the south. He
ran, he leapt, he flew, he was seen and gone again like the
lightnings in the sides of heaven; and where he stayed, there he
pulled down the side of the sky, so that it was shaped like a bowl.

'When that was done, he looked at the Company of Fools and
Deaf Mutes, and saw that they were swimming in the sea. He
said in his heart, "There shall be the First Land." He called to
them "Reach down, reach down-o-o! Clutch with your hands.
Haul up the bed-rock. Heave!" They reached down; they hauled
up the First Land from the bottom of the sea. The name of it was
Aba-the-Great, and there was a mountain that smoked in its
midst. It was born in the Darkness.

'And Naareau stood on Aba-the-Great in the west. He said to
his father, "Na Atibu, it is dark. What shall I do?" Na Atibu
answered: "Take my eyes, so that it may be light." Then
Naareau slew his father and laid his head on the slope of the
mountain that smoked. He took his right eye and flung it east:
behold! the Sun. He took his left eye and flung it west: behold!
the Moon. He took the fragments of his body and scattered them
in the sky: behold! the Stars. He took Riiki the Great Eel; he
flung him overhead; and behold! his belly shines there to this
day, even the Milky Way.

'And Naareau planted in Aba-the-Great the beam of wood that
had lifted the sky: behold! the First Tree, the Ancestor Sun. The
spirits of the underworld grew from its roots; and from the
whirlpool where its roots went down to the sea grew the An-
cestress, Nei Nimanoa, the far-voyager, from whom we know
the navigating stars.

'And when it was light, Naareau made Aba-the-Little in the
west and Samoa in the south. He planted in Samoa a branch of
the First Tree, the Ancestor Sun, and ancestors grew from it.
They were kings of the Tree of Samoa, the Breed of Matang, the
company of red-skinned folk, whose eyes were blue – Auriaria

and Nei Tituaabine, Tabuariki and Nei Tevenei and Taburimai. And Auriaria was king of the crest; and his children were Kanii and Batuku who reigned beneath the Tree.

'And Naareau plucked the flowers of the tree of Samoa. He flung them northwards and where they fell, there grew Tarawa, Beru, Tabiteuea, and a multitude of islands between south and west, not to be numbered. All the lands of the earth were made by Naareau the Younger. Who shall know the end of his knowledge and his works? There is nothing that was not made by him.

'So at last all things were finished according to his thought. He said in his heart, "Enough. It is finished. I go, never to return." And he went, never to return.'

9

CENTRAL GILBERTS

George McGhee Murdoch at Abemama

A second application I had made for permission to go to the front was turned down at the end of 1916. Our second daughter, Rosemary Anne, was born at Tarawa in January, 1917. A month later, the four of us left Tarawa for Abemama, the headquarters of the Central Gilberts. My orders were to take over there from that famous old-timer George McGhee Murdoch, who was waiting to retire from service.

My great advantage as a beginner at Abemama was that George remained nearby after handing over to me. He had been allowed, against the usual Colonial Service rule, to settle down in retirement on an island of his own district and open a trading station there. Kuria, where he lived, was one of the High Chief of Abemama's tributary islands (Aranuka was the other) and only twenty miles away.

Kuria is a tiny lagoonless strip of sand not more than five or six miles long, but broader than most Gilbert islands. Its deep and silent coconut forest is over a mile across in some places, and the minute population – less than two hundred souls in those days – were unable to gather the rich crops unaided. George's coming was a godsend to them, for he brought in his own labourers from other islands and worked the land on a fifty-fifty basis, he paying all the costs. He did not make much out of it for himself, but I never saw a man in retirement happier than he was. He had married his third wife not long before retiring – Mamie – the big, plump, laughing daughter of a white trader and a Gilbertese mother, who treated him at once with the reverence due to a god and the kindly firmness of a mother for her rather difficult son. Mamie delighted his declining days – or maybe declining is the wrong word here – by presenting him with a new baby about once a year for I don't remember how many years in succession. The compound of his trade-store above the shining beach was always a hurly-burly of incredibly active infants as freckled and Scottish-looking as himself. He would sit on his beautifully neat front verandah gazing out at the wild tangle of them with infinite satisfaction, murmuring, 'Why did I not spend all my life at this . . . just gathering copra and making babies? Can ye tell me that, now? D'ye know of any finer activities for a man? Ye say ye do not? Well . . . have another wee drink.'

It was an easy trip across to him in the 35-ton ketch *Choiseul*, which Burns, Philip and Company kept based on Abemama to collect the copra of the three islands. I used to go and spend a night with him every six weeks or so, to draw on hs vast fund of local knowledge. He was not very forthcoming with me at first, mainly because he felt I made an unworthy successor for men like Charles Workman and himself. Heaven knows I felt the same too, but when I admitted it he didn't like that either. He was pleased when I lost my temper and shouted, 'All right, I'm a pup. So were you and Mr Workman pups when you started. Now you're superior. What about helping me to be superior too by the time I'm sixty like you.'

'Now that's what I call talking, laddie,' he answered: 'You come to your old uncle, and he'll teach ye . . . he'll teach ye,' and from that time on we were friends.

He was a little sandy-grey man, as wiry and alert as a fox-terrier, always spotlessly turned out in starched ducks. There was mastery in his jutting beak of a nose, and the deliberate, waxed bristle of his sergeant-major's moustache betrayed, perhaps, an over-conscious will to dominate, but caution and humour too shone in the pale blue twinkle of his eyes from under tufted brows. He had needed all the controlled strength that was in him to make what he had made of his life between 1871 and 1917. He never told me his personal history as a continuous tale, nor did he ever set out to speak directly in my hearing about his past, but from time to time he would turn aside into odd, stark little scenes out of it in the course of talking about other people. I have had to make what order I could of the scraps he released.

He was born at Greenock in 1887, the son of a small painter and glazier. He grew up, in his own words, a sickly bairn with a continuous running cold until, at twelve years old, he began coughing blood. By the next year, his condition had worsened. His parents could afford no more medical treatment for him, and would not accept charity. So, on the doctor's advice that a long sea-voyage might do him good, they got him employed at short notice as captain's boy in a barque sailing out of Greenock for New Zealand.

The captain, according to George, was a very fine man except when drunk, which was nearly all the time. With the drink in him, he was a fiend of hell. What aroused his fury most about George was his weakness. The little boy was thrashed whenever he coughed, for being the bad bargain he was. A favourite game was to swipe him back-handed across the mouth. This caused him to spit blood in a way that made his master laugh. Most of his top front teeth had been smashed by the time the barque reached New Zealand.

The sick child deserted ship at Auckland with a spare shirt and his next most valued possession, a toy monkey on a stick, wrapped up in it. He had found on the way out that the warmth of the tropics eased his coughing. Someone had told him too of the blessed climate of the Gilbert Islands, and he had made up his mind to get there somehow. He spent three months in the strange city looking for his chance. I never heard what he did to keep himself alive; all George would say about it was, 'I did not beg, I did not steal, and the monkey was grand company; my mother gave it to me the day I left home.' He found a job at last as captain's boy in a barquentine trading up to the Marshall and Gilbert Islands. And so, in 1871, at fourteen years old, he sailed with his man's experience, spare shirt and infant's toy for the Central Pacific.

The next fragment is the story of how Benjamin Corries befriended him in the Gilberts. Benjamin was a sternly religious but not teetotal Yorkshireman of about thirty-five who ran a successful trade-store on Maiana, the island between Tarawa and Abemama. He was horrified, when the captain brought George ashore with him one day, to learn that although the ailing boy could neither read nor write and knew not a single Bible story, his master proposed to do nothing to cure his ignorance. Ben could not let things go at that. The fate of a child's soul was in the balance; his duty lay clear before him. The night before the ship was due to sail, he went aboard, drank the captain under the table and brought George ashore with him.

The captain landed with a search-party at daybreak, but by then the boy was hidden in a village five miles away with a brother of Ben's native wife. Other men of her family were gathered at the trade-store. They stood round to see fair play while Ben fought the captain first and the second mate next to a standstill on the beach. The ship left the same morning, without George.

He was allowed to idle day-long by the lagoonside at first, bathing whenever he liked and fortified by enormous doses of shark-liver oil that Ben himself forced down his throat twice daily. In three months he was spitting no more blood, in six his cough was gone and he had grown plump. Every evening, Ben gave him two hours' teaching in the three Rs at a table under the palms by the beach. There was no heavy discipline until his lungs were healed; but after that, the exquisite copperplate script he learned from Ben was beaten into him, according to his own phrase, with the buckle end of a leather belt. 'The Books of Genesis and Exodus were my first and second reading primers,' he used to say: 'Beginning with those, I read every chapter of the

Bible aloud to Ben straight through to the last o' Revelations. He would expound our readings next day as I worked with him in the trade-store. I was rising eighteen before we came to the end, and that finished my schooldays. He never thrashed me after that except in fair fight, as man to man, when I argued with him about the Scriptures. I didn't argue often, for he had a fearsome hard fist. Ay, Ben was a militant Christian.'

At twenty, working now on a good wage as Ben's book-keeper and store-manager, George married a girl of Maiana, who bore him two children, Agnes and Charlie. Before he was twenty-five, he had saved enough money to set up business on his own account. He started small, with Ben's kindly help, at the south end of Maiana, but his ambition from the first was to get across to the rich island group of Abemama, Kuria and Aranuka, over which the redoubtable Tem Binoka, made famous by R. L. Stevenson a little later, ruled as absolute monarch. It was a bold ambition, for Tem Binoka wanted no white man snooping in his kingdom and bearing tales about his murderous ways to the British, American and German warships which policed the Gilberts under the Pacific Islanders Protection Conventions. He had refused many an applicant before George came into the picture.

But, as George saw things, the others had all taken the wrong line. Their sole aim had been to set up local trading stations, buy the High Chief's copra dirt cheap and sell it to the trading ships for their own profit. 'But Tem Binoka was a shrewd man,' said George to me; 'he didn't see why he should let folk step in like that just to do him in the eye under his own nose, so to speak. What he needed was a private agent of his own clever enough to do everyone else in the eye on his behalf. Your old uncle was the very man for the job. I became what he would have called his factor, had he been a Scot. I managed the whole of his heritable estates and, believe me or not, it was a mighty profitable deal for him.'

George organized production and marketing on Tem Binoka's several thousand acres of coconut land as it had never been organized before, taking a commission on his sales to the trading ships. He made a pretty thing for himself – enough to send his beautiful little girl Agnes later on to the best schools of California and his son Charlie to school and university in Australia. But he gave much for what he earned; he was always greatly more to the High Chief than his man of business. It was he who, operating as a kind of secretary for foreign affairs, maintained friendly relations between Tem Binoka and the tough New Bedford whalers who, in those days, found Abemama lagoon a convenient base for hunting the equatorial whale. It was his influence too that converted his formidable chief from resenting the visits of British warships as threats against his throne to tolerating them as tokens of Queen Victoria's friendship, and brought him in the end to submit to the British Protectorate with resignation instead of hate. The Protectorate would doubtless have been established whether Tem Binoka had wanted it or not, but the peace in which it came to Abemama, Kuria and Aranuka was uniquely George McGhee Murdoch's gift to the Empire.

I could never get George to say much about R.L.S's stay on Abemama in 1889. There must have been some deep misunderstanding between the two men. The great and gentle romancer never knew that, but for the intercession of his masterful little fellow-Scot, Tem Binoka would have refused to allow the party from the *Equator* to settle ashore. It was not George but Benuaakai, Binoka's cousin and close friend, who told me this. I do not suppose that George was particularly interested in Stevenson as a writing man – he never had much time for pen-pushers, as he called them – but he had heard or divined for himself that his compatriot had *te kangenge*, the wasting sickness that the Gilberts had cured in himself, and this, according to Benuaakai, was the ultimate argument he used to beat down Tem Binoka's resistance. It makes a strange picture – the gross-bodied and ruthless island potentate, who held the lives of his own subjects so cheap that he would shoot them down from tree-tops for the amusement of seeing them fall sprawling, nevertheless touched by the pleading of his little white factor for the health of a sick stranger. How deeply and urgently George did touch him is implicit in Stevenson's own account of the building of 'Equator Town' for the visiting party in two days, under Tem Binoka's personal supervision. I like to think that, had the great writer known all the facts, he would have dealt as kindly with George – adventuring now and then, perhaps, as pleasantly far into the field of sentimental conjecture about him – as he did with the High Chief. But, to prove the full value of his helpfulness, George would have had to reveal something of the real nature of his unspeakable employer, and he was too loyal for that.

So, R.L.S. remained always for George the pen-pusher who did not like his face, and George figured in R.L.S.'s record as nothing better than 'a silent, sober, solitary, niggardly recluse' without a name, who lived on sufferance at Ahemama 'far from court, and hearkening and watching his conduct like a mouse in a cat's ear'. George said to me once, 'Maybe he would have liked me better if he had known I was legally spliced to the mother of my children. But how could he know? Outside old Ben Corrie and me, there weren't many white men in the Gilberts who indulged in the luxury of marriage, those days. After all, with his own leddy in the house, it would not have been decent to receive me had I been living in sin with a village woman.'

'But why didn't you make sure he knew, Mr Murdoch?' I asked (I never presumed to call him George to his face).

'There are things a man doesn't run around explaining about himself,' was all he troubled to reply.

Three years after the Stevensons left, the British Protectorate was established, with George operating as one of the principal agents for setting up tentative native courts on the Gilbert Islands. 'From that time on,' his own account ran, 'I transferred my services from King Binoka to Queen Victoria. Binoka was sore with me at first, but he settled down to it and stayed my friend. I ordered myself a belt with a big crown on the buckle, and I stuck another crown in front of my helmet. Solid silver, they were. I told him the Queen herself had sent them to me for a present. Whenever a new law came out, I invented a special message from the Queen to him requesting his *pair*sonal collaboration in the matter. He was impressed and pleased. I made a by-ordinary good citizen of the old reprobate before he died.'

George's modest title under the new administration was District Agent and Tax Collector, but his tremendous business was to supervise the working of the Native Courts he had nursed into being, to bring peace and order without the use of force into the life of the young lagoonside villages, and to get the wild white beachcombers of his day – very far from always without strong measures – to toe the line of British law. His official colleagues at the outset were his old benefactor, Ben Corrie of Maiana, and another Yorkshireman, Alf Hicking of Tabiteuea, but these soon returned to their own job of trading, and he alone remained, at a salary of £150 a year, to teach succeeding generations of newcomers their business as administrative officers in the Gilbert Islands. His vast knowledge of native custom and his sympathetic understanding of the people were behind every enactment of importance to the islands passed between 1892 and 1917. His pay rose to £200, £250 and finally £300–400 a year in the slow course of time; his title was changed to District Officer; he became a Deputy Commissioner for the Western Pacific – in other words, a magistrate with power to try cases in which Europeans were involved – and this gave him the right to wear a civil uniform of the fifth class.

'I was a proud man,' he told me, 'when I first put on those trappings. I cannot say they precisely suited my style of beauty . . . and the wee sword had a habit of tripping me up, times; my mother would have looked at it poking between my wee legs and said, "George, ye look gey like the monkey on a wee stick I gave ye"; but she would have been fine and proud of me, ay, she would that. It was the idea of the thing. I wish she could have lived to see me climbing that sword.'

But the high climax of his career came in 1912 when, forty years after he had strayed the streets of Auckland, a penniless child with death in him, he was appointed to act for twelve months as Resident Commissioner.

'Ay,' he said, 'I felt grand up there at the Residency. I used to stand looking out over the sea and say to myself, "George McGhee Murdoch; look at how you started . . . and here you are, in charge o' one o' His Majesty's territories overseas." Mind ye, though, I did not get too big for my boots, for I knew that Charles Workman would have made a better job of the pen-pushing than I did. They should have appointed him to act really. But there – they've given him his chance over at Nauru now. Looking back, I'm glad they did not pass me over.'

Lonely Station

The Government station at Abemama, which George had made, was an enclosure of about ten acres of coconut-grove above the lagoon beach. It was placed where the twenty-mile capital C of the land was broken, almost at its middle point, by a tidal passage between lagoon and ocean. Down on the beach-head were the boat house and a flagstaff. Due west from the flagstaff, six miles across the blue flame of the lagoon, lay the surf-smothered barrier of the ocean reef, stretched from tip to tip of the C, with two or three palm-tufted islets riding on it near the passage where the ships came in.

Inland among the palms stood the District Officer's quarters, a three-roomed thatched house built wholly of native materials, its servants' quarters grouped nearby. A generous government had furnished it free, gratis (and, incidentally, for almost nothing) with floor-mats made in the female gaol; string beds – meaning beds sprung with string, not springs – manufactured by the station carpenter; six Austrian bentwood chairs; a squatter's chair; a kerosene lamp that the faintest breeze blew out; a kitchen table for the kitchen; another kitchen table for the dining-room; a china basin with ewer (not a single crack in either); and two japanned chamberpots. There was, however, also a stationery cupboard in the office, which we eventually appropriated for a wardrobe, and that, with one or two additions of our own, spelt luxury enough for us. It is astonishing how a few packing-cases with cretonne frills, and books, and photographs in silver frames, and a cheap vase or two here and there, can make a home, and I think District Officers' wives more than most others have a genius for charming miracles out of these simplicities. They have to.

Scattered around us through the trees were a small box of an office, a beautiful maneaba, and two handsome gaols, one for men, one for women. The last was to prove useful to Olivia for purposes far from penal, as I shall reveal more fully later. The dwellings of the Native Magistrate, his Chief Kaubure, Chief of Police, and Island Scribe were ranged with those of three or four station police down against the tidal passage. A small medical visiting station and dispensary under the charge of a Native Dresser stood over by the wind-blown ocean beach a furlong to eastward. There was a Roman Catholic mission station a mile or so along the lagoonside road. The resident missionary, Father Trautwein, and two teaching Sisters were the only other Europeans on the island, except the captain and engineer of the ketch *Choiseul*, who were at sea most of the time. It was a lonely life for any white woman prone to sitting down and twiddling thumbs, but Olivia was not a twiddler. I dare not claim that her methods were always strictly legal, but she certainly was addicted to go-getting.

She began, irreproachably enough, by combing the villages for sick children and establishing a kind of nursing-home-cum-mother's-education-centre in one of the houses of the servants' quarters. There was no doctor on the island for fifty-one and a half weeks of the year, but the Dresser at the visiting station supplied simple medicines from his stock and, with the writings of Dr Truby King as her main stand-by, she had extraordinary success with her patients and pupils from the start. She was the first white woman to live on Abemama since R.L.S. had been there with Mrs Stevenson for those few months in 1889; many mothers brought their ailing children to her out of sheer curiosity at first, but in the end it was her cures that kept them coming.

Most of her cases called only for sensible hygiene or care about diet, but there were emergencies which demanded a certain inventiveness. One day, the Dresser brought along a year-old baby who, he thought, must be very near death. It looked as if he were right. The little boy's entire back and buttocks were red-raw, stripped of skin by some spreading infection. For two months in hospital the rawness had continued to eat outwards from an original rash in the small of his back. He had screamed and struggled with the pain of it at first, but now he was so weak that hardly a movement stirred him. His body was wasted beyond belief.

We had one of those medical guides issued by the Board of Trade for the use of sailormen beyond the call of doctors. But that volume was, perhaps naturally, silent on the subject of infantile skin complaints in the Line Islands, and our Truby King book did not specialize in this direction either. So Olivia had to proceed empirically. Her general guess was that some kind of food deficiency (I don't remember talking much of vitamin starvation in those days) had at least as much to do with the little boy's state as bacterial infection. Which substance he lacked, nature alone knew, but cod liver oil, pumpkin mash, brown rice water, young coconut jelly, and the yeasty precipitate of fermented coconut toddy seemed to promise a hopeful variety of answers. The technique was to get as much as possible of every one of them into him in the course of each day, leaving the ultimate choice to nature's commonsense. As for the skin trouble, Olivia guessed it needed soothing as well as antisepsis, and attacked it with an unguent of her own invention. Her prescription for the mixture was – castor oil, one tablespoonful; glycerine, one tablespoonful; tincture of iodine, ten drops. The stuff was ladled over the small boy's back and buttocks and covered with cotton wool. Whether it was the vitamins, or the ointment, or both that triumphed in the end we had no means of knowing; but in two months the baby had put on nine pounds and was crawling around gaily with the skin as sleek as satin on his back.

Our back premises were conveniently situated for Olivia's less innocent purposes up against the enclosure of the female gaol. That commodious building consisted of a single forty-by-thirty-foot room enclosed in heatproof walls of packed coral lime. Its deep-eaved thatch of pandanus leaf was raised on studs five feet above the top of the wall, so as to allow a continuous play of fresh air beneath the roof. It was the most heavenly-cool building on the Government station and, as Olivia observed in our third or fourth month there, absolutely wasted for the most part, because Abemama women were so law-abiding.

I personally felt that the chronic emptiness of the gaol owed less to the freedom of Abemama women from original sin than to a certain chivalrous prejudice of the Native Court's against consigning ladies to the lock-up. But it was no part of my functions to interfere with the Court's acquittals on points of fact, and I did agree with Olivia that the beautiful empty gaol offered amenities as much to be desired for sick women as for sinful ones. As a result, Olivia collared it, after about a month's feeble resistance on my part, as a centre for the pre-natal care and education of ailing expectant mothers.

The Native Magistrate was delighted with the arrangement, and co-operated in a way that threatened to cause embarrassment at first. His argument (as we heard later) was that, as the gaol had been converted from an aridly penal institution into a first-class school for expectant mothers, it was now worth practically any young woman's while to be locked up in it. He accordingly directed his village kaubure and policemen to take more vigilant cognizance than they had formerly taken of offences committed by females of child-bearing age, in order that these, by being sent to prison, might take advantage of the course of instruction initiated by Olivia. We first learned of his commendable enthusiasm when, after a session of the Native Court that I had not attended, a flood of eleven cheerful young women (convicted of offences ranging from abusive language to assault upon a policeman) suddenly presented themselves to the wardress, with garlands of flowers on their heads, for immediate incarceration.

Olivia had at the time five patients comfortably housed in the gaol, and said she could not possibly move a single one of them out on the spur of the moment. The floor-space admitted of only seven more inmates, allowing an area of ten by ten for each person. The immediate problem was, therefore, to reduce from eleven to seven the number of the new candidates for admission. I felt that this might solve itself by natural erosion in the course of my routine review of the sentences inflicted. But the hope was a vain one; all the sentences were in perfect order and, beyond that, not a single young woman showed the least wish to appeal. On the contrary, one and all said they wanted to stay as long as the law allowed them, and longer if possible, so as to learn everything Olivia had to teach them about how ailing expectant mothers ought to be treated. The two who had achieved three months each for joint assault and battery upon a policeman burst into tears and protests at the cruel idea that justice might in their case be tempered with mercy. They regarded themselves as scholarship-holders, so to speak, among the ruck of girls whose crimes had earned them only a week or two of prison.

I could, of course, hardly admit their main argument that, having been sentenced in due and proper order to terms of imprisonment, they now had an absolute *right* to use the prison as their education centre. But, on the other hand, an absolute obligation was upon me to see that the sentences duly and properly passed by the Native Court were carried out. So all the ladies had to be taken in. The wardress was surprised and annoyed at my weakness; it meant an unprecedented amount of work for her, and besides, she regarded the gaol as belonging now solely to Olivia, herself and the ailing expectant mothers. She made me feel as if I were quite the worst criminal in the piece. I had some initial difficulty with Olivia too; she said the idiotic working of the law would be very bad for her patients. However, we managed to get round the problem of over-crowding at once. The convicted ladies most kindly agreed to sleep in the clean thatched working sheds that stood shaded by palms within the gaol yard. It was, therefore, only innocent folk – that is to say, the wardress and patients – who occupied the actual lock-up at night.

The Native Magistrate was delighted with that arrangement too, because, as he said, it not only provided for the proper segregation of the criminal population but also made everyone feel free in spite of being in prison. I felt the same myself, but ventured to warn him that if the wave of female delinquency continued on Abemama at that rate, it would be a pity, because it would force me to drive the ailing expectant mothers out of gaol. He replied with a cautiously worded conjecture that we had seen the worst of it, and, strangely enough, we never had more than three convictions a month after that. Furthermore, there were no new cases whatever until all but two of the original eleven had left us weeping for the sorrow of their enlargement and promising to return as soon as possible.

I abstained, after due reflection, from reporting the matter to headquarters. The truth is, I found it more than difficult to make out a convincing case for the summary misappropriation of one of His Majesty's Proclaimed Gaols in furtherance of a little scheme of the District Officer's wife's, however benevolently inspired. The facts, as set forth in writing and staring at me from the paper, seemed to shout of jiggery-pokery from first to last. Olivia would not admit this – she said the facts were all right: it was only the crude way I put them – but she did suggest another good reason for keeping things off the record. Her basic contention was that the Colonial Office wouldn't want to hear of her doings because it made a point of ignoring the existence of District Officer's wives for any purpose whatever. That was so grimly true that her reminder made a man of me; I did not see, in the long run, why I should bring my own wife to high official notice only to have her (and, incidentally, myself too) condemned as a law-breaker. My conspiracy of silence with her was, of course, as deeply immoral as her theft of the prison, and I do not recommend any such goings-on for imitation by married District Officers in this age of swift political communications and retributions.

Yet, I cannot forbear from claiming that the issue was an extraordinarily happy one for all parties concerned. The village police and kaubure, inspired by the advantages which the prison offered to female offenders, became at least moderately zealous in bringing their womenfolk to court for breaches of the peace. The womenfolk, eager to learn what Olivia had to teach them, knew that all they had to do to qualify for a course of instruction was to indulge in the pleasure of cracking a village official on the head or some other equally rewarding crime. The ailing expectant mothers, surrounded by constantly renewed drafts of these interested and willing helpers, ailed so luxuriously that it was difficult to get rid of them, even when they ceased altogether to ail. The end result was the dissemination of a very reasonable knowledge of pre-natal hygiene and infant welfare among the women of Abemama. As a respectable retired official

I naturally hold no brief for lawlessness, but I have often wondered how much the prestige of British administration in the wilds owes to the sane derision with which District Officers' wives, bent on good works and getting them done, sometimes treat the pettifogging man-made regulations that hog-tie their intimidated husbands. The total gain will never be calculated on earth, for the husbands are usually as shy as I was about furnishing official reports, but it must bulk enormous in the books of the Recording Angel. I hope so, anyhow.

My being the husband of a healer like Olivia and the successor of a man like George Murdoch sometimes led the villagers to expect more medical help from me than I was qualified to give them. It was a matter of history on Abemama that George had once removed a man's leg above the knee rather than stand by and let him die of the spread of gangrene from a compound fracture. I saw the patient's stump twelve years after the event and asked George, the next time I saw him, how he had tackled the job. His answer was typically laconic: 'Anaesthetics, laddie? Well, not precisely anaesthetics. But I had six grand men to hold him down. You can't allow too many gymnastics in an operation like that. Instruments, ye say? I had a scalpel for the soft parts, and a hacksaw for the bone, and a spirit lamp to sterilize them with. I had some catgut forbye to tie up the big blood-vessels, and some coal-tar to dip the stump in when I'd sewn the flaps o' skin over it.'

This was all I ever got out of him personally. It was O'Reilly, the Medical Officer, who told me that he had picked up a lot of anatomy in the course of years by going to look at operations in Tarawa hospital. I had watched a good many operations at Tarawa myself, but I never felt that my observations qualified me for surgery to the extent of amputating limbs. Nevertheless, there were certain things one could not possible refuse to attempt in the absence of anyone more competent to do them. I was faced with one of them in our third month at Abemama, when a middle-aged villager was carried into my office and laid on the floor with a request that I would at once cut the 'sting' of a sting-ray out of his leg.

A sting-ray is a dangerous fish to catch on hook and line

because of its whiplike tail armed at the tip with a pair of bony, brittle, five-inch, barbed spines as sharp as needles. If it is hauled incautiously close before being despatched, the whip sizzles from the water and, in a flash, one of those spines is left buried in the fisher's body. The brute seems to aim at the stomach as a rule, and many a death from peritonitis is the result. My patient was lucky to have escaped only with a sting lodged in the big outside muscle of his thigh. But even that was perilous; there is a filthy slime on the broken-off spine, which quickly leads to septicaemia if the thing is left embedded in the wound.

'But why cut it out?' I said. 'Why not just pull it out with a pair of pinchers?'

'If you pull it out,' they replied, 'the barbs will break off inside him, and then, in a day or a week, he will die of the poison. The doctor always cuts them out whole and cleans the wound with the brown medicine that burns.'

I supposed they meant iodine by the brown medicine that burned. I had iodine, but, as I protested, I was not a doctor, and had nothing to stop the bleeding with.

They looked at me sorrowfully: 'The flesh will bleed. But the sting is buried in a muscle, and muscles, as you know, do not bleed.'

I did not know anything of the kind; the fact was entirely new to me, and I only half believed them until the Hospital Dresser confirmed it. 'Very well,' I said to him in a last wriggle, 'you know a lot more about it than I do – you get ahead with it.'

'Sir,' he replied, 'if I cut him and he dies, I shall be dismissed, for I have no certificate for performing operations. But if you cut him and I sew him up, I shall not be dismissed even in the event of his death, because I shall be able to say to the Doctor, "Behold! Grimble cut him and I tried to save his life by sewing him up".'

That seemed to settle it to everyone's moral satisfaction. I felt that not even the Colonial Office could have defined its own attitude towards a District Officer's political liabilities more clearly; so I gave in. After applying a tourniquet with what seemed to me much skill, the Dresser handed me a lancet which he used for opening boils and had sterilized in the flame of a spirit-lamp; he stood by with swabs for whatever bleeding there was (which seemed to me a lot), while my victim's friends kept the incision conveniently gaping by tension on his thigh from either side of it. The pain of my clumsy efforts must have been frightful for him, especially when I had to fish in the wound with the tweezers for broken bits of barb. The sweat poured out of him, but he lay from beginning to end without a gasp or a wince. The Dresser saved his life, as arranged, by sewing him up, while I went outside and was sick.

I was a little more experienced in midwifery than surgery, thanks to the teaching of Native Medical Practitioner Sowani. Mighty-limbed, six-foot Sowani, son of a Fijian father and a Tongan mother, prince of fishermen and king of canoe-racers, was also the pride and glory of the Gilbert and Ellice Islands Medical Service. He had been trained as a Native Practitioner at the Suva Central Hospital and sent up to Tarawa in the early nineteen hundreds. There he served for the next thirty-five years, absorbing all the surgery European Medical Officers had to teach him. Doctors came, doctors went – and sometimes there were long gaps between appointments to that obscure, ill-paid, exacting service – but Sowani went on forever, the constant factor of safety at Tarawa Hospital. According to our Senior Medical Officer O'Reilly, himself a fine surgeon, there was no major abdominal operation that he could not perform as well as the average European practitioner and, in the field of obstetrics, no case of abnormal presentation that he could not handle better than most.

It was necessarily the cases of abnormal presentation that Sowani introduced me to at Tarawa. No Gilbertese woman of those days would dream of calling for medical help in normal circumstances. Childbearing as a function had no terror and little discomfort for those lissom-bodied mothers. When the hour of labour came, their single fear was for the evil magic that enemy sorcerers might direct against them, and that was a thing their mothers and grandmothers knew better how to circumvent than any imported medical authority, they thought. Beyond this too, the Gilbertese women's deep modesty about being seen wholly naked – even by their own husbands – worked always against the intrusion of doctors. It was only when the village midwives' skill and counter-magic had failed to bring a child to birth, and the mother was near death, that the medical department was ever given a look-in. And there was one particular kind of case – beyond the help of any human power, as they believed – that white doctors were never invited to attend. I suppose it might be called a false pregnancy in medical parlance, but there was rather more behind it than that term usually implies.

As I was struggling one morning in the office with accounts, the queer high-pitched wailing of a woman began to distract me from my work. It did not strike loud on my ears, for it came wavering through the trees from the Native Government quarters a hundred yards off; what forced it on my notice was its insistence; it fluctuated between two monotonous semitones and there was hardly a break in it. I fought it with irritation for half an hour, but, as I listened, the strange quality of it began to make me uneasy. I got up at last and walked over to the Native Government lines.

I found the wailing girl in the home of her father, one of the station policemen. She sat there naked, head back, eyes shut, her mouth stiffly agape, as if levered open by an unseen hand to make way for her desolate cry. The cry itself seemed, queerly, not to be hers at all, but rather a sound forced through her throat by some alien thing inside her. But perhaps that was only my morbid reaction to the terrible distension of her stomach. From immediately under her ribs she was so swollen that the taut skin, stretched as it seemed to bursting point, shone like satin.

Her mother tried to cover her with a sheet when I entered, but, without a moment's interruption of her keening, she flung it away. She had first stripped off her clothes, the old woman said, when her stomach had begun to swell the night before. The swelling had started after she had woken with a wild scream, round about midnight. Since then, she had sat naked and bolt upright, impregnably silent and grinding her teeth while the distension grew and grew, until this morning, an hour ago, when she had started to wail.

'But why didn't you call someone last night,' I asked: 'the Dresser or me? You knew she was ill.'

The old woman remained dumb. I turned to the father. 'And what did *you* do about it?' He hung his head mutely too. I scribbled a note to the Dresser, telling him to bring sedatives – I couldn't think of anything better – and rounded on the parents again; but I could get only one thing out of them before the Dresser arrived: 'Nothing can be of any avail against this sickness,' they said, 'for it is the work of Terakunene. She called his name when she awoke.'

Terakunene was the sword-fish spirit, the procurer of women for men. It was to him that a rejected suitor turned for revenge upon the girl who refused him. His help was enlisted, according to tradition, through a hair of the girl's head. If the unsuccessful suitor could possess himself of one, he tied it around his thigh, just above the knee, and wore it so for three days, fasting alone in some solitary place by the ocean beach. On the third evening, just after dark, he built a small fire of sticks, sat before it with his face towards the sea, plucked the hair from his thigh, and, waving it back and forth over the flames, muttered north, west and south in turn:

Terakunene Terakunene-o-o
Go thou to make her answer, even that woman Nei Ioa.
Go thou to make her come to me.
Go thou to madden her if she comes not.
Go thou to kill her if she comes not.
(If she comes not) she shall be mad for me,
She shall swell with thy child for me,
She shall be dead for me.
She shall be dead!

With the last 'dead', he threw the hair into the fire. The belief was that unless the girl gave him his will of her within the next three days, the sword-fish spirit himself would visit her on the third night. She would wake mad from a dream of his embraces, shrieking his name, her belly swelling with his child. On the third night after that, she would die.

The Dresser arrived with bromide, the only sedative he had. It proved useless. I would have tried putting her to sleep with morphine, but I had none. (I went nowhere without it in the years that followed.) We tried whatever we had for windy colic and digestive troubles, but the Dresser's stock of medicines included nothing but the most elementary made-up mixtures, and she fought madly against every attempt to dose her. We got very little into her – but I doubt, in any case, if more would have made the least difference. She ceased to wail that evening and slept a little from time to time, but refused all food. The distension continued unrelieved. She died the third night. Within an hour of her death her stomach was normal again. The parents had predicted that. They said Terakunene's monstrous children were born only when the mother was dead.

If Terakunene magic did come into this case, as the parents and villagers believed, it is probable that the poor girl's revengeful lover told her he was about to set the sword-fish spirit on her; in that event, self-hypnosis, quickened by her inheritance of age-old dreads, could conceivably have done the rest – or so I have been told. But I never found a scrap of evidence to show that Terakunene magic had indeed been used. The parents clung hard to the fact that she had woken up screaming the spirit's name; but this proved nothing save that she had had a nightmare. For the rest, her sickness had followed the course traditionally ascribed to the working of Terakunene spells; but village traditions and inferences drawn from them do not make medico-legal evidence. My personal belief is not that the symptoms of the disease were brought on, in this or any other case, by magic, but that the magic and the people's belief in it were simply the by-products of a myth which attempted to explain the symptoms. What the terrible sickness was is more likely to be discovered by medical investigation than by psychical research.

By good fortune, one of the abnormal cases I had seen Sowani deal with at Tarawa was what he called in Gilbertese a double-hand presentation. I was glad of the experience a year or so later on the island of Nonouti. I knew – or thought I knew – roughly what was in store for me when word came that a double-hand case was waiting in a village up-lagoon for whatever help I could afford. The girl who brought the message said that the baby's down-stretched hands had been born eight hours before, but nothing the midwives could do would bring the head and body to birth. Nobody supposed I could succeed where they had failed, but as the mother would certainly die if nothing else happened, and the village kaubure had said they might be punished if she died as a result of their trying any more, perhaps I would like to see what I personally could do about it. It seemed an ungracious message at first hearing, but in point of fact, its intention was infinitely courteous. The midwives merely wished to assure me in advance that if I did not succeed in my effort nobody in the village would blame me for failing.

I was on my back with dysentery at the time, but I could not possibly ignore such a summons. I sent the messenger off at once with a promise to be there anon, and had myself rowed, with such paraphernalia and antiseptics as I possessed, up-lagoon to the village. But I did not feel good-tempered on the way. Amoebic dysentery is a fretful, weakening business and I thought Fate might have timed things better for all concerned, especially my grudging self. I mention this because of the pretty, golden-brown girl who met us on the village beach. She signalled us in from where she leaned, crowned with a white-wreath and smoking a pipe, against a palm tree at the beach-head. She was evidently there to guide me, but she did not move from her restful position when I stumbled up the loose sand towards her. That irritated me in my peevish mood. I was angrier still when my groggy legs gave out and I fell sprawling. I shouted, 'Here, come and help me up,' with never a 'please' or a smile.

She was dressed only in a short kilt of smoke-cured water weeds and it was easy to see, as she came to pick me up, that she was pregnant. When she got closer, I saw that her face was pallid and deeply drawn. That in itself reproved my rudeness. But it was her kindness that most abashed me. 'Alas!' she cried as soon as she saw how weak I was, 'you are ill, Man of Matang. Alas! They should not have called you!' and, putting her arm around my waist, made me walk with mine about her shoulders while she carried my bag for me.

I knew that by 'they' she meant the sick woman's midwives and told her – I am glad to remember – that they had been quite right to call me. That seemed to reassure her. We struggled rather feebly together up the glaring beach and rested in the shade of the palms by a cook-house on the flat. It occurred to me there to tell her that I did not yet know the sick woman's name. She looked at me searchingly for a time and then, her wan face breaking into a strangely beautiful smile, 'She is called Nei Maie,' she answered. 'Have you ever seen her?' and added with a sudden shout of laughter when I said No, 'Do you think you can drag the baby out of her?'

The coarseness of her phrase about another woman's misfortune and the callousness of her laughter made a too shocking contrast with her dignity and kindness of a moment before. My anger flared up again. I drew away from her: 'You laugh, woman – you will yourself be bearing a child before long? Nei Maie is near death, and you laugh? Or is it that you do not know how near death is to her? Are you wicked or perhaps only a fool?'

She laughed again in my face, with plain merriment this time: 'I am not wicked. I am not a fool. I know that woman is nearly dead. But I do not pity her. Why should she be afraid of dying? Perhaps she would like to die.'

She had the brilliant laughter of her race, carefree and golden-voiced, but I was too outraged to respond. 'We waste time,' I said. 'Bring me quickly to the house.'

We walked down the lily-bordered village street, she chuckling from time to time, I aloof from her ruthless humour, leaning nevertheless heavily upon her shoulders. The villagers called cheerful greeting to us as we passed. After a hundred yards or so, she stopped at a house with no one in it, saying, 'I pray you, be seated here a little, while I go and prepare that woman for your coming.' She leaned forward over the raised floor, put my bag down, and pulled a mat to the edge for me to sit upon. Then, 'We shall meet again,' she murmured and slowly walked to a house across the road, hung with leaf screens. Before she lifted a screen to enter, she turned her beautiful smile once more towards me and called, 'We think the baby is dead. But that woman does not in truth want to die. Perhaps she is indeed afraid, a little. O, that you could drag the baby out of her!'

The repetition of that crude phrase, and the wambling of my

stomach, and the swooning heat of midday once more overcame my temper. 'Hurry, you hussy!' I bawled at her, and she disappeared, her smile wiped out, behind the screen.

Nei Maie's mother called me into the house over the road ten minutes later. I had lain all the time thinking with renewed self-pity how very ill I felt. I had the grace to forget it, though, when I saw Nei Maie. I did not see her face, because they had covered it for modesty's sake with a sheet, but she looked like a dead woman, lying prone on her mat, the midwives seated at her head and feet fanning her. Her lax limbs were flung wide as if in a gesture of mortal exhaustion. I thought with rage of the callous laughter of the girl who had met me on the beach.

I tried to do things as I had seen Sowani do them at Tarawa. I was helped a little in my geography by having read Playfair's tome on abnormal presentations. But where Sowani had finished his work in under an hour, it took my fumbling, frightened hand over two hours to get the baby in a position to be born. My memory of what I did is one of blind groping against masses that my touch could not identify and resistances that I dared not, for fearful ignorance, force. And through it all, save for a few small shuddering whimpers, Nei Maie lay still and silent.

I gave her ergot and the baby was born at last. Though it was not living, there was no trouble with the after-birth, or haemorrhage, or temperature, or any other complication; the mother was, in short, saved. That was important, but it is not, for all that, the point of the story. Doing last things for my patient before leaving, I suddenly remembered the girl on the beach. I felt pretty righteous by that time, and it seemed to me that a slating for her heartless crudities would do her a lot of good. I asked Nei Maie's mother who and where she was: 'I wish to speak to her before I go home,' I said, 'for she talks with a bad tongue and there is no kindness in her.'

The old woman looked at me but did not speak. I repeated my question, with more information about what the girl had said.

'But, Sir, you have indeed dragged the baby out of this woman,' she replied with a smile, 'and we thank you for it.'

'But who is this girl? That is what I am asking you,' I insisted pettishly. There was a long pause before she answered, 'She is my daughter.'

'Then where is she? She must be near at hand. Bring her to me.'

She suddenly took my hand in hers and smiled into my eyes: 'Sir, I have only one daughter, and she lies here before you. Please do not be angry with her.'

10

TARAWA AGAIN

Mautake's Patrol

My service in the central Gilberts faded out rather drearily with three months of dysentery (the only real plague of Europeans in the Gilberts was *amoeba*) from which I was rescued by the providential arrival of a ship at the end of 1917. The doctor on board ordered me to Ocean Island for repairs and, within a month from then, I sailed for Sydney with the family, on sick-leave, weighing a little over seven stone. I went with permission – at last – to get myself recruited for war service; but they told me in Sydney to get rid of my appendix instead, which I did, and that put an end to my last chance of joining up. I returned to the Gilberts alone early in May, leaving Olivia behind at Bowral, New South Wales, for the birth of our third daughter, Monica Hope.

*

When I got as far as Tarawa, I found there would be no ship to Abemama for three or four months. I was glad of that excuse to stay a while, for things were in a queer state there. The District Officer who had replaced me in the Northern Gilberts had now been sent down to the Ellice Islands, and the Native Government was facing up alone to serious unrest about land-ownership.

The situation was due, in a way, to my own silly fault. Passing through Tarawa on the way to Ocean Island five months before, I had told my great friend Mautake-Maeke, the Chief Kaubure, an exciting piece of news; a proposal of mine to establish a Lands Commission in the Gilberts had been approved. The matter was not confidential, but no official date had yet been fixed for starting work (and, as a matter of fact, no beginning could eventually be made until 1922); I should have known better than to talk about it so prematurely, especially at Tarawa.

Tarawa was always at high tension about land-ownership. It dated from the dramatic day I have already told of, when the coming of H.M.S. *Royalist* had interrupted a war between the House of Teabike and the House of Auatabu, the two factions that had split the island for centuries up to 1892. Had *Royalist* arrived a single day later than she did, the House of Teabike would have become, by right of conquest, overlords of every square yard of land on Tarawa. But the Royal Navy saved Auatabu alive, and Captain Davis very rightly ordered that land ownership on the island should remain as it had been before the war began. The leaders of Teabike, thus disappointed in the eleventh hour of certain victory and its fruits, never really got over their frustration. Their faction was by far the richer of the two, but they went on wanting everything.

From 1892 onwards, the people of Teabike flooded successive District Officers with claims for the 'return' of the land which they had just not conquered, and, unfortunately, many of them got their way. This excited counter-claims from Auatabu – hundreds of them – going back to wars a hundred years forgotten. No less unfortunately, many of these succeeded too. Soon, it was as if the *status quo* ruling of Captain Davis – the only one that set a logical, remembered date for the judgement of any case – had never been made. By 1915, the land-affairs of Tarawa were in a state of chaos, and a spirit of estrangement charged with all the bitterness of the old wars reigned between the six middle villages of Tarawa, where the Auatabu folk lived, and the twelve villages to north and south of them, which belonged to Teabike.

It was Mautake-Maeke's own father, 'Old Maeke', as we used to call him, who had started the trouble I found on my return from Australia. Maeke was a leading chief of the Teabike faction. He had been Island Scribe in his day and there was nothing he did not know about the bitterness that the old land-jealousies could arouse. But he was old and could not resist a dig at the other side. He launched a whispering campaign about my proposed Lands Commission. His story was that I intended to dispossess the House of Auatabu of all the lands it would have lost but for the coming of H.M.S. *Royalist*, and hand these over lock, stock and barrel to the House of Teabike.

His whisper was put out in Betio, Teabike's village at the south end of Tarawa. It gathered force there, and went forth as a shout of triumph across-lagoon to Buariki at the north end. Buariki's maneaba roared with the news. The lie swept like a storm from north and south through the other sixteen villages. The people of Auatabu rushed to their maneabas to discuss it. 'Alas! this is a true word,' they said, 'for Mautake the son of Maeke is the friend of Grimble, and it is for love of him that the Man of Matang will take our lands away from us.' In the end, they swore a joint oath never to submit to the rulings of any Lands Commission, and the men began to prepare their shark-tooth spears for war: 'We will stand up on a day before Grimble's return,' they agreed, 'and kill the men of Teabike or die in the attempt. It is better to die than live on without an inheritance. And the signal for our rising shall be the killing of Mautake the son of Maeke.'

All these things had happened in early January, four months before my return. Since then, Mautake had done all he could to give the lie to Maeke's boast. Disowned as a traitor by his own folk and constantly stoned as the arch-enemy in his passage through the villages of Auatabu, he had maintained an unceasing patrol from end to end of Tarawa's length, trudging more than forty times alone the thirty-mile road between Betio and Buariki and lying unguarded in the village maneabas wherever sleep took him. Not a man would come out to meet him anywhere, so he made a town crier of himself. 'Listen to me!' he called as he passed, night or day, between the silent houses. 'Listen to me, all people! I come to tell you, I, Mautake the son of Maeke, that the House of Teabike lies. You will hear the truth from Kurimbo (Grimble) when he comes. Wait for Kurimbo.'

For three months and two weeks his courageous constancy

held them all in leash. But there came a night in a village of Auatabu when voices answered him out of the dark, 'Mautake-o-o! It is thy turn to listen. Return to us but once more, and thou shalt die, and none shall see thy face again.'

He replied without hesitation, 'It is good: I shall be with you tomorrow.'

He had been a pagan until then, but the next day he went to Father Guichard of the Sacred Heart Mission. 'I am going back to that village at once,' he said; 'my ancestor the Moon will protect me. Nevertheless, if perhaps I am killed and my body is thrown to the sharks there can be no straightening of the path of my ghost past Nakaa's net. Therefore baptize me, so that I may go the Christians' road to paradise.' The Father baptized him after hesitation, as a man on the point of death.

He returned to the village that night. Walking between the black shadows of the houses, he discarded his usual message for another: 'Here I am, you people, Mautake the son of Maeke. You said you would kill me if I returned. Let it be so if you will: I sleep in your maneaba tonight. I will die so that you may better remember these, my last words, the House of Teabike lies; wait for Kurimbo.'

When I arrived, three weeks later, it was not he but Father Guichard who told me of how he had gone to be baptized. What happened to him in the village was revealed to me later, in a way so typical of the Gilbertese idea of drama that I dare not pre-empt the climax. The immediate, personal account he gave me of the part he had played treated his lonely patrol as nothing but a piece of ordinary official routine.

Neither resentment against anyone nor any sign of hankering after praise came out of him. He was the perfect official, absolutely uninterested in himself as the hero of a piece, bent only on getting the thing settled and forgotten for everybody's happiness. His only reply to my thanks for what he had done was, 'There is peace for a little now, but the path is not yet open to the end. Perhaps, if you will call a meeting at Abaokoro, we shall find the end together.'

Abaokoro was the Native Government Station on Tarawa's upper arm, where it sood like a buffer state between Teabike's

209

six northern villages and Auatabu's six central ones. Living there, eleven miles across-lagoon from the white man's official headquarters at Betio, a District Officer could feel himself wholly encompassed by the life of his people. So I settled down galdly in the thatched transit-quarters at Abaokoro, while Mautake did his last patrol alone to call the people together.

A week after that, I took my place at the table in the vast Native Government maneaba under the scrutiny of two thousand pairs of watchful, unsmiling eyes. There was dead silence as I plugged my painful way through the things I was bound to say of Teabike's lies, and Auatabu's violences, and the nasty mess they had piled up for my return.

As I talked into their rigid silence, I remembered rather wryly how, three years earlier in that very maneaba, the old Native Magistrate had predicted that my words would one day blow upon them like a strong wind. It was not happening so this day, I thought. But yet it came through to me somehow that the minds behind those veiled eyes were not unfriendly to Mautake or myself. Something in the air – I don't know what – said quite distinctly that the force that held them so grimly unresponsive was the precarious balance of some kind of apprehension that they felt for each other.

What I did not know was that every man in that packed crowd had a knife handy for self-defence under the mat at his feet. Mautake knew, but he did not tell me until afterwards. I think his judgement was right. Had I known it at the time, I should almost certainly have taken the gesture for a prelude to attack, not defence, and tried to be heavy-handed about it, with who-can-say-what consequences. As things were, I did get the right impression: their fear of each other was what I had chiefly to guard against, and I managed to avoid saying anything that might set them fighting for shame of seeming fearful.

Mautake himself invented the way for me to set Auatabu's doubts about the Lands Commission at rest. 'If you ask them now to agree to a final judgement,' he told me before the meeting, 'they will refuse, for they have sworn to have no truck with a Commission. Another thing must be offered to them . . . something that is not final. Do not say to them, "I come to settle disputes;" say to them instead, "I come to listen to disputes so that I may advise you whether there is any sense in all these big words or not." Be very sure to say that your advice will not stand as a law to bind them. Make it clear that you only want to show men of good sense what kind of dispute the Lands Commission is never likely to listen to, so that many may be saved from making fools of themselves when the day of final judgement comes.'

It was a brilliant idea and I followed it to the letter. Everybody was bursting to talk, but nobody wanted to commit himself. I could almost hear the tension in the maneaba relaxing – like the hum of a dynamo running down – as I explained the notion of a council composed of village elders and myself which promised to treat them to nothing but advice. A relieved murmur swept through the place as I finished. But there was just one more thing that Auatabu wanted . . .

Nobody rose to speak; only a voice called from far back in the crowd, 'Mautake-o-o!'

'Stand and speak!' answered Mautake.

Still nobody stood, but the voice came again, 'Mautake! Will Kurimbo not be afraid?' and stopped short.

Mautake smiled: 'What marvel is this? Afraid of what?'

'Will Kurimbo come to us in our village and sleep there without the men of Teabike around him?'

'Which village, O man without a name?'

'Any village of Auatabu.'

'I will bring myself to Tabontebike tomorrow night.'

'Not with thee, Mautake-o-o! Not with any man. Alone. We of Auatabu would speak with him alone.'

Some voices were raised in protest, but Mautake silenced them: 'Kurimbo has walked much with the men of Teabike in Betio,' he said. 'Is it not right that those of Auatabu should now see him among them?' Then, turning to me as if I had heard nothing of this, he repeated, 'The men of Auatabu ask if you will pass a night alone among them, and I know not what to reply . . .'

In the circumstances, there was nothing left for me to say but what he himself had said to Auatabu four weeks earlier: 'I shall be with you tomorrow.' That ended our first day's business, and the people returned to their villages.

The next evening, an orderly took me down to Tabontebike by canoe, strung up my mosquito-net in the maneaba there, and left me with some tins of food and a book of Hazlitt's essays for company. It was perfectly obvious that nobody intended to do me any harm, but I couldn't help wondering exactly why the men of Auatabu wanted me all alone like that. My puzzlement increased as midnight passed and nobody came to visit me. But I fell asleep at last, half-smiling at the inveterate Gilbertese appetite for drama that nothing could ever hustle to a premature climax.

The stage certainly seemed set for drama when they did arrive. A sound of creeping steps awoke me. I lifted my net to find a dozen of them surrounding me. By the dim light of my hurricane lamp I saw spears in their hands. They stood wordless while I arose, trussed the slack of the net up over its canvas roof, and sat down again on the sleeping mat.

I won't deny that the spears struck me as sinister. The sight of them made me feel strangely naked in my pyjamas. But I did manage, as soon as I was seated, to give them an ordinary greeting. I got an immediate reward for that. The quick heartiness of their response, '*Ko na auri-o-o*' all together, swept away any notion I may have had that they had come to do me in.

'Sit down,' I said, perhaps a trifle breathlessly, and they sat. I handed tobacco around.

It was only when pipes were going strong that their leader spoke, and I learned why they had made such a point of my being alone. They wanted to tell me a story. 'It was thus, with spears in our hands,' said the spokesman, 'that we came to kill that friend of thine, even Mautake the son of Maeke, when he dared to return that night and sleep alone in our maneaba . . .'

I remembered as he talked how Mautake's cousin, Teriakai, had said to me once, 'If you stay still in the sea, the tiger-shark will charge you. If you swim away from them in fear, they will smell your fear and chase you. If you swim without fear towards them, they will be afraid and leave you in peace.' I think it is the same with angry men as with tiger-sharks, except that, with human crowds, awe rather than fear is the thing that lonely courage inspires. That, at least, was the meaning of the spokesman's story for me . . .

'We had sworn among ourselves to kill him if he returned,' he said; 'and so, when he came, we took up our spears. And when it was past midnight, we crept to our meeting-place near this maneaba. But I came with sadness in my heart. I said in my heart, "I do not want to kill this man", for I was kunainga (awed), as it were in the presence of a spirit. Yet if I had been alone, I should surely have killed him, because I had sworn to do so. Each man of us, alone, would have killed him, for shame of breaking the oath.

'We gathered in the blackness under the trees, because the moon was bright. There were twelve of us. And we knew that Mautake would be lying in the boti of Maerua, the place of his fathers within the maneaba, with his feet towards the west. So we said, "Let six of us stand on his north side and six on the south, and strike all together when the word is given.' I myself was to say the word. I did not refuse, because I was ashamed. And we went to the side of the maneaba by the boti of Maerua.

'We stood by the side of the maneaba, but behold then a marvellous thing! The moon stepped between two clouds, and it was light. We saw each others' faces. I looked into the eyes of my friends, and I knew that their hearts refused that work, even as mine did, because they also were kunainga. And because the first word had been given to me, I said, "Men-o-o! What are we about to do? Our hearts refuse this work!" One answered me, "It is true. Our hearts are heavy." Others said after him, "It is true. This man is, as it were, a spirit and we are kunainga in his presence." Others said again, "If this man is so ready to die for what he has told us, perhaps his word and not the word of his father is the true one." So I said, "Men-o-o! Let us free each other of our oath." And we freed each other, and were glad, and returned to our houses.

'And many among us said after that night, "Perhaps Mautake has indeed not lied to us. Perhaps Kurimbo will indeed not take away our lands and give them to the men of Teabike." So we stoned Mautake no more when he walked through our villages.

'And there were some who said, "Let us tell Mautake now that we will listen to the Lands Commission." But others answered, "Hold! That is too great a word. Let us wait first and hear what Kurimbo says when he arrives."

'And others said again, "Yes, and even if Kurimbo speaks us fair when he arrives, how shall we know his inward thought? How shall we know he is our true friend after what we have done to Mautake?"

'So, when Mautake came to call us to the meeting at Abao-koro, this was the way of it: we agreed among ourselves that we would go to the meeting, but we said to one another, "We will seek a sign from Kurimbo, whether he is our friend or not. If he is not our friend, he will refuse to come alone to us. But if he does not refuse to come alone, then we shall know that there is no anger against us in his heart." And behold! you did not refuse. So we know you are our friend.'

Dawn made a garden of wild rose and daffodil in the sky as they sailed me back to Abaokoro. We shared my bully-beef and biscuits among us for breakfast on the way. I don't know when I have ever enjoyed a meal more than that one.

I went straight to Mautake from the landing. He was glad to hear my story of the night's happenings, but he only smiled when I talked of his courage: 'I knew myself safe in my boti of Maerua,' he explained. 'Sleeping there, I was in the hand of the Moon, my Ancestor. And was I not right to believe in his love?' (The moon was male for the Gilbertese.) 'Did not those men of Auatabu relate how he showed their faces and hearts to each other, even as they came to kill me. And if it had not pleased him to save me alive, was I not safe from Nakaa's net after the Father had baptized me?'

But the people of his father's house could measure just how much cold nerve it had taken to risk what he had risked that night. The men of Teabike were proud to reclaim him as son and brother. The men of Auatabu, assured now that I bore them no secret grudge on his behalf, clamoured for the beginning of the Council of Advice that his statesmanship had conceived.

Hundreds flocked to our court. Thousands of lies were told. Wars two centuries old were dragged up. Victories nobody had ever won were named. Mythical marriages, bogus adoptions, impossible gifts of old were invented. Aged ladies tottered in to orate about the angers and jealousies of their mothers and grandmothers before them. Customs and usages totally unknown were trumped up to prove inheritances that had never been enjoyed by man. It was scandalous. The answer to nine hundred and ninety-five grievances in every thousand simply had to be 'Sir (or Woman), it has given us a real treat to hear you, but really . . . this will never, never do for the Lands Commission.'

But they talked. They talked themselves dry. All the goading, gnawing prides and envies of five generations came surging out of them in that grand three months of free-for-anybody before the packed audience of the maneaba. You might think it could only have doubled the fury of ancient bitternesses to encourage such goings-on, but it did just the opposite. Mautake knew his people. The freedom to let themselves go, unrestrained, before the whole listening world of their island, friends and enemies alike, was what mattered to them most of all. It was as if the deepest need they felt was to purge themselves of a century of clotted rancours, regardless of consequences, in one last tremendous orgy of words.

As claim after egregious claim was found wanting, Auatabu's fear of what the Lands Commission might do to them wilted and died. The audience grew more and more hilarious. In the end, men of both factions began to laugh at their own claimants instead of at each other's, and to cheer the other side instead of the home team. The new friendliness spread outside the maneaba. Soon, families who had been at continuous enmity since the battle of Baretangaina in about 1870 were fraternizing. 'The porpoise is dead, the whale is sunk,' sang Tata-Teribabaiti, chief poet of the House of Teabike, the admired of all Tarawa. His song was the climax and crown of the council's work. It was at once a paean of praise and a satire on the overweening claims, now laid to rest, of his own faction. It ended with a jibe at the Teabike leader (his name does not matter) whose family had aspired to make themselves High Chiefs over Tarawa:

'It is over' – Tata made him say – 'and where shall I go now?
It is over, you people: I shall get me a ship and disappear over the
  horizon.
For all is said, the first word and the last.
I shall go out there, where the porpoise and the whale are sunk;
I shall be High Chief of the ocean and King of all the fish –
Unless – alas! – the *Royalist* comes again to prevent me.'

And then, to round it off, the poet's own *envoi*:

Behold! the back-and-forth, the dartings, the stabbings of my words are
  done!
For the talk is ended, the judgement judged
And there he goes now sailing over the horizon.
The porpoise is dead, the whale is sunk,
The thunder-cloud is fled from the sky,
The storm is over: a small, cool wind blows between the villages.
A cool wind-o-o-o! O-o-a!

The poem was reckoned by the experts of Teabike to be a
masterpiece of diction and, beyond that, a glorious joke against
themselves. They set it to the music and statuesque gestures of a
bino (sitting dance), put one hundred and twenty of their finest
performers to practise it secretly, and produced it one gala night
in the Native Government maneaba before an enthralled audience of two thousand. The thing swept Tarawa off its feet for
admiration and laughter. For the next six months, nothing but
that bino was danced in the villages of Auatabu and Teabike. So,
the song of a poet confirmed the work of peace that Mautake's
courage had made possible, and his initiative inspired. 'And that
is as it should be,' said Tata, 'because, look you, the poet is the
servant of brave men.'

The Whistling Ghosts of Arorae

The work of the Council of Advice was hardly well finished
when a ship of the Japanese trading company in the Marshall
Islands brought unexpected news to Tarawa. The company had
decided to send no more of its vessels to pick up copra in
the Gilbert group south of Butaritari. What worried me about
this ultimatum was that a number of the longshore traders

down south were in the habit of holding the copra for the Japanese concern, which paid better prices than others. They had to be warned at once that their only buyers from that time on would be the rare British ships that came their way, and I was the only person there to do it. It was lucky, in the circumstances, that the 35-ton ketch *Choiseul* had come up from Abemama on her own business some days before and was waiting to take me back to the Central Gilberts. I chartered her that day for a quick run to the Southern Gilberts instead, and went on board the same evening so as to be sure of an early start next morning. Thus it was that I fared forth to meet the whistling ghosts.

Our first landfall was Onotoa Island, 270 miles from Tarawa. There was no ship's passage into the lagoon in those days, and only one canoe – the Native Magistrate's – was waiting for us outside the reef. A steep westerly swell was running; the reef was a-lee; it was tricky work manoeuvring my transfer with a suitcase and a steel despatch-box from the ketch to the canoe. I mention these points to leave it clear that no conversation passed between the ship and the canoe except the exchange of curt orders and responses about my transhipment. Certainly, nobody in the ship's crew shouted anything by way of gossip from the northern islands. I could not possibly have missed hearing it if they had.

There was no talk in the canoe until we had shot the big surf in the boat-passage, but when we had made calm water the Native Magistrate said suddenly *apropos* of nothing, 'We hear Tabanea is dead.'

The Tabanea he meant was my old friend the professional sorcerer of Tarawa. The death of a man like that could not fail to set the whole group talking, for there was not an island where he had not a crowd of customers for his peerless love-potions and amulets. But he wasn't dead, I told the Native Magistrate; I had seen him only the week before, heartily enjoying the great song and dance at Tarawa.

It did not seem to impress him, though; he chatted on as if I had not spoken; 'They say he died the day before yesterday, in the evening, of *te bo maiaona* (a blow from above him).'

'What's a blow from above him? Who says? What ship brought the news? Certainly not ours,' I countered irritably.

It appeared that a blow from above him meant what we might call a seizure or stroke. He did not state who had spread the rumour, but said no ship had brought it. He was bound to say that; ours was, in fact, the only deep-sea craft in the Gilberts at the moment; the other was down in the Ellice group.

'So there you are,' I wound up rather pompously, 'it's just another silly bit of village tittle-tattle.'

'*Tao eng* (perhaps, yes),' he murmured, '*tao eng*' – meaning roughly, 'Oh, well, let it go at that' – and changed the subject.

The whole thing had slipped out of my mind by the time we landed. I was so used to village rumours of that sort. Nobody else mentioned Tabanea to me for the forty-eight hours I stayed on Onotoa; probably the Magistrate had warned everybody that the subject irritated me: in any case, it was not until I got to Arorae, the last island of the Southern Gilberts, that the next thing happened. It never would have happened if I had spent only a day or two there, as elsewhere. But I found trouble in the place; the nature of it does not matter here; the point is, it forced me to stay. The ketch left with a promise to be back in a month or so.

Arorae lies out in the blue, 100 miles from Onotoa. It is a lagoonless wisp of coral sand and coconuts, open on every side to the towering Pacific swells. When westerly gales sweep up at it, the huge surf bellows week-long on the weather reef like a million driven bulls raging at the thresholds of the villages. The westerlies blew hard for most of my stay. I couldn't get away from that tortured roar, or the yelling of the coconut-crests in the wind. The ceaseless, smothering din did something to my relations with the people; somehow, it seemed to be always between us. I felt very lonely among them. Perhaps that made me a good subject for a game of brown man's bluff.

Bluff or not, it began when I had endured nearly a week of the place. My one familiar friend on Arorae, a retired Tarawa police-man, married to a local woman and on a visit to his in-laws, came to look me up. Tarawa men adore a comfortable chin-wag, especially in their own dialect when they are among strangers. I fancy that was what tempted him to be so extra-communicative that evening. As soon as he was well seated on the guest-mat, he began newsily, 'So Tabanea is dead.'

I smiled, 'Now, now . . . you got that bit of gossip from Onotoa . . . by our ship.'

He denied this blankly. He said he had heard it the Sunday before last. I pointed out that his timing made nonsense for me: our ship had not even arrived at Onotoa by this date. But he persisted that our ship had nothing to do with the case. He had heard about Tabanea's death the Sunday before last from his wife's very aged and absolutely infallible kinswoman, Nei Watia.

'Nei Watia has another name as a baptized Christian, but, for this kind of thing, one must always call her Watia,' he explained.

'What kind of thing?' I naturally asked.

He was too wrapped up in his main theme to answer that at once. The old woman, he drove on, had mentioned two important details: Tabanea had died just before sunset, of a blow from above him.

I rubbed it in that the phrase was precisely the one that the Native Magistrate of Onotoa had used, but he overrode the irony: 'Naturally the words are the same,' he said, 'the news-bearers do not speak with two voices. What they reported in Onotoa they reported to Nei Watia also, here in Arorae.'

This was at least good entertainment, so I asked for more about Nei Watia's exceedingly single-voiced news-bearers.

It appeared they were alternatively called *Taani-kanimomoi* – The Whistlers. He said the Whistlers were the ghosts of dead relations . . . not the very long dead ones . . . the more recently dead. These made a constant habit of returning to the Gilberts. Their domain was the air (he called it 'the layer of wind' – as it were, the invisible plane) just above the level of the coconut-crests. At that height, they flew up and down the islands seeing and hearing everything that happened. They came lower from time to time and passed the news on to anyone alive who understood their speech. Not many people did understand it, because they spoke in whistles; but Watia was an adept; she had power; she could actually order her particular ghost to come along and answer questions whenever she wanted.

I took his talk for a big boast. It was only by way of calling his bluff that I asked whether his infallible relation-in-law would undertake to ask her ghost a question from me. But, far from piping down, he put me on the spot instead.

'*Aongkoa* (Of course)' he replied at once. 'Is it indeed your wish that I should ask her?'

I found it was not particularly my wish, but I could not withdraw. The upshot was that he came back the next night with an invitation for me to go with him at once to Nei Watia.

I followed him through the bush to a stony, treeless space above the weather beach. It was a wild night; the place was shuddering and thundering with the fury of the surf; but the moonlight flooded it starkly between racing cloud-shadows. A solitary screened shack stood out in the open, fifty paces away. I saw the glimmer of a faint light through the plaited screens. He pointed: 'There is Nei Watia,' he said; 'I cannot go in with you,' and left me standing there. I watched him plunge back into the blackness of the bush.

The thatch was so low that I could not stand upright inside. A hurricane lamp was burning on the floor. An incredibly aged face was glaring up at me round the light, almost from floor-level. It had a cutty pipe in its mouth; its lips were moving but I heard no words. I stood there mute until a skeleton hand flailing above the face ordered me to be seated. I squatted, cross-legged as she was, on my side of the lamp, fascinated by that ruinous, wild-haired mask. The lips moved again, but the roaring of the night drowned her voice. I craned an ear forward. Then with atrocious suddenness the mask was convulsed and lunged up at me. She tore the pipe from her gums and shrieked into my face, '*Tabanea is dead!*' Nothing but that. I had not recovered from the shock of it when the whistling began.

A single note, strident, like a cricket's, sounded from behind my left ear. I whipped my head around. Nobody was there. A second chirrup fell from the roof. I sprang to my feet; my head struck the ridge pole; the witch screamed with laughter; but I hardly noticed it, for the whistling was at once all around me. It wasn't harsh now, but multitudinous. It crowded in on my ears wherever I turned, as if a host of tiny invisible birds were twittering up there in the shadows of the roof.

I dived out into the moonlight and pelted round the shed. In that white glare everything was visible. There was nobody on the roof, no tree, no sizeable rock within fifty yards where anyone could be hiding. Back under the thatch, I fell on hands and knees to stare into the crone's face. Her gums were clenched, but still the twittering went on overhead. There was no break in it even when she shouted at me, 'The Ancestor waits. What is your question?'

The Ancestor might have been her father for all I knew. I did not ask, but shouted back at once, sprawling there on my knees, 'When will the Japanese ship be returning to Arorae?'

She stared at me for a long moment: 'You have told us the ship will not return,' she said at last.

'Yes, yes, grandmother,' I replied, 'but perhaps I was wrong. What does the Ancestor say?'

Her answer was to twist her face over her huddled shoulder and howl at the roof, 'The Man of Matang asks when the ship of the Japan men will return.'

The twittering ceased. For half a minute I heard nothing but the noises of the night. Then there came a morse-like succession of strident chirrups, followed by a dozen phrases of something like birdsong that faded gradually back into the clamour of wind and sea.

'The Ancestor has spoken,' muttered the witch; 'count twenty-three days from tonight, and the ship will arrive.' That ended the session.

'Well – so much for the whistling ghosts and their news!' I said to myself outside. 'A mere trick of ventriloquism.' Just how she could have whistled and talked at the same time, or thrown a chirrup with her mouth shut, I couldn't imagine; and I was puzzled to think why she should have said the ship would come when I said it wouldn't. I decided she had been caught in my little trap 'perhaps I was wrong'. 'What an old hoax – she and her precious Ancestor!' I thought, clinging to the hoax idea rather desperately as I groped my way home through the screaming darkness of the bush.

But the fact is, Tabanea was dead, and he had died in the evening, and the cause of his death was a blow from above him – an embolism, the doctor called it. He was found lying in his dwelling-house at just about the time I went on board the ketch at Tarawa. The ketch lay anchored eleven miles down-lagoon from his village. Obviously, the crew *could* have heard the news before we left next morning. But, knowing how fond I was of him, they wouldn't – they couldn't conceivably – have kept the thing to themselves on our southward run, had they heard it. It was the very first news they rushed to tell me when they came back to pick me up.

Also, the Japanese ship did return. The prediction was a little out in point of time; she arrived on the twenty-second day not the twenty-third. She came to pick up two copra-lighters which she had left at Arorae.

11

PRIEST AND PAGAN

When a man is dying, the main concern of Christians is that he should be at peace with his Maker before he goes. In pagan rituals, the emphasis is not usually upon what happens before death: the rightness of the ceremonies performed immediately after death is what matters most for the safe passage of the departing ghost to paradise. The two kinds of belief are poles apart, but either can raise problems for the living.

Father Choblet, a French priest of the Sacred Heart Mission in the Southern Gilberts, approached his particular dilemma from the Christian angle; Tabanaora, a simple villager of Tarawa, tackled his from the pagan one. But both acted out of love for a fellow human soul, and each brought to his solution a courage which, as I think, will tolerate no distinguishing tabs of race or religion.

Father Choblet's parish was Beru Island, a hundred miles south of Abemama. He was 5ft. 1in. high and a human dynamo;

also, he didn't like bureaucracy. The debonair way he had of interpreting rules and regulations used to raise the hair off my scalp sometimes. But yet, there was a kind of reasonableness and integrity in most of his illegalities that somehow managed to illumine the real intent of the law instead of undermining it. His defiance of the inter-island travelling regulations was a case in point.

The regulations, as they stood then, prohibited canoe-voyages between the islands from the end of September to the end of March every year. That period, in the Central Pacific, is the season of unpredictable westerly gales. The Gilbertese are adventurous sailors; the islands lie anything from twenty to one hundred and twenty miles apart; a frail outrigger canoe caught midway between two of them in a roaring fifty-miler has about as much chance of survival as a snowflake in a blast-furnace. Hundreds of fatalities stood behind those regulations, and nobody knew more about them than Father Choblet. But he had to make a choice.

One morning, a westerly gale was working up to full fury around Beru Island when a small trading steamer slipped under the lee of the land and sent a boat ashore. The huge surf smashed the boat on the reef, but the crew struggled safe to land. One of them brought a letter to Father Choblet from the island of Nukunau, thirty miles to eastward. I saw the letter myself some years later; it had been scrawled in Gilbertese by a native mission-teacher: 'Father Franchiteau is dying here,' it ran, 'there is no other priest; he implores you to bring him the Last Sacrament.' That was all.

It was Father Choblet's canoe-boys who told me what happened next. 'When he came and ordered us to launch the canoe,' they said, 'we thought he had gone mad. So we spoke to him softly of the Government's laws about travelling. That made him laugh, laugh; and then he did not laugh any more, but told us about Father Franchiteau. Yet still we thought he was mad, for there was death in the sea for all of us that day. When we told him of our fear he turned away, saying, "All of us? Who spoke of all? I am going alone," and he put his little bag on the canoe. Then suddenly he looked to us like a spirit. He is a very small man, but he grew big, and we were not afraid any more. We told him that. Then he confessed us, and gave us absolution, and put his arms around us, saying, "Come with me." So we all put out to sea, singing songs with him.'

Only a Gilbertese canoe-man could tell you just how they fought through the terrible surf, but they did. None of the crew could ever remember clearly how they got within sight of Nukunau before dusk, but they did. They weathered over twenty miles of that raging sea before the canoe broke in half. And after that, as Father Choblet explained to me, it was mere child's play. They only had eight more miles of boiling Pacific between themselves and Father Franchiteau. All they had to do was to cling together to one half of the wrecked canoe, sing more songs, and trust Providence to lend a hand – which it did. It sent them a six-knot current that swept them straight into a bay of Nukunau a little before sunset. It took care that none of them was battered quite senseless in the frightful maelstrom of the weather reef. It provided that their torn bodies should win to shore on that twelve-mile coastline, less than half a mile from the mission house where Father Franchiteau lay dying. He was conscious when they staggered in. He died with good cheer a few minutes after receiving the Viaticum. It was only after the burial service the next morning that Father Choblet's tiny frame could take no more and collapsed.

The bureaucratic sequel is worth recording. Officialdom, of course, simply had to take notice of the affair. The Father had incited three Gilbertese boys to break the law and risk almost certain death in doing so. He was not himself subject to the native regulations. Only the boys could be prosecuted, and, legally speaking, the religious motive of their errand gave them not a leg to stand on in defence. I was not the District Officer who saw that they were brought to court. It was George McGhee Murdoch who had the honour. He made Father Choblet the chief witness against them and insisted that the Native Magistrate should fine them £1 each on his evidence. It was a serious sum for them. The Father made a scene in court about it, and I don't blame him. But George made up for it when the court rose, for he called the boys back and publicly presented them with a reward of £2 each, 'Just for their guts,' as he explained to the Father. The fines went into Caesar's pocket, which is to say, Public Revenue; the rewards came out of his own slender purse.

*

It was George who first told me the story of Tabanaora's duel with the tiger-shark, but I had most of the intimate details from an old mission-teacher of Tarawa. He told me that Tabanaora – a cousin of his – was a baptized convert of the Boston Missionary Society's at the time. Other eye-witnesses of the fight denied it. The internal evidence might mean one thing or the other. But, whichever way it was, the thing he did was nothing if not typical of the spirit of his own people. Family love lives as deep in the Gilbert Islander as his courage.

Tabanaora was the eldest of eight brothers who lived in a northern village of Tarawa. He was a man of thirty or more when Tebina, the youngest, came up for initiation into manhood. He himself had schooled Tebina, through twelve long months of ritual segregation, to face the stern ordeal. The boy went through the terrible test by fire without the flicker of an eyelid. Tabanaora's love soared (in the words of my old friend) as proud as the frigate-bird up against the noon-day sun. But his joy was short-lived, for Tebina was killed by a tiger-shark the very day after he had been pronounced cured of his burns.

The shark took him after sunrise, as he stood fishing with rod and line, breast-deep on a sandbank by his home village. He was seen from the shore to fling up his arms of a sudden and go under. That was the last of him. A dozen canoes went to search the bank, but no trace of his body remained.

It was not only grief for his personal loss that weighed on Tabanaora, but fear for the boy's after-life too. Baptized Christian or not, he still believed in Nakaa, the guardian of the gate between earth and paradise. There at the gate he sat forever, waiting to strangle in his net the ghosts of those unhappy dead whose way into the life beyond had not been ritually straightened. The straightening of Tebina's way was impossible – and he was doomed to everlasting extinction – unless at least

225

one limb of his body could be recovered for the death rituals.

But Tabanaora had a hope to buoy him. The shark would probably return at the same hour next day to the bank where it had made its kill. Such is the habit of the brutes, and he built upon it. He prepared himself for what he had to do next by fasting all day alone in his screened hut by the lagoonside.

At sunset he emerged and crossed the narrow breadth of the land to the ocean beach, carrying with him his ten-foot spear of fire-hardened wood. He laboured all night by torchlight, to the thunder of the surf, arming the spear's edges from hilt to tip with the razor-sharp teeth of tiger-sharks that he himself had slain. Shark eats shark, as everybody knows. At dawn he stood on the beach naked, to call a blessing on his finished handiwork. My old mission-teacher gave me the exact words of his prayer: this is the literal translation of them –

> Rise, Sun, rise with fortunate face.
> Rise, Sun, the Ancestor.
> Rise, Ancestors, Auriaria and Tabuariki.
> Rise, God and Jesus-o-o!
> O, Sun and God and Jesus, bless my spear.

So fortified in the strength of all the powers he believed benign, he turned and strode through the morning stillness of the coconut grove back to the quiet lagoonside. He walked without speech or pause into the shallows. The villagers crowded to stare in silence from the beach-head as he waded and swam with his spear to meet his brother's killer.

The shark gave him no time to wait and think. It was already on the prowl nearby. His feet were hardly planted on the sand-bank when its dorsal fin was seen racing straight in at him from behind. The watchers roared a warning. He whipped round, saw, side-stepped, and thrust. The point of the spear glanced off its leather hide. But he was safe for a few moments: tiger-sharks cannot turn quickly; the monster surged past, to reverse direction thirty yards off.

Its approach was more cautious this time; it began to circle him slowly, and that was just what Tabanaora wanted. It gave him the chance to measure his distances as the circles gradually narrowed. When the charge came, he was so sure of himself that he did not even trouble to side-step. He stood stock-still in the path of that rising, rolling lunge. As the vast jaws opened, he hurled his whole weight forward, stiff-armed, to plunge the spear's point between them. That and the shark's own rush carried the saw-edged shaft tearing eight feet deep into its vitals. The impact heaved him high; he clung on. The spear snapped by the hilt; he went under – but only to come up unhurt and stand with folded arms while the shark thrashed itself to death over the sand-bank.

He hauled it ashore by the tail, triumphantly intoning the Boston Mission's rendering of *Onward Christian Soldiers*. It was dragged to his house-place under the arching palms, where he cut it open with incantations to Nakaa and the ancestral shades. The remains of Tebina his brother were in its maw. There was enough of them, by his reckoning, to ensure the straightening of the boy's path past Nakaa's strangling net, through the gate, and so into Bouru, and Mwaiku, and Neineaba, those lands of ancient desire beyond the western horizon. The pious rites began at once. Both the divination by leaves and the divination by stones on the third day showed them to have been wholly successful.

Tabanaora's fight happened before the Flag came to the islands. Of course, if it had happened under British rule, this story, like Father Choblet's, would have had its bureaucratic sequel. Not that anyone ever invented a law to prohibit duels with tiger-sharks; but Tabanaora's night-session on the ocean beach would have constituted an infringement of the curfew regulations. Very serious. Nevertheless, I conjecture that his District Officer would have managed to square the law with justice, as George Murdoch did in the Choblet case. That is why District Officers were invented, bless their hearts – to see (at their own expense, naturally) that Heaven gets its dues no less than Caesar.

But what I like best of all to remember about Father Choblet's act and Tabanaora's is the common denominator of their courage. It is an exact one. The priest knew that he himself would die unshriven if he failed to reach Nukunau; the pagan knew there could be no saving his ghost alive if the shark devoured his body. Each of them risked suffering the very horror from which he was trying to protect his brother man. Each trusted the god or gods of his choosing to see him through. When that kind of love and kind of faith are wedded in action, I think they make their own special passport at the bar of whatever heaven.

12

SOUTHERN GILBERTS

House that Vanished

The trouble that had kept me five weeks at Arorae was a quarrel between the whole people and an acting District Officer, which ended in his return to Ocean Island. That raised acute staffing problems in the group. New officers simply could not be found in 1918. In the end, the Old Man was left with no recourse but to see if I could run the ten central and southern islands together as a single district. The plan meant a change of headquarters from quiet Abemama to Beru, the island most centrally placed for the purpose and, politically speaking, the capital of the south. I never got back into our Abemama house except on visits of inspection, for the sequels of the Arorae trouble held me in the southern islands until Olivia's return with the children in late October, 1918.

*

The history of our doings at or near Beru began at sea, five miles out from the weather reef, an hour and a half before sunset on an evening of ferocious westerly squalls. There is no ship's entrance to Beru lagoon and the bottom is dangerous for half a mile outside the boat-passage. The captain of our ship was justified in standing well clear of a lee shore in weather like that; but we felt he had rather overdone it when we contemplated the landing-craft he had set at our disposal. He said the rickety launch and two boats towed behind it were all he could spare for the accommodation of Olivia and three infants; three nursemaids; a cook; a houseboy and his wife; a native clerk and his wife; my orderly, his wife and child; myself with five boxes of office necessities and a steel safe; forty-eight chickens and twelve guineafowl in cages; crated provisions for six months, including a ton of Navy biscuits for staff; the staff's personal luggage and bedding; the children's cots and bedding; our family's personal luggage, household effects and bits of furniture. Also six goats.

We sixteen humans were huddled one on top of the other into the stern-sheets of the launch. Olivia was perched on the knee of Sila, the cook, while I sat in the lap of full-bosomed Faasolo, his wife, Joan's nursemaid. The dunnage was piled in the boats, mountains high, with the goats balanced on the peaks as if back in their native highlands. The sea was brutally steep and the squalls brought driving rain that had soaked us through before we left the ship's side. The captain lost his nerve in the last minute, when he looked down at the wallowing, overloaded craft: 'Don't you think you had better take a third boat?' he yelled overside, as if we hadn't asked for one.

'Tell him,' said Olivia to me, 'I wouldn't accept another boat from him if he were the Emperor of Morocco.' I did so with pleasure. 'And now, home, James!' Olivia said to the Gilbertese launch-boy.

Chickens cackling, goats bleating, children wailing for wetness, misery and fear, we lurched off on the five-mile run to the boat-passage. If the ancient engine had conked out – as it showed signs of doing – before we reached safety, we should have been swept helplessly by sea and wind down on the raging reef, for there wasn't a hope of getting oars out in those packed craft. But it did not conk out, and suddenly, in the middle of a blinding rain squall from the south-west, when nothing but the sea-sense of our steersman held us true on our south-east course from ship to passage, we found ourselves in calm water. Guided by ear alone, with visibility zero, he had turned suddenly due east through a break in the crashing surf at exactly the right moment. 'Moment' is no exaggeration; a mistake of ten seconds more or less would have destroyed us. But Gilbertese steersmen do not make such mistakes.

It was low tide. Beru lagoon is very shallow inside the passage, and the boats could not go far in, so Olivia, the children, their cots, their nursemaids, and I transhipped into canoes that had come to meet us. We took a few tins of milk and soup with us. The others stayed behind to deal with the rest of the stuff.

'There's the kitchen roof,' I said, pointing to a thatch just visible between trees two miles across the water; 'we'll soon be there now.'

Our spirits rose. We began to organize as we went along. I had seen the District Officer's quarters on my first recruiting trip three years before, as Charles Workman's doggie. It was a three-roomed wooden bungalow by the lagoonside, with deep verandahs, back, front and ends. A fine big kitchen, neatly built of native timber and thatch, had been added to its north end, and an office, also native-built, opened off its south verandah. The Old Man had granted me a special warrant of £50 to do the whole place up. We saw it already in our mind's eye freshly painted in and out, gleaming white under a gay red roof between the golden-brown of its native annexes.

The blustering night was upon us before we reached shore. 'We'll put the children in the middle room,' Olivia decided: 'We'll have the one next to your office for ourselves, and that will leave the one nearest the kitchen for a dining-room.' We said how marvellous it was, after all our goings and comings in strange houses, to be able to plan surely, cosily like that again. It looked to us almost as if Providence had set the stage – the comfortless ship, the screaming squalls, the perilous passage into safety – to sharpen our delight at having a home of our own waiting to take us in now . . . at once . . . just over there, where that light was glimmering through the sodden darkness.

'We'll get a roaring fire started right away in the kitchen stove and warm the children by it while we're waiting for the things to come ashore,' I said.

'Yes, and we'll hot up some milk for them and have a tin of soup for ourselves, to keep us going,' Olivia answered, as another rain squall plunged down on us.

It was black dark on the beach, but the Native Magistrate and Chief Kaubure were there with a hurricane lamp to guide us. It was natural for us to ask them to lead us first to the big native-built kitchen, with its promise of immediate warmth and food. They ushered us in through a side door. The place was letting in the rain; there were holes in the thatch and pools of water on the cement floor. But there were dry spots here and there. The only real trouble was the stove.

There was, in fact, no stove. The Magistrate said something about it having been taken to Onotoa by my predecessor. However, that was no moment to be bemoaning details. The children were crying with cold and hunger. The first thing to do was to get a fire started somehow. The Magistrate and Chief Kaubure brought in dry sticks from somewhere and soon had a blaze going on the floor, with a kerb of big coral rocks around it. We took the babies out of their dripping clothes, wrapped them in blankets and stood their cots around the glow. The smoke was appalling, but there was warmth. 'And now for a saucepan and some milk,' said Olivia.

But there was no saucepan either. Everything of that kind had gone to Onotoa with the stove. My predecessor had made Onotoa his headquarters for the past year or more. The fact was known to me and I was the goat for not having foreseen the natural consequences. However, as Olivia said, we had our own utensils, and in the meantime a kettle would do for the milk if anybody had one. The Magistrate did have one, and the children got their warm drink with some biscuits we had brought for them. But before we got down to the soup, a thought struck Olivia: 'Perhaps we shouldn't move the children tonight. There's room in here for a double bed if we push out one of the cots. I'll share it with Joan by the fire; I'm pretty cold myself; there'll be no smoke when the fire burns clear.'

It seemed to me an excellent idea. The storm had blown itself out, the rain had stopped and I saw stars through the holes in the thatch. I believed I could squeeze a single bed into a corner for myself. We put the soup on and called for beds. They arrived eventually, on loan, from houses in the Native Government lines. The beds belonging to our own quarters had, unfortunately gone to Onotoa along with the stove and saucepans.

The substitutes so kindly lent to us were solid wooden affairs, rough plank tables on short legs, and they made rare hard lying; but, as Olivia said, it didn't affect the children, and we two could soon get the station carpenter to run us up some nice string ones like those at Abemama. Meanwhile, there were our people arriving with the heavy gear – we heard their shouts from the beach. The idea was for me to go and see everything laid out on the front verandah before turning in. All we needed in our queer emergency quarters were the bundles of sleeping mats, bedding and mosquito nets. Everything else could just wait until morning. It would be marvellous to wake up fresh at daybreak, have a dip in the lagoon, and get down to the big, thrilling business of home-making.

I went out by the way we had come in and made straight through the trees for the canoes, eighty yards away. The night was now still, but very dark. It was fumbling work getting all that stuff dumped on the beach from the canoes by the dim light of hurricane lamps. I picked out the bundles of bedding and sent them back to the kitchen. 'Now get the rest taken and spread out on the front verandah,' I told my orderly.

He was a Tarawa man and strange to the place: 'Where is the verandah?' he asked.

I pointed inland: 'Up there, as straight as you can go.'

He went through the screen of trees with a lamp to get the lie of the land and I returned to report all well to Olivia. Our troubles were over. This had been a real adventure . . . fun to write home about when we had settled in and all that . . . but thank heaven it was only for a night. We were just getting ready to turn in when the orderly appeared at the door: 'I cannot find the verandah,' he said simply: 'I have searched south, I have searched north, I have searched middle. In the south there is another thatched house like this, very old and dirty, but in the midst between that and this there is no verandah.'

'You'd better go and see what he means,' said Olivia. She smiled, but she already knew in her heart as well as I did what the answer was. There was in very truth no verandah in the midst between. It had accompanied the stove, and the sauce-pans, and the beds to Onotoa. So had the rest of the house and everything in it except two kitchen chairs. We were, in short, stranded on Beru, homeless but for the chairs and two ruinous native shacks eighty feet apart.

*

But morning came and we bathed in the lagoon. The waters sparkled emerald-clear over the white sand bottom. We seemed to be swimming in limpid green light. In the cool of early day, the palms towered still and patient, like tall saints with folded hands gathering strength to face the burning noon. Their peace came dropping slow upon us as we walked back up the beach. 'After all,' Olivia said, 'we can have a really beautiful native-built house now, with great big rooms. I've always wanted to live in one of our own design. Then you can use that special warrant of £50 to buy a stove and a sink, and a roof-tank, and a new bath, and a cistern, and some chairs, and a wardrobe . . . oh, and I don't know what-not else instead of paint for that rotten old wooden bungalow.'

We began to design a grand new home that day. It was easy to consider ourselves on picnic until it was ready. The kitchen we were in was turned into a sitting-room-dining-room-office and the other shack, formerly the office, became our collective bedroom and night-nursery. The domestic staff lodged out in the Native Government lines, our cooking was done mostly in a native earth-oven. We had two squatter's chairs for comfort among our bits and pieces, and the station carpenter was asked to make us two string beds as soon as he could. Everything went blithely from the word go, except that Olivia and I were attacked by a queer irritation of the skin. But, as the children didn't get it and we felt very fit, we dismissed it for what George Murdoch always used to call 'just another of these dog-diseases of the Pacific.'

The beautiful headquarters and training school of the London Missionary Society were at Rongorongo, five miles up the curving shore. Their neat buildings by the beach looked neighbourly towards us over the water. The resident staff of five English workers – two married couples and a single lady – made generously helpful friends for us from the first week. There was Father Choblet too, the hero who had risked death to bring the

Last Sacrament to his brother-priest at Nukunau, a giant's soul in the frame of a gnome, vivid, humorous, passionate, truculent – '*Je suis français de la Vendée, moi!*' he used to shout at his most redoubtable moments – brave as a lion, kind as an angel. His station and the house of two teaching sisters of the Sacred Heart lay only two miles north of us. We had had no such glut of European contacts ever before in the Gilbert group. The children were bursting with health. The only small nuisance was that skin-irritation.

I scratched an itching eyebrow one morning as I was writing, and a tiny speck fell on the paper. It was alive. I had never seen that particular insect before, so I showed it to my orderly. He laughed: 'That is what we call *te uti-baraaki*. Where did it come from?' But the smile went out of his face when I told him. 'Alas!' he cried, 'this is an evil thing. It eats its way under the skin, and lays eggs, and multiplies exceedingly, and the itching thereof is beyond bearing, and, before it can be rooted out, it is necessary to shave the hair from those places where it abides.'

We were suffering, not to put too fine a point on it, from crab-lice caught from the wooden beds so kindly lent to us. We swarmed with them. That was the second and last time I ever saw Olivia weep at the mischances of domestic life in the Gilbert Islands. The first had been at the ruin of our dinner for the Old Man at Tarawa. 'It's the tiniest little things that irritate most,' she said, and I thought she was right in this particular case. We slept on the floor until the string beds came along, a fortnight later.

*

We never discovered if the Old Man had known there were no quarters for us. He was a queer bird, but probably he hadn't. In the absence of a District Officer at Beru, the only places he would have landed at on visits of inspection would have been the two Mission Stations. Incidentally also, he could not have got a clue to the situation from anything he found at Onotoa, because the timbers of the missing house were never reassembled there in recognizable shape. They simply disappeared. It was just another of those Gilbert and Sullivan twists that added zest to life in the islands, as Olivia said, and we left it at that. One did not, in any case, put one's Chief on the spot in those days.

Our new house was to be built, according to plan, entirely of native materials, round three sides of a square, its courtyard turned inland. A big lounge between two bedrooms was to face the lagoon, and in the wings we were to have another bedroom, a day nursery, my office, the kitchen, and the bathroom. But a home like that was going to take five or six months to finish, whereas we wanted to be out of the shacks by Christmas Eve (which was also Olivia's birthday) only two months ahead. Work was therefore concentrated on the three front rooms first of all. These were ready a week or so before Christmas and we settled in happily, leaving the two shacks to be used as a kitchen and an office until the new ones came along.

The weather was not very good to us, as the westerly season was now at its zenith; but the driving rain taught us just where more leaf-screens were needed to make the house cosier for Christmas, and those took no more than a few minutes each to plait. We were all snug by Christmas Eve, with the weather doors and windows blinded against possible storms. 'The great thing is to be ready for trouble,' said Olivia on her birthday morning: 'Thank heaven we are out of those wretched shacks. They'll probably lose their roofs if these tremendous squalls go on.'

The squalls were indeed tremendous. News came in of village houses blown down, and I began to regret having felled a good many of the trees that had screened the house to westward; they had spoiled our view over the lagoon, but the lack of them now exposed us to the wind's full force. However, the weather abated in the afternoon, and by dinner-time all was quiet. We filled the children's Christmas stockings and turned in, more than ever serenely rooted in our new home.

But at midnight another squall awoke us. It hit the house with the impact of a solid mass. We heard the walls cracking with the strain. The whole universe shrieked, and so did the children. I leapt out of bed and tried to light a hurricane lamp; but the house was full of whirling gusts; I could not. Olivia groped her way through to the children in the pitchy darkness. I groped after her with the unlit lamp. As we went, screens that filled the front doorway exploded inwards and driven spume from the lagoon flooded the lounge. The whole house was staggering and groaning. In the children's room, Olivia stood feverishly holding out her nightdress for shelter while I lit the lamp. But top gusts put even hurricane lamps out; the flame flickered perilously. We knelt on the floor, she spread her lifted nightdress over it, I opened my pyjama coat around it, to keep the flame alive. We must have made a marvellous Christmas Eve tableau like that. But we didn't feel marvellous when we looked overhead. The roof above us was whipping madly up and down. We saw lashings snap. Fragments of thatch were torn away as we watched. There was a ripping, rending roar; the whole roof suddenly vanished before our eyes into the screaming night. The lamp went out. We knelt in gross darkness, with our wailing progeny about us, while the gale lashed down upon our roofless heads.

*

But we thought our new house the grandest thing in the Gilberts when it was finished. Not a fragment of European stuff went into it except a corrugated-iron kitchen roof for a water-catchment. Lime burned from coral rocks made the base it stood on. The walls were of coconut-leaf midribs lashed upright side by side. Door and window frames were of moulded coconut timber. Lattice work of ivory-white pandanus-root slats filled the windows and garnished the tops of inside walls. String made of coconut fibre held the whole together with intricate and beautiful patterns of cross-lashing. The cool, twilight interior was a study in dun-browns, silver-greys and old-ivory, so complete in its own beauty that it refused all wall-decorations save here and there a patterned native mat and an etching or two, sparsely distributed. We got our stove, and bath, and roof-tank, and cistern, and what-not-else at last, thanks to an extra-special warrant the Old Man granted. The roof was built doubly strong after that educative Christmas Eve, and life went swimmingly from then on in our adorable home by the lagoonside.

Of the five islands officially called the Southern Gilberts, Tamana and Arorae, with 2,000 souls between them, were 100 per cent Protestant; Onotoa, with 1,500, nearly 100 per cent; Nukunau, with 1,500 and Beru, with 2,400, 80 per cent each; and William Edward Goward, the local head of the London Missionary Society had been, politically speaking, their dictator for twenty-odd years up to 1918. I never came to know him well, as he retired just before we settled at Beru; but he remained with us in the spirit; the impress of his tremendous personality had moulded every village teacher of his making to his own unbending shape, and I had much to do with the formidable politico-religious organization he left behind him.

At nearly sixty, he was a stocky, pink-faced, white-haired figure – rather like Lloyd George, I thought, but Olivia said more like Bismarck – in radiantly laundered ducks, flaming with energy, stubborn as a mule, puritanical as a Pym, arrogant as a cardinal. His village visitations at Beru were royal progresses. Flocks of beefy, white-skirted native pastors, teachers and deacons followed in his train. His parishioners lined the village streets and bowed as he passed. His word was, quite literally, law: he said pagan shrines must be destroyed, and they were destroyed; he said that Gilbertese women must wear drawers, and drawers for women it was; he told the people they must choose only deacons of the Protestant church as village kaubure, and only Protestant deacons were chosen; he told the deacon kaubure how to vote in cases before the Native Courts, and they voted no other way – or were sacked by the Magistrates, at his order, if they did.

To be honest, Government lassitude was responsible for most of this. The administration of the Southern Gilberts had always been neglected, for the very reason that Mr Goward's masterful hand rested so inflexibly upon them. From that angle, the Empire owes much to him; he was, in his own way, the major force for peace and discipline there for a great many years. If, in the course of his good works, which were legion, he managed to establish government by the elect in lieu of government by the elected, it was mainly because officialdom abandoned him too much to his own devices. It certainly was never the fault of the London Missionary Society as a body. His successors in office helped me much, from behind their own scenes, in getting the Native Courts to operate without fear or favour of denominational parties. It must have been extremely difficult for them. They had to deal with a staff of Samoan and Gilbertese pastors fashioned by the old chief in the formidable likeness of himself. To these ironsides, the liberalism of the new regime could have seemed nothing short of blasphemy, and I remember with gratitude the courageous firmness of the leaders who taught them otherwise.

One of the first things I had to do was to secure a reasonable representation of Roman Catholic opinion in the Native Courts. It was *prima facie* bad in principle, I suppose, to identify the representation of the people with denominational religion. But there were no overt non-Christians in the Southern Gilberts to complicate the issue. For the rest, the general run of villagers, Protestants and Roman Catholics alike, had few feelings for right or wrong, justice or injustice, outside those dictated and limited by their sectarian prejudices. That was the worst of all the results of the Government's *laissez faire* policy; it affected the administration of the law. As the Native Courts sat in judgement on members of both the warring sects, clearly the only thing to do – and quickly – was to give the Roman Catholic minority at least some voice in their deliberations.

*

Eventually, as retirements permitted, we worked up to a ratio of one Roman Catholic kaubure to every three Protestants in the Native Courts of Beru and Nukunau (Koata, the Native Magistrate of Onotoa, had already turned Roman Catholic of his own accord, which was convenient) and the arrangement showed good results. But the early days were not without their troubles on Beru. The very first of the Sacred Heart Mission's flock to be appointed kaubure, whom I shall call Timoteo, rather failed – from my angle, at least – to get the real hang of the thing. A policy of non-sectarian administration was, after all, the great idea. Father Choblet said he saw what I meant, but . . .

238

Timoteo was one of his village teachers, and a very good one too. I haven't the least doubt that the Father, by ways and means known to his cloth, had made very sure that that individual and no other would be freely elected by his parishioners. However, everyone else was doing the same thing on Beru, so why not he? '*Il faut être toujours réaliste,*' as he was always fond of saying when annoyed. The election (or selection) took place when I had been about three months there, just before I left on a tour of the central islands.

When I got back four weeks later, Iuta, the Native Magistrate, a gentle little Protestant, greeted me on the beach with a very long face: 'Alas! I am about to be dismissed from office, for I have deeply sinned,' he said. 'Why, what *have* you been up to, you old villain?' I asked. I could not imagine a man like him guilty of any crime worse than over-kindness.

He did not brighten up: 'I have suspended Timoteo, and the Father has told me that you will at once dismiss me for that evil act. And he has said also that if you do not dismiss me, he will make the Old Man on Ocean Island dismiss you. And he has said also that if the Old Man of Ocean Island does not dismiss you, he will make the Old Man in Fiji dismiss him. And he has said also that if the Old Man in Fiji will not listen, he will make the King dismiss him, and the Old Man at Ocean Island, and both of us. Therefore it is expedient for you to dismiss me at once, lest worse things happen.'

It appeared that, from the day of my departure, Timoteo had looked upon himself as an officially authorized crusader for his own church. 'The day has now come,' he told the Protestant villagers, 'for the truimph of the one true faith over darkness. Here I stand to prove it, all you heretics.' When they politely ignored that, he began to shout it up and down the village street, mentioning names, articles of faith and the penalties he, as kaubure, would cause to be inflicted upon all unbelievers. But it was only when he made a habit of bawling insults mixed with curious dogma outside the Protestant school that public patience cracked, and even then the report went not to Iuta, but to the Father: 'Relieve us of this madman, we beg you,' it ran, 'for he talks very vilely, and of

239

a religion that we do not wish to know, being Christians.'

Though it was perhaps unhappily worded, it did at least throw the initiative, with extraordinary forbearance, whole into the Father's hands. He, however, read it as a gratuitous insult, and took it to the Native Magistrate, demanding the immediate official vindication of Timoteo. His claim was that Timoteo had done nothing but testify like a good Catholic to the faith that was in him. But Iuta investigated the facts and wisely suspended Timoteo. After further inquiries of my own, I found nothing for it but to ask the Father to put up a less militant candidate for the office.

He said that he didn't want a fresh candidate. Timoteo was the best qualified of his flock to speak out for the Catholic church as a kaubure. Timoteo must be reinstated.

'But Father,' I protested, 'he wasn't appointed to speak out for your church or anyone else's. That's the whole point. The government isn't a proselytizing organization.'

'*Mais soyons réalistes au moins!* Regard those others. Are they not all deacons of their church, *et quelle église, ma foi!* And do they not bawl their canticles day and night, to pierce the ears of my poor people?'

'Yes but . . . Father, they don't demonstrate in official uniform . . . with official threats . . . shouting insults outside your school. They do their singing and praying reasonably, in chapel.'

'Insults, you say? Reasonably? O, but the insults and unreason I have supported from that Buddha! *C'est à fou-rire . . . c'est inouï!* I implore your justice. I demand the reinstatement of Timoteo.'

'That Buddha' was his engaging name for Mr Goward. It was true that the news-sheet published by the resolute old gentleman had made outspoken attacks on the Roman way of thinking. But the Sacred Heart's publications had superbly held their own at that kind of thing, and, in any case, the sacred freedom of the press had nothing to do (as far as I could see) with the case of Timoteo.

'I simply can't appoint a Roman Catholic kaubure just to give you the pleasure of getting a kick-back at Mr Goward,' I pleaded.

'But he is a good Catholic . . . the best in my flock. His influence cannot fail to be good. Regard the principles. I beg you . . .'

'Yes but . . . Father we're arguing from different premises. You *must* look at the facts . . .'

And so on: facts, premises, principles – we went round and round in that age-old contention between passionate priestliness and bureaucratic beastliness. 'You have lifted me up only to throw me down,' he shouted as he left: 'You have destroyed my prestige. You have trampled upon my church as the Boches trampled on defenceless Belgium.' He confirmed the last phrase in writing, and never would retract it. But he did nominate another man, who turned out excellent.

And he never ceased his loving kindness. A bunch of bananas from his garden (he was a great gardener as well as a great man) arrived with the scorching letter he wrote me. Every one I ate made me feel more like a worm. The reproachful looks of Sister Yves when I went up to call on him two days later shamed me still more. She stood on the beach to meet me: 'The Father regrets not being able to welcome you today, as he is indisposed,' she said, and then, seeing my crestfallen looks, 'He has suffered much, you understand, but perhaps he will be strong enough to see you if you return next week.'

I did return. He was his sanguine, dominant self again by then. 'As a human being with human sentiments,' he opened, leaning forward to hold my hand as he sat, 'I permit myself to say that you have done me a great wrong. As a Christian and a friend – though you are not of my church – I forgive you nevertheless.'

My cantankerousness found that difficult to swallow whole. I asked him if he would also forgive me if I went on thinking I had done him no wrong at all. He leapt to his feet, addressing heaven with upflung arms, '*O juste ciel!* How I have prayed for patience to support this monster!' Then, as suddenly as he had arisen, he sat down again, doubled up with laughter, pointing at me. When he came out of it, he took both my hands, speaking very quietly: '*Voyons*, let us speak no more of it. Let us be good friends.' I don't think I have ever had an acuter sense of receiving an honour.

We argued and grew hot many times after that. He tried to dictate to me about divorce and to interfere with the marriage laws. His rudeness when angry was staggering. He used abusive epithets like knuckle-dusters. He enraged me once by saying the Great War had been God's judgement on England because her Kings refused to bow to Rome. Yet his fanaticism was lit by sparks of amazing sanity. One of his dicta was that the disestablishment of his own church in France was the best thing that ever happened to her, because it made her fight for her living. I never met a more intricate, arrogant, humble-minded, lovable mass of impassioned unreason and cold hard commonsense. We quarrelled, but never fell out; he called me a heretical, bureaucratic pragmatist, I called him narrow-minded and interfering; but he was not narrow-minded; always at the end, it was his tempestuous laughter that ended the bout and made us friends again.

*

I had returned from my tour of the central islands with a slight attack of dysentery, which neglect did not improve. Emetine was not yet being used in the Gilbert Islands (I don't know why); I had lost faith, for myself at least, in the sickening ipecacuanha treatment, and all patience with my proneness to the disease. It seemed to me that the less notice I took of it, the sooner it would pass. But amoeba refuses to be treated like that. By the middle of March I was sulkily on my back again, and feeding on slops. Colitis came along; I got more and more cautious about diet; at the end of April, I was living on two glasses of milk and water a day, very weak, and savagely sorry for myself.

Father Choblet was constant in his visits. I remember his talking to me much at that time of how, in seven or eight years from then, he hoped to return to his beloved France again. He always explained with care that he had no wish to stay there long; Beru remained always his road to Heaven and he wanted to come back to die; but he felt that Providence might not grudge him a short visit to his family after, say, thirty-five years of exile. It was when his agonized human loves spoke to me so piteously through the iron disciplines of his dedication that I knew the real, the towering, stature of the man concealed within the cassock, and saw for the first time blindingly how little the trappings of the churches and the dogmas they stand for must matter to Heaven, or should matter to humanity, beside the simple worth of the men they hide and divide. When I had been ill for two and a half months, I said to him out of the gladness of my revelation, 'You know, Father, I don't think religion necessarily embellishes a man; it's always the man who embellishes his religion.' But that started a furious argument, which he ended by saying I was too sick to think straight. In any case, I was a heretic and therefore not worth listening to. 'And as for the sickness,' he finished, 'well, you are not a member of my congregation, but you are my friend . . . I wish to speak as a friend.'

I knew that opening gambit of his; it meant he was about to tell me something insufferably true about my ego. He did. I leaned back sulkily on my pillows to take the withering blast of it. He began mildly enough by saying that the time had come when I ought to make an effort to eat something. According to his diagnosis, I was starving myself to death instead of fighting back at the disease. But his last words had a sting in them: 'Your mind is sicker than your body,' he told me; 'Despair . . . that's your trouble . . . and despair is a mortal sin as well as being cowardly.'

It stabbed the deeper because I had a feeling he was right. Only that morning, I had decided I couldn't last long at the rate the colitis was going. But I mumbled something about being at the end of my patience, and fed to the teeth, and justifiably so, and be damned to everything. That set him really talking Choblet.

'Impatient? Fed to the teeth? Justifiably?' he barked, '*Mais ça me fait rire! C'est tordant, ça!* Ha-ha! Regard how I mock you, and take another look at yourself. There is Providence – Divine Providence – waiting at your elbow with a lagoon full of fish – kind foods – strengthening foods – and what do you do? You talk to me of justification when you haven't even the courage to use divine help. Impatient . . . Justified, are you? Well, I have some

better words. Pusillanimous, that's what you are . . . and a prig
. . . a pusillanimous prig!'

There was much more of it, but that is the gist of what he
shouted as his tiny figure in its white soutane hurled itself
hopping and gesticulating around the room. He only stood still
to laugh at my furious retort. 'You can treat me to bad names if
you like: you are a privileged invalid. But you know I am right.
That is why you swear so,' he smiled when I dried up. He left me
with the quiet advice that I should begin my cure by eating a
little boiled fish with more confidence in the mercy of Providence and less fear of stomach aches.

The contempt in that gorgeous phrase 'pusillanimous prig'
shamed me into trying. It hurt at first, but Nature (or, if you
like, Providence), given a fair chance, began to fight on my side.
I was on my feet in a fortnight. Father Choblet's whip-lash
truths about my spirit, in effect, saved my body.

*

A month later, it was his turn to fall ill. I knew nothing about it
until a laconic note from Sister Yves came like a bolt from across
the blue lagoon. He might have ptomaine poisoning or appendicitis she thought. He was in terrible pain. He could not go
on much longer without help. He himself believed the end was
very near. Could I possibly come to him?

The only medicines left in my depleted chest were half a
bottle of castor-oil and five morphine hydrochloride tablets of a
strength I have forgotten. There was a hypodermic syringe too,
with a rusty needle. I took the lot. He was doubled up and
groaning when I got there. His murky box of a room was stifling
hot. A solid mass of villagers swarmed around his bed, robbing
him of air. I told them impatiently to give breathing space. He
raised himself a little, to whisper, 'Ah, be gentle with them,'
and fell back again. He had not slept for three nights and days,
they told me. His temperature was soaring, his pulse racing and
feeble; he was semi-delirious. He called it appendicitis himself.
Maybe it was; I don't know. But I do know that the pain that
racked his body meant almost nothing to him. One thought

alone obsessed and ravaged his mind. There was no brother-priest at hand to bring him the Last Sacrament.

He babbled his tortured thoughts to me between paroxysms. He had risked his life in raging seas three years before to save Father Franchiteau from that selfsame horror of dying unshriven on Nukunau. He had succeeded miraculously . . . but now . . . 'I was too proud of my success,' he told me, 'I was too proud. This is my punishment. I die alone, without Viaticum.' His fevered thought turned to the added centuries of purgatory it might cost him; 'I shall not see France from purgatory,' he muttered: '*Hélas! mea maxima culpa!*' It was not despair but a humility beyond belief, which accepted the imagined savagery of his God as justice perfected.

It did not occur to me that I could save his life. My only hope was to ease his passing. I knew the morphine could do that, but he would have refused it as a mere anodyne. So I lied to him. I told him the injection was the very latest thing for abscess of the appendix. The effect was electric. It was like pressing a button and starting a dynamo. Hope leapt from him as instantaneous as a spark. As I pushed in the blunt needle he began to talk of God's infinite mercy in bringing him low, so that he might see his sin, and then sending this drug to save him.

I wanted him to die thinking like that of the ultimate decencies, not the man-made horrors of his God. Nothing else seemed to matter. So I embroidered the tale with more lies. I was not, and am not now, ashamed of any of them, because they did confirm him in the belief that Providence was back at his elbow. I had proof of it. Though my first timid dose of the drug – a single tiny tabloid – brought him little relief from pain, he lay there for an hour gasping gratitude to Heaven and poking fun at my glum face. His joke was that, as an instrument of Providence, I ought to look a lot happier. Confidence swept out of him like a rushing wind; it raced alive through the gloomy little room and infected the villagers still crowded at the doorway: 'The Father will live,' they shouted, 'he will live!' and rushed out to tell their friends – all save one, who ran in to hold my hands. He looked weeping into my eyes for a moment and went out without speaking. It was the poor Timoteo I had had to sack three months before. But emotions made no certainty for me. I could not share the faith and hope that radiated from the bed.

I had to make a choice in the next few minutes. Should I spend the last few tabloids of morphine in one big, comforting dose or eke them out in two small ones? A single hundredth of a grain had barely eased him; one of his most urgent needs was sleep; I did not think that two would put him under. I gave him all the rest. Perhaps I hoped he might die sleeping; I was so certain he could not live. As he floated serenely into unconsciousness, I slid two tablespoons of castor oil into him. I couldn't conceive it would help much, but it couldn't do him any harm, I thought.

He woke in six hours with the pains clutching at him again. He asked, writhing, if it was time for another injection. I had nothing for his help now save more lies. It struck me of a sudden that the pure power of his belief might put him to sleep again, if I could give it something to cling to. I had heard of such miracles; it seemed worth trying. I said, 'Father, I'm going to double the dose this time,' and made a big show of putting tabloids in the syringe and filling up with boiled water to melt them. 'I'll have to reduce again next shot,' I told him as I injected pure water into his arm: 'Can't afford to risk an overdose.'

And it worked, or, rather, his faith did. His body relaxed; he was asleep within two minutes, and remained so for another three hours, until the castor oil took charge. The pains were less after that, but still heavy. I injected more water, and once more he plunged into sleep like a small boy. The temperature left him and his pulse rallied while he slept. I told him when he woke that he would have to bear the rest of his aches unaided for twenty-four hours, as I dare not give him another dose earlier. 'But I have no more than a little tenderness left,' he said: 'Let me have a drink of water, and I will sleep . . . I am still very sleepy.' Even the tenderness was gone by the time he woke again.

So he lived to face the rest of his strange destiny. Maybe there was nothing so wonderful about his cure, after all. His temperature might have come from a chill, his pains from some kind of colic, for all I know. In that case, the castor oil was all he needed to put him right, with perhaps a spice of heretical companionship to keep his pecker up. But he would naturally have none of that. He said it was stupid and wicked quibbling. The whole thing was so clear to him: I had need of him with his truths (plus boiled fish) in my extremity; he had needed me with my lies (plus castor oil) in his; *ergo*, and inevitably, Providence had sent each to the other properly equipped at the proper moment. The proper moment was when faith was most ready to work. I said, 'What about the faith of an agnostic?' and that led to some of the finest linguistics I ever heard him use. He won the argument by pointing out that I wasn't an agnostic but a heretic Christian, anyhow, which I was proud to accept.

*

The story leaps forward eight or nine years (I forget exactly how many) for the sequel. I was Resident Commissioner when his joyful letter came to tell me that, at long last, he was going back to France, and for a whole year. He had been thirty-six years without a holiday. The way leave had come to him was of itself providential, he said. He had not liked to ask for it, as there was always so much work for everyone, but he had not been very well of late, and the Bishop had ordered him out; so now he could dwell without contumacy on the thought of seeing his folk before he died. He would be coming to Ocean Island by the next opportunity, to wait for a passage to Australia.

He arrived three months later, shrunk to almost nothing in his soutane, and leaden-skinned, as if the blood in him had changed to some grey liquid. Only his face seemed not to have shrunk, but its features were strangely altered. The fine-bridged nose had broadened between the eyes; the ears and the high arches of the brows were somehow thickened. They thought in the group that he had some kind of anaemia.

But what did it matter what he had, he smiled. The good doctors of France would soon put him right; he would see his people for a blessed year; there would be the good peasant food of La Vendée; he would return roaring like a lion for more work, and he didn't know how many more arguments with me and my bureaucracy. He left me at the front steps laughing, '*Trente-six*

ans! Bon Dieu! Mais tiens . . . bon Dieu . . . it was well said, that!
Bon Dieu . . . Bonté Suprême!'

But it did matter what he had. Of all the sicknesses that
possibly might have forbidden his twelve thousand mile way
home, he had the most dreadful – leprosy. I did not see him for a
week after the doctor's heart-breaking verdict. He wanted to be
alone. From things he said later, I humbly guessed at the bitter
struggle he had had with the fury of despair. But he came out of
it superhumanly serene. 'I clung too much to the happiness I
vowed to renounce,' he told me: 'That was a sin. I should have
begged Monseigneur to let me stay. There is work for me to do
among the lepers. God has been merciful in allowing me to
redeem my sin.' No lies this time had helped him back to his
faith in the goodness of Providence.

We built a two-roomed house for him, at his own request, in
the asylum where our forty or fifty lepers lived. We would have
put him elsewhere had he wished, but he wanted to be with the
others. The settlement was a new one, laid out as much like a
village as possible, in a cheerful spot not too far from Tarawa
hospital. One or two cases had begun to respond to gynocardate
injections, but results were so rare, known failures so many.
Hopelessness deepened by the awful lassitude of the disease
itself was our constant enemy. It robbed even the vivid, fighting
Gilbertese of their will to live. They withered in their new home
as they had withered in the old one, hoping for a quick end.
They did nothing but sit and wait. There was never a smile in
that camp of the walking dead. I feared much for the Father.

But I need not have feared. I was able to visit him at Tarawa
five or six months after he had settled in. The first thing I
noticed was a beautiful new order in the settlement. No
coconut-leaves littered the ground between houses as before;
crinum lilies grew in neatly kerbed borders along the paths. The
place had the air of a village proud of itself. There was industry
everywhere; I saw men making nets, women plaiting mats.
People chatted from house to house as they worked. And there
was laughter. They called cheerful greetings to me, where once
they had sat as mute as the doomed. The asylum had become a
real refuge, alive and glad of life.

'Here, what have you been doing with my lepers?' I said to the Father when I sat in his house.

'Ah, you have noticed? But did you not know? I am the new District Officer, Leper Asylum. And, *ma foi*, my people listen to my advice better than to any bureaucrat's,' he laughed.

That was beyond all argument. I asked him how he had got them going.

'I began by doing my duty as a priest. The rest followed,' was his reply; 'When the soul is awakened, life is worth living. But you have to be a good Catholic to understand that, *cher hérétique!*'

I sidestepped that one by asking him how he was. He said the doctor reported progress already, but added, *'mais vous savez, je ne me tracasse plus de tout ça. Je suis bien content de la paroisse que m'a donnée le Bon Dieu.'* He was absorbed in his job. Providence had turned up trumps for him again.

The Prisoner

We had managed to get a message through to Tarawa in early March, 1919, that Olivia expected another baby in August. Word came back in May that the Senior Medical Officer and Nurse Armstrong, a recent addition to his staff, would be arriving in early July to do a thorough health-survey of Beru while awaiting our family event.

I remember well how pleased we were at the idea of having a doctor at hand for a whole month or even longer. It was not that either of us was ever particularly anxious about falling ill. The post-war spate of pseudo-medical journalism that was to succeed in creating so many recondite diseases for nervous minds to dwell upon had not yet afflicted us. In our comfortable ignorance, we recked not at all of psychoses, and still expected castor-oil, bread poultices, iodine, and aspirin to cure most ailments. They usually did, too. Olivia had a score of questions to ask about the cases she had contrived, as usual, to collect from the villages for treatment in our back premises. Also, I personally wanted advice about Obadaia, a difficult prisoner in the men's gaol, who was doing sentence of a year for a rather serious assault.

The average Gilbertese prisoner of those days – sensible man – seldom took his incarceration as a great hardship. A few weeks or months in the lock-up meant nothing locally in terms of social stigma. Why should a man be penalized for paying on the nail for his mistakes? was the reasonable public view; and also, what the Government called hard labour was a glorious joke. No government that prized its reputation for humanity could, in fact, possibly dare to load any prisoner with the merciless stint of daily work a free man's family demanded of him in his village. So, a fellow could always count on a nice rest in gaol, and recalcitrants were very rare indeed. But Obadaia was one of the few.

He was a craggy Hercules of a man, much taller and more negroid than most of his race, outstandingly intelligent, a well-known wrestler, and immensely fit-looking. He had stabbed another villager through the arm and brought him very near bleeding to death for paying undue attention to his wife. The girl, a good deal younger than himself, was innocent of offence and lived quietly with his mother while he was serving his sentence. But mortal jealousy gnawed him. He was sullenly idle. I had only once seen him snap out of it. That was when we were installing our new kitchen stove and he worked along with the cook under Olivia's direction. For two days he was all smiles and did everything at the double. But when he went back to ordinary prison routines again, he returned to his black brooding and began to sham sick. At least, I thought he was shamming; he could never manage to look ill, or run a pulse or a temperature; but he said he had frightful pains inside him, and I wasn't a doctor, and in the end the daily repetition of his tale began to make me anxious. The solution of his problem and mine got itself strangely tangled with the birth of June Angela, our last child.

Olivia kept very well until the last week of June. Nothing had happened before the birth of the other three children to make us expect trouble this time. The fair-weather season was at its best; chills were almost impossible to catch; there were no influenza colds in the villages. What did hit her I cannot say, but she came back from a sunset walk one day saying she was giddy and thought she had a bit of a temperature. The thermometer said rather more than a bit over 104 degrees.

Both of us guessed that if the fever stayed up there for long there might be a premature birth. Maybe we could have prevented that from happening, had we known how; but we didn't know, and aspirin failed to bring the temperature down. All we could think of doing towards midnight was to get a few things ready at once against any event. Olivia said there was no need to pull long faces about it, anyhow; I myself had been a seven months' child; my mother had told her so: 'And just look at you now!' she ended. 'As merry as an undertaker!' Thus encouraged, I went out to prepare for the worst.

The main thing was to sterilize everything likely to be used, including gallons and gallons of water. It was the water that brought Obadaia into the picture, because I had to organize watches of prisoners in the kitchen to keep heaps of it continually on the boil. I admit that the use of His Majesty's guests for domestic purposes was strictly forbidden, but I did not happen to be thinking much of rules and regulations at the time. The prisoners themselves – there were nine of them, all in for mere peccadillos except Obadaia – were quick to respond when I woke them up in the gaol and explained the situation. Obadaia took the lead at once: 'Men-o-o!' he called, 'we are asked to save Missis and her baby! We prisoners! We bad men! How wonderful is this thing we are given to do! Let us make a plan now.' And there, crowding around a hurricane lamp in the big, dark prison-house, they eagerly resolved themselves into an organizing committee. It was arranged that they should work in four-hour watches of three men each, the first to go on duty at once, headed by Obadaia.

I left the midnight watch at work in the kitchen. When I returned in ten minutes to see how the fire was going, Obadaia whispered, 'Sir, is Missis asleep?' I told him she was, but burning, and muttering, and very restless. He returned back to the stove without comment, and I left again, for there was a big job of reading to get through. I had to study as quickly as I could everything Playfair had written of the way babies were normally born. All my little experience in the villages so far had been with abnormal presentations. I dared not think of those. Time was too short, in any case, to read of every morbid possibility. It came back to me then how, at Cambridge, one had feverishly mugged up spot subjects just before an examination. This seemed rather like that, save for one thing – the cost of a mistake.

As I settled to my reading in the lounge, Olivia's fevered mutterings came to me brokenly across the hissing, clicking whisper of the trade wind through the palms outside. In the night, when the cheerful rumours of life going forward are stilled, anxious ears are not easily stopped to noises that come so lonely out of the dark. But, one by one, Playfair began to answer the frightened questions of my ignorance. He wrote in a way a layman could understand. His simplicity captured and held me absorbed for four hours, and drove spearheads of confidence through the legion of my fears. He engaged me so wholly, I noticed no change in the night's voices until I laid the book aside. The wind still hissed and clicked in the palms, but Olivia muttered no more. She seemed to be humming instead, on a deep, quiet note. It was strange, but there was such contentment in the sound, it did not alarm me; it held some restful quality of sleep itself. I went into her room.

But it was not Olivia who hummed. Though the fever still burned in her, she lay silent in an untroubled sleep. The sound seemed to come from nowhere and everywhere. Wherever I groped it was around my ears, neither nearer nor farther, like a vibrant mist hung on the darkness. It was not until I brought in the lamp that I found Obadaia sitting on the step of the verandah doorway. He had been there for three hours, he said. His heart had been heavy when I told him Missis was not sleeping well, and he thought I would not mind if he came and sang to her the way his grandmother had taught him. There were no special words to his song, only a trick of making what he called a ghost-voice that floated over sick people and gave them dream-less sleep. Olivia had reacted to it very quickly, and had not stirred since. He could guarantee her sleeping on without evil dreams until daylight, he said, if I would let him go on.

I thanked him for what he had done, but he had lain twisted with one of his pains only that morning; if it had been genuine, he ought to go and get some more sleep now, I told him. His stern face was lit with a sudden smile: 'Listen!' he answered, 'how the trees are crying in the wind! This morning an ill wind blew through my heart and it also cried . . .' He broke off, looking me in the eyes, and I left it at that, more touched by the beautiful discretion of his phrase than shocked at the confession of malingering. So he sat on in the dark crooning his strange, wordless lullaby while the kitchen watch was changed, and I pored once again over the passages I had marked in Playfair (Volume I, Normal Presentations), and Olivia slept her dreamless sleep till break of day.

She herself, on waking, volunteered a word about how she had slept: 'It was queer. I kept on having nightmares and waking up mumbling and grumbling half the night. Then I remember thinking I was wide awake and hearing a kind of quiet humming sound all round me, and everything seemed marvellous. I suppose that was a dream too, but I didn't have another after that. I still feel wonderful, as if nothing could possibly go wrong.'

It seemed best not to tell her yet of Obadaia. Her temperature was only a few points down, and I thought she might have further need of his help.

The kitchen watch went on, but I sent Obadaia off to get some food and sleep. He said he wanted nothing but a drink of tea, and begged leave to lie under the trees near the house, if the law allowed it. The law did nothing of the kind, but I did, on condition that he would stay off shift until nightfall and eat something solid at midday. I saw nothing more of him until that night, when he returned to duty in the kitchen.

I doubt if many women in the civilized world have ever made a trial trip into self-anaesthesia as Olivia did. A Dr Woinarski of Melbourne (bless his memory) had told me how it worked when we travelled together from Ocean Island to Australia. You begin by putting an ordinary glass tumbler into your patient's hand, as if she were going to drink, and tying it in that position with a bandage. Then you take six strips of thick blotting-paper an inch broad by six long, soak them in chloroform, pop them into the glass, and cover them over with a very loosely packed wad of cotton wool. This last lets the fumes through and at the same time prevents contact with the burning liquid. Your patient holds the glass close to mouth and nose, and breathes in the fumes for as long as she can keep her hand up. When unconsciousness comes, the weighted hand falls away and she breathes nothing but fresh air. If she comes to, she lifts the glass again, and the same thing is repeated.

There were several bottles of chloroform in stock at the medical visiting station. I asked the Native Dresser to bring one along and time me while I tried the idea out on myself first of all. He reported that my tumbler-hand fell in about half a minute, and that I stayed under for about forty seconds. After that, as Olivia agreed, the important thing was for her personally to get the hang of it; which she did with distinction and much good cheer, though her temperature was over 104 degrees again, towards seven o'clock of the second day. 'This will make it all as easy as falling off a log,' she remarked when it was over: 'I think I'll have another sleep before the great event. It won't be long now.' If, from that time I felt any fortitude, it was only because hers sufficed for both of us.

She slept almost on the moment, but not restfully until Obadaia came to magic her once more. I watched the effect this time. She had lain twitching and flinging on her back for half an hour before I called him. Three or four minutes after he began, she turned on her side and seemed to be engulfed at once in peace. She stayed so until near eleven o'clock when Obadaia got up from the doorstep. 'I think it will not be long now,' he whispered. 'It is expedient to make all things ready,' and went back to the kitchen. I followed mechanically. His prediction had been so much the same as Olivia's, it did not strike me to wonder how he had guessed until I was halfway through the final preparations. 'The thought came into my heart as I sang,' he answered. Somehow I was sure that that clinched the matter, and so indeed it fell out.

I carried a sterilized tray of sterilized things in sterilized hands out of the kitchen and stood it on a sterilized cloth in the room.

254

Child never had a more completely aseptic welcome into this bacillary world than June Angela received. She arrived four hours later, an hour before sun-up, lobster-pink, a million years old, almost without finger-nails, and weighing just over three pounds. There were no complications.

'Well, that's that,' Olivia murmured, as I handed the baby over to Faasolo, Joan's Ellice Island nursemaid: 'Queer job for a District Officer, I must say!'

Kind Mrs Eastman and Miss Simmons arrived from the London Mission station up-lagoon soon after and took charge of her. I slept for the next twelve hours.

Mother and child were doing well when I came out of it. 'I've been thinking,' Olivia said: 'This is really rather lucky. I'll be up and about again by the time Doctor arrives. Now, what I'm going to tell him is . . . ' It was all about her ailing expectant mothers.

For the next three weeks there was nothing but sunshine from Obadaia. We were building a sea-wall of coral blocks at the time, which made heavier chores than usual for the prisoners, but he did the work of any other four of them together, laughing and splashing while he heaved great foundation blocks around like a boy-giant happy with his playthings. Iuta, the Magistrate, was concerned about the uproarious noise he made; he felt that such a flow of gaiety was indecent in a prisoner. I thought myself it was simply Obadaia's way of showing regret for past malingering. Iuta said perhaps-yes, but there was something else behind it, he was sure. He turned out to be right, though I never told him how. The whole thing was too complicated for explanation on the official plane.

There was that malingering, to begin with. I went out to the sea-wall workers one day to say something to Obadaia. He was not among them. They said he had gone to lie down in a clump of salt-bush not far off, being tired. I found him sitting alone there clasping his stomach and gasping.

When a man wants to swing the lead, he does not go off and hide himself to do so. I had him carried to the house.

The doctor, who arrived the following week, found he had

advanced chronic appendix trouble and operated at once. He never had been shamming. The only lie he had ever told me, I thought shamefacedly, was when he had confessed himself a malingerer, so that I might let him go on crooning to Olivia.

His young wife was there holding his hand when I went to see him in hospital. I told her in front of him how much he had helped Olivia, and how we had all misjudged him before that. But instead of smiling she hung her head and whispered, '*Ti maama* (We are ashamed),' and again after a long silence, but looking at Obadaia this time, 'Ti maama.'

'Ti maama,' he whispered back at her, 'but I cannot tell the Man of Matang.'

'You must tell him,' she insisted: 'If you do not, I will.'

'Still your heart, woman,' he pleaded, 'and I will tell Missis when I am no longer sick.'

'You will tell him now, because of your love and honour for Missis.'

He yielded to that. Clinging tight to her hand, he began hesitantly but gathered strength as his tale went on: 'Sir, you remember? I slept under the trees at daybreak of the second day, after I had sung to Missis. And when it was noon, I awoke, and all were gathered in their houses to eat. A thought came to me then, an evil thought. I said in my heart, "Perhaps that woman my wife is not faithful to me, now that I am shut up in the calaboose." I said again, "I will go and search in her eyes, and if I see lies there, I will kill her." So I went, and no man saw me go. I came up to the house of my mother from among the trees. None saw me arrive in the village, for all men were sleeping after the noon-day meal. And I went in . . .'

He broke off, looking at his wife: 'It is enough, woman. I have told him of my sin against the law.'

'It is not enough,' she said inexorably, 'for those other things also are forbidden to prisoners, and I sinned with you in doing them.'

He sighed heavily and looked at me again: 'I went in. I woke my mother. I said to her, "Let down the screens of the house." When she had done that, I said, "Leave me alone with my wife." She left us alone. I looked into this woman's eyes, and I knew there were no lies in them. I stayed with her, and we lay until the evening. The tale is done.'

'The tale is not done, Man of Matang,' she said, staring at the floor.

He groaned: 'Is it not enough? Will you have me locked in the calaboose for ever?'

'Peace,' she murmured, 'I also shall be locked up, for I sinned with you.'

'So I returned when it was dark,' he went on drearily, 'and sang to Missis again. When that was done, I lied to the policeman; I told him that the Man of Matang had ordered me to sleep near at hand on the side verandah. He answered, "*Aia!*" I went to the side verandah. And when everyone was waiting for news of Missis, I crept away. I went back to my wife, and we lay again until the morning . . .'

'I have greatly sinned,' he added after a long pause. 'Yet since that time I have had no more evil thoughts, and I have worked with a glad heart, because I know this woman is true to me.'

Naturally, my thought ran first to the moral of his disastrous story for the moral-minded: this seemed to be that a District Officer should never, never accept personal favours from prisoners. It subverts all discipline. What interested me most at the moment, however, was the moral courage of Obadaia and his wife and its inspiration: 'Tell me your thought,' I said to the young woman; 'Did he sin most against the Government, or against me, or against Missis?'

'If he had sinned only against the Government and you,' she assured me solemnly, 'it would have been a thing for secret laughter between us . . .' She made it admirably plain; to hell with the law and its minions; his sin had been a personal sin against Olivia – using her illness as a stalking-horse for prison-breaking and illicit love-making with herself.

'And how many months in prison do you expect to get for your part in the crime?' I asked her.

'I thought perhaps a year, for I said to him, "Come back to me tonight, or I shall die," and he came back, and I was not ashamed until he left me alone again.' She wept.

The abundantly clear point in all this welter of facts and

motions was that, but for my being the husband of the object of their devotion, I should never have been burdened with their confession. My only obligation in the circumstances was to pass it on to Olivia, which I did. She, in turn, very properly decided that she had no right to impart it to the District Officer. She therefore abstained from mentioning the subject in my office. In any case, we both agreed, it was largely June Angela's fault for catching everyone on the wrong foot as she did. So the thing never reached the official plane. As for Obadaia, what with his good-conduct marks and all, his sentence ran out while he was still in hospital. Or, rather, Olivia saw to it that he was kept in hospital until his sentence ran out.

RETURN OF A STRANGER

My old enemy, 'Amoeba', was at me again two months before Christmas, 1919. This time, the only medicine available was a 1-ounce packet of Epsom-salt, which proved unhelpful. For fear of another crack like 'pusillanimous prig' from Father Choblet, I gave an earnest trial to that dietetic idea of his that had lifted me out of the last bout. But perhaps I lacked faith, or started eating too early, or ate too much or too little boiled fish, for it didn't seem to work. Nevertheless, Providence, by the Father's reckoning, remained active. On Christmas Eve, a totally unhoped-for schooner turned up and removed what remained of me to Ocean Island for treatment.

The event undoubtedly was providential for me as a person, but it didn't look like that for anyone else. The schooner was a small one, crammed with native passengers. There was not even deck space aboard for the four children and their nurses. Olivia stayed with the family on Beru. Fate had celebrated her birthday-cum-Christmas Eve the year before by ripping the roof off our house; this year it left her with a roof but without a husband in her solitude.

The captain promised to return and pick them all up within six weeks. Had he been able to do so, he would have found Olivia busily engaged, without benefit of medicines, in fighting an attack of dysentery on her own account and nursing Rose-mary, aged three, through a raging temperature that seemed to come from blood poisoning. Rosemary had splintered her shin in a tumble. The splinter, as Olivia remarked afterwards, clicked back nicely into place under manipulation by a village boneset-ter, but the sore festered. I fancy that the need of keeping it poulticed day and night was Olivia's main incentive for regard-ing herself as cured of her dysentery. Perhaps, too, a light diet helped her. It had to be light. The promised ship did not turn up for four and a half months. By the time it arrived, she had been twelve weeks without such luxuries as flour, rice or potatoes. She was not fat in May, 1920, when she at last came through to me at Ocean Island.

The Old Man had departed on long leave before she arrived, and that had meant a fortunate turn of the official wheel for me. My luck was that Charles Workman had recently been made Resident Commissioner, Solomon Islands, while Geoffrey Smith-Rewse had been seconded to Nauru as Acting Administrator and every other local officer senior to me by service had either retired or resigned. The Old Man had said to me in January that there was nothing for it but to leave me hanging around at Ocean Island as offsider to anyone the High Commissioner might send up to take charge in his absence. I was glad enough of that prospect at the time. A spell of Ocean Island's fresh foods and iced drinks seemed to me exactly the medicine for all of us.

And then, out of the blue, came the astounding order from Fiji that I was to be offered the chance of acting as Resident Commissioner for three or four months, before being packed off on long leave myself.

I well remember how the Old Man reacted to this grotesque proposition. Grotesque was his word for it. I agreed with him in principle but pleaded that, as a matter of practice, I should much like to accept the offer. He replied with one of his saturnine, double-barrelled sniffs and drew me into the dining-room: 'Look here,' he said, rolling back the mat and pointing to some deep dents in the floor boards: 'Do these remind you of anything?' They did. They had been made by the rain of boulders that had crashed through the roof when I blasted his back yard.

'Now,' he went on, 'I'll leave you with a word of advice. It's this – remember it. When you want to dynamite your official seniors, don't attack them from overhead. Their heads are quite invulnerable. Lay your shot near where they do their thinking – under their seats. That gets them every time. You may perish in the process, but what does a genius more or less matter to the Colonial Service, anyhow?'

I was still trying to work out the exact implications of this utterance for me when he emitted a short yelp, something like a laugh, clapped me on the shoulder and finished: 'Well, the ball's in your hands, Grimble. But none of your funny games before I leave, please.'

So it came about that Olivia and I woke up one morning to find ourselves in charge at the Residency. It was almost six years to the day since we had climbed the front doorsteps as not very welcome intruders into the Central Pacific. That first taste of larger responsibility set a term, I suppose, to my chequered apprenticeship as an administrative officer.

We sailed for home, via Sydney, in August. The arithmetic of our voyage is worth a word in passing. Six years of service entitled us to a passage grant of free transport from Ocean Island to Australia and, in addition, to a payment of £60 down towards the cost of our onward fares to England. My few months as Acting Resident Commissioner had not added to my wealth because (to use the jargon of the financial regulations then current) the substantive holder of the post – the Old Man, in fact – was on full pay leave, and none of his salary was available for the acting incumbent. But we had managed to save £280 out of our pay of £400–£500 a year between Tarawa, Abemama and Beru. Of this, £120 was spent on boarding-house fees in Sydney, where we had to wait three weeks for a ship, and on winter clothes for the children. We found that second class fares to England via Suez would mop up rather more than the remainder of our capital, including the grant of £60. We accordingly travelled round the Cape in a ship designed for the transport of emigrants from England to Australia, and left Sydney with £80 still left of six years' savings to paint London red with.

Our ship was held up for a week in Adelaide by a dock strike and for ten days in Durban by a coal strike. All the children caught whooping cough in the endless hugger-mugger of that horrible craft. Three of them picked up impetigo of the scalp, which was to take months to cure. Poor Rosemary's poisoned leg gave trouble all the way; osteomyelitis was what she had, the surgeon said; and, to put the lid on it, she went down with measles a few days before we reached Tilbury. The others did, too.

We descended upon my father's and mother's house in late November, three months and a week after leaving Ocean Island. The six of us, regarded as a single import, grossed exactly 55 lbs. heavier than the combined weight Olivia and I had exported from the United Kingdom in 1914. But after all, as Olivia remarked, we were still alive. Also, the whole of my full pay during the trip was due to us. That would look after the children's doctors' bills. So, we were still ahead of everything by that £80 in the bank.

I sought conversation with numerous uncles in the early days of my leave. I thought a few first-hand impressions of what they loved to call our far-flung possessions in the Pacific would be sure to hold them spellbound. But somehow the talk never got as far as impressions. It almost invariable developed something like this:

Uncle: 'Hullo, my boy, glad to see you back. Sit down. Have a cigar. Now, tell us what you've been up to all these years out there.'

Self: 'Oh, I've been –'

Uncle: 'You don't look too well on it, whatever it was. Did you keep up your riding?'

Self: 'Well – no – you see – there aren't any horses there. But I –'

Uncle: 'What? No riding? Hm! Now, the other day, Jackie Jack-Jackson said to me – (*Jackie's dicta on fox-hunting as an aid to health here omitted.*) But you must have got a bit of fishing.'

Self: 'Oh, yes, I had plenty of that. The tiger-shark –'

Uncle: 'What? Tiger-shark? Now, the other day, I was talking to a feller back from Ireland. (*Ensuing tale of a fight to the death with an eight pound salmon omitted.*) But I suppose you had a shot at the tigers in those jungles.'

Self: 'Well – no – you see – there aren't any jungles or tigers. But I did –'

Uncle: 'Good God! No big game? Then what in the world *were* you doing with youself in your spare time?'

Self: 'Well – you see – a district officer is kept pretty busy as a rule. He –'

Uncle: 'Oh, yes, now I see. Those cannibals and head-hunters, eh!'

Self: 'Well, no – you see – there aren't any cannibals in the Gilberts.

Uncle: 'And all this time we've been calling you the king of the cannibal islands. Just fancy! No cannibals.'

Self: 'Well – you see –'

But the total loss of horses, salmon, tigers, and cannibals was usually more than enough for my uncles. They weren't unkind about it. They felt the shame of the thing as deeply for me as for themselves. It was out of pure tact that they hurriedly looked at the clock and remembered they had men to see about dogs, and ushered me out with floods of talk about those damned radicals.

Kind Mr Johnson had retired from the Colonial Office some years before I got back to England. I never ventured to ask anyone else in Downing Street to explain exactly what that terrifying phrase 'qualities of leadership' meant to high official-dom. I did go to the Colonial Office, but not to ask questions. My notion was that the people in the personnel department might be glad to hear a few facts about living conditions in the Gilberts, if only for the forewarning of new recruits against avoidable dangers, such as being left without medicines where there was no doctor. I had got a good deal said about things in general to the beautiful young man on the other side of the desk, and was just beginning to expand on particulars, when he interrupted me.

'My dear fellow!' he exclaimed, 'you're not asking me to put all this on record, are you?'

I answered, meekly enough, that this had been the idea, and tried to explain why. But he interrupted me again.

'But – my dear fellow! I mean to say! Good heavens! If we told our applicants even a quarter of these facts in advance, we'd never get a bally recruit!'

I borrowed £150 at the end of my leave to pay my way (emigrant class again) back to the Pacific and leave the family in funds until I arrived there. I did not see them again for seven years. But that is another story.

MONTEROSSO AL MARE, LA SPEZIA, *March–November*, 1951
CHESTER, NOVA SCOTIA, *February–April*, 1952